THE DARK SIDE OF MANAGEMENT

What isn't management and why doesn't it matter? This compelling book leads the reader away from the stories told by managers and management theories to show the secret history of the field.

In characterizing the progress of management as a war on workers, this book offers a controversial and revealing alternative intellectual history of this overwhelming discipline. The author employs a unique range of theories and sources, including the founding fathers of management, US labour and social history, and earlier intellectual figures such as Marx and Weber alongside the contemporary insights of Foucault and European and American workerist and post-workerist thought, to shed light on the world of management.

This book is key reading for researchers and students across the social sciences. With a controversial and stimulating approach, it also engages readers with a general interest in business and management issues.

Gerard Hanlon is Professor of Organizational Sociology at Queen Mary University of London, UK.

THE DARK SIDE OF MANAGEMENT

A secret history of
management theory

Gerard Hanlon

Routledge
Taylor & Francis Group

LONDON AND NEW YORK

First published 2016
by Routledge
2 Park Square, Milton Park, Abingdon, Oxon OX14 4RN

and in the USA and Canada
by Routledge
711 Third Avenue, New York, NY 10017

Routledge is an imprint of the Taylor & Francis Group, an informa business

© 2016 Gerard Hanlon

British Library Cataloguing in Publication Data
A catalogue record for this book is available from the British Library

Library of Congress Cataloging in Publication Data
Hanlon, Gerard.
The dark side of management : a secret history of management theory / Gerard Hanlon.
pages cm
Includes bibliographical references and index.
1. Management. 2. Industrial management. I. Title.
HD31.2.H36 2015
658--dc23
2015001787

ISBN: 978-1-138-80189-9 (hbk)
ISBN: 978-1-138-80190-5 (pbk)
ISBN: 978-1-315-75458-1 (ebk)

Typeset in Bembo
by Taylor & Francis Books

For Gabriel

CONTENTS

PREFACE

In 1956 Reinhard Bendix wrote a wonderful book entitled *Work and Authority in Industry: Ideologies of Management in the Course of Industrialization*. It examined the rise of management as a set of practices involved in the construction and legitimation of new hierarchies through the work organization. It is a shame it is not widely read any more because it highlights how contentious and ideological management is. This book is an attempt to take Bendix seriously, to add to his scholarship through a different political lens and to extend his remit from the work organization to the whole of society. This lens makes this a book about management as class struggle from above – about the imposition of authority and the resistance that precedes it.

The most dominant discourse of the twenty-first century – management – is ultimately materialistic because it seeks to alter social relations so as to ease the path of capitalist accumulation and to transfer wealth from one class to another. Management is not, and never was, a discourse between different 'best' ways to organize production or about functional solutions; it was and is a political endeavour to order and reorder, break down and rebuild, modify and mould, legitimate and justify social relations between people. At the centre of this is a neo-liberal project to force market-based solutions, competitiveness, self-care, individualism, utility, formal rationality and property rights on to a recalcitrant population. In this sense, I argue management is the first neo-liberal science because the work organization becomes a site both to ensure such individual competitiveness and to legitimate and extend property rights through ownership, selection, training, promotion, deskilling and a host of other practices. Rather than being neutral, objective or scientific, management is a very particular brand of politics.

Central to the book is the idea of management as merely a symptom of labour's resistance. Without labour, there is no management in the modern sense. Labour gives birth to management, and after its birth management futilely seeks to escape labour or to individualise and destroy its collectivity in order to make the subject more dependent or vulnerable. The life of management comes through labour conflict. Furthermore, it is the *refusal of labour* – by which (following others) I mean labour's resistance to the control of capital and management – that shows capital and management how they can develop. To give some brief examples, open innovation is based on open-source software; the education and health systems of most of the industrialized world start with labour, not with capital; and hospitality industries survive only on the cultures within which they exist – cultures often created in opposition to capital. Refusal of capital is essential to capitalism, and management is a symptom of this refusal. So Drucker is wrong when he says management is the most productive force; refusal and labour are the productive, innovative forces. What follows will use these insights to examine management as class struggle from above.

As with any book, there are blind spots. Although I recognize the centrality of many struggles – gender, race, colonial, immigrant, ethnic, sexuality – I touch on them only indirectly. I plead guilty to not foregrounding these forms of analysis and instead centralizing the issue of class. I also accept that I am largely, although by no means exclusively, undertaking an analysis of reading management *theorists* rather than focusing on their *practices*. There might hence be a temptation to assume these management theorists could achieve what they argued for – of course, they never did and we should not simply accept them at their word. Nevertheless, their work is important because it demonstrates the *ambition* of management. The sheer scale of what management theorists sought is breathtaking and we would benefit greatly by taking management writers seriously. They sought, and still do seek, the total subsumption of society to capital, of life to work, or of polity to economy – so that early management theorists harbour early neo-liberal ideology. That large elements of management are also neo-liberal is one of my contentions.

I use Marx's term the 'general intellect' to discuss what others might call 'culture', 'socialisation' or 'society'. In one sense, it is all of these, but I wish to retain the term in order to maintain a focus on how management's reach has always stretched beyond the workplace and how labour has resisted, ignored and acquiesced in this reach, and hence how the general intellect has never been a neutral space but rather is one that is already heavily structured by labour and by *management* struggle.

I must thank Sinead Waldron and Terry Clague at Routledge for encouraging me to pursue this project and for forgiving my many editorial weaknesses.

Lastly, no book ever emerges on its own. Directly and indirectly, many people have helped me to think thorough these issues. I sincerely want to thank those who indirectly made this work possible. Specifically, I want to thank Peter Armstrong, whose formidable intellect, class consciousness, rigour and kindness to me have been an inspiration over twenty-five years. I also would like to mention Gibson Burrell, who developed the Management School at the University of Leicester. Thanks to his generosity. I learned so much there. Gibson always affirmed we should read more and write less – sound advice. Finally, I would like to express gratitude to all of those scholars – such as Tom Keenoy, Hugh Willmott, David

Knights, Mike Reed and Stephen Ackroyd – who carved out critical management studies, a space from which I have benefited even as I dispute much of it.

I would like to express thanks to the following friends who read, commented on or engaged with the work in a variety of direct ways: Elena Baglioni, Arianna Bove, Liam Campling, Denise Ferreira da Silva, Emma Dowling and Tim Edkins for all their generosity, assistance and helpful interrogation. I also want to thank friends at the University of Leicester – Stephen Dunne, David Harvie, Simon Lilley, Eleni Karamlai, Dimistris Papadopoulos and Martin Parker – for always making a place for me where I could try out my ideas. Equally, I would like to express my heartfelt appreciation to Mats Alvesson, Sverre Spoelstra and Nick Butler for enabling me to study with them at Lund University. It was in this two-month period at Lund where the first draft of this book was written. This was possible only because of the generosity of Mats, who somehow managed to find funding for me. All three, and their colleagues, were exceptional hosts, and Sverre in particular gave me unlimited time and companionship.

I have also shamelessly benefited from the very many and very different discussions I have had with my good friends Peter Fleming, Matteo Mandarini and Amit Rai. Their fingerprints are all over what follows and it would have been a much poorer book without them. Stefano Harney introduced me to many of those mentioned above, always returned me to the political, encouraged my pursuit of the early neo-liberals and put me on to Lippmann. He is at the core of this book, even though I guess it is anything but what he would have written – go figure. For all of these people, if the traffic were remotely more two-way, I would feel better. Needless to say, all errors and misunderstandings are those of the author.

In many ways my family are embedded in this book – from my mother's ambition for a better life and my father's refusal of authority or constraint, my brothers' search for something different in a country where they did not speak the language, and my sisters' more typical Irish migration to the US and their steely determination, alongside Niall and Kerry, to mould their lives into what they desire. In their different ways, all of them have refused, and though each of them is far away, they are ever-present to me. But mostly, this is for Gabriel, his cousins Jack and Liam, and his younger brother Dylan, in the hope that they too will fiercely refuse and strive to make something beautiful of their lives.

Gerard Hanlon

London, May 2015

PART I

Introducing the violence of management

INTRODUCTION

Managing the free gifts of the general intellect and the division of labour

Management as a symptom of refusal

What is the division of labour based upon in contemporary capitalism? In the Western industrialized economies, what do most of us sell in the labour market? The answer is ourselves – we increasingly sell our subjectivity. No longer do we trade technical, professional or expert skills; today we sell personality. And what do we get with the sale of our personalities? The answer, it seems, is personal dependency. What else can it mean to be authentic, or, as Peter Fleming (2009) expresses it, 'to be your self at work'? To comment on this is simply to recognize that Mills (1951: 255) was correct when he noted that 'personal traits become part of the means of production'.

More recently, workerists, post-workerists and cognitive capital theorists, neo-liberal human capital theorists and human resource management theorists, relationship marketing proponents, open innovation advocates, sociologists, economists and a host of others have recognized this. In different ways, all recognize that where value comes from has altered. No longer is it simply located in the factory – although it is there, too. Today, it is located in the subject, or what Gary Becker calls 'human capital', what Marx terms the 'general intellect', or what Robert Lucas names 'external effects'. That is, it is located in you and me or subjectivity alongside the routine of our labour or the captured labour of the computer on which I am typing or the paper you are reading. Although many have noted this change in value production and perhaps more value capture from the factory and the technical division of labour to the 'personality market', few have linked it to the growth of personal dependency. Indeed, many see it as individualizing, liberating or an escape from deadening labour and routine. This book is an examination of this transition to new forms of personal dependency as management, itself merely a symptom of labour's collectivity, reacts to it and attempts to dismember it and grow dependency through individualizing and isolating the worker. This is a dependency that is at the heart of the neo-liberal drive of management and of the state through their linking of self-care to work – even, or maybe especially, degraded work – or to property ownership wherein rights allocated to the latter far outstrip those of the former. (Even liberal thinkers such as Ferdinand Mount (2013) are beginning to discuss this shift in rights and obligations in favour of property.) As such, it is central to management, which in its origins shares the same fundamental principles as neo-liberalism – indeed, in the final chapter I discuss it as the first neo-liberal science.

What follows will locate these changes much earlier than many contemporary scholars have chosen to do. Rather than see the growth of personal dependency as rooted in the transformations of the 1960s and 1970s, I will contend it emerged with industrial capitalism. I begin by examining nineteenth-century America, with its prioritizing of personal independence, and then move on to examine how the independence of the craft worker and farmer was undermined to create the mass industrial worker. This shift was driven by an increased technical division of labour and the growth of mass production that simultaneously collectivized labour, thereby enabling it to protect itself from the market via unionization, collective protest and so on. But then this transition undercut this collectivist strength through the individualizing and 'liberating' effects of the personality market, the later assault on organized labour and globalization. In so doing, it created the thing early Americans most feared – personal dependency. This push towards personal dependency and the attempted liberation of capital from labour is the story of what today we call management.

The book will examine the struggles and recompositions that gave rise to this change. It will do so through a close reading of the founding texts of management thought. Most particularly, it will analyse the work of F. W. Taylor and Elton Mayo, the founders of scientific management and human relations, respectively. Through this excavation, I will argue that the division of labour and its management is fundamentally an exercise in dependency and authoritarianism. This is primarily, but by no means exclusively, a form of class struggle wherein those at the top – whom the proto-fascist theorist Robert Michels (1915) terms 'the elite' – use the management of the division of labour to secure their social position and become a new aristocracy, not unlike the oligarchs currently arising in America, the UK, Russia and China. Fundamentally, the management of the division of labour is an attempt at the technical and social deskilling of workers because the worker is always a political problem that needs to be addressed.

Oddly, this is not a very radical suggestion. In his formidable book *An Inquiry into the Nature and Causes of the Wealth of Nations*, Adam Smith acknowledged this very point. Smith's first chapter is entitled 'Of the division of labour' and it is here that he describes the dividing of pin-making into the series of simple and routinized tasks that were revolutionizing production at the time. He argues that the increased division of labour would afford the capitalist three advantages: it would simultaneously deskill and increase the dexterity of the worker; it would save time through specialization and by locating workers in the same space; and it would enable machines to replace labour (Smith, 1981: 17). However, later in this same tract Smith highlighted how, if left unchallenged, the division of labour would also create new illegitimate hierarchies. He argued that although individuals were generally born with equal amounts of talent, the children of the philosopher and the factory worker would experience such different lifestyles because of their parents' occupations that by their seventh year their paths would radically diverge (Smith, 1981: 28). Smith implicitly acknowledged class was at the centre of the division of labour, its management and its new hierarchies. Furthermore, he acknowledged that his own project turned labour into a political problem because

> The man whose whole life is spent in performing a few simple operations, of which the effects too are, perhaps always the same, or very nearly the same, has no occasion to exert his understanding, or to exercise his mind in finding out expedients for removing difficulties which never occur. He naturally loses, therefore, the habit of such exertion, and generally becomes as stupid and ignorant as it is possible for a human creature to become. The torpor of his mind renders him, not only incapable of relishing or bearing a part in any rational conversation, but of conceiving any generous, noble, or tender senti-ment, and consequently of forming any just judgement concerning many even of the ordinary duties of private life.
>
> *(Smith, 1981: 782)*

Managing work and the division of labour are thus about creating new forms of subjectivity, authority, hierarchy and individual and collective ways of being, and hence new forms of political problem. As we shall see in what follows, Marx, Braverman, Durkheim, Weber, Michels, the first neo-liberals and early management theorists all made central the issue of the division of labour and the management of work to their construction of their various imagined communities.

What follows places the growth of the modern division of labour and management within the development of capitalism and the two forms of control that emerged out of the Enlightenment. In *Caliban and the Witch: Women, the Body and Primitive Accumulation*, Silvia Federici argues that two basic modes of thinking about social control emerged out of the Western Enlightenment and that both were central to the despotic attack on women, the commons, the racialization of ever more labour and the (often female) knowledge vital to maintaining the (semi-)independent ways of life that were being savaged by capitalism, the market, colonialism and science. One form, most associated with Hobbes, focused on external control wherein the state acts as both the creator and policeman of acceptable behaviour. The second is linked to Descartes and stresses conscience and the human will so that it 'allows for the interiorizations of mechanisms of power' (Federici, 2004: 149).

Management, I will contend, combines both strands of control, which it then put to work in the service of capitalism. As such, despite what management may tell itself, I will argue that – far from being a break with a past that was itself located in the expropriation of knowledge, slavery, colonialism and the degradation of women, non-whites or the working class – it is an extension of the reach of this discipline and control. It is not the story of Smith or Montesquieu's civilizing process (Hirschman, 1977). Rather, it is a history of violence. The choice of scientific management and human relations is not random because they both represent ends of what I see as Federici's continuum – a continuum of the physical to the psychological, perhaps (Mills, 1951: 110 also alludes to this tradition).

Taylor and Mayo fit into this dual form of control and both have had a profound influence on management knowledge over the last century or more. In 1955, Peter Drucker (2007b) described Taylor as perhaps making the United States' most profound intellectual intervention since the Federalist papers. He credited Taylor with significantly contributing to today's mass consumption society. More recently, Eva Illouz (2008) suggested Mayo was the most important management theorist of the past century. She claimed he was responsible for feminizing management and the workplace and that he thereby changed how we interact, how we accept authority, and how we legitimize power within and between institutions such as the work organization and/or the family. Similarly, every management textbook holds forth that Taylor and Mayo made important contributions to our understanding of modern management and, as a result, of social control within modern life. Even though their theories were never fully implemented, simply by outlining the potential of managerial ambition they helped to shape the actual management control structures we have created and resisted over the past 150 years. And yet, I would suggest that management theorists' work and what it represents is understated or misunderstood because we ignore its links to violence, expropriation and authoritarianism. Remedying this is a major theme in what follows.

I will argue three things: first, Taylor and Mayo complement each other; second, they centralize concepts that have remained vitally important to management thought and practice in the century or more since they wrote; and third, management itself is ultimately a tactic for implementing neo-liberalism. To simplify, if we understand these theorists, we understand much of contemporary management, its role in society, the growth of the personality market, the neo-liberal collapse between work and life or polity and economy, the brutality of organizational life, and increasing personal dependency. The concepts examined in this book include the moral and political agenda of management, the invoking of science and objectivity to support what are political ends, the attempt to remould the individual subject, the creation of new lines of authority and power, the reconfiguring of the organizational form to create today's externally regulating bureaucracy – 'the most efficient type of social organization yet devised' (Mills, 1951: 78) – and the increasing sophistication of management techniques of internal discipline. Underlying these concepts are very real areas of struggle based in the pursuit of profit through the control of labour; the rise and rise of instrumentality and formal rationality; the manipulation of the work ethic; the expropriation of knowledge; the legitimization of management's right to manage the workplace and beyond to the whole society; and the sifting and shaping of populations through the emergence of biopolitics. In different ways, all of these topics are central to the creation of the twentieth and the twenty-first centuries, and they have been, and importantly still are, deeply embedded in management thought and practice. An understanding of this thought and practice enables us to understand better our contemporary experience – an experience located in violence, primitive accumulation, expropriation and value capture.

As we will see, Taylor and Mayo continuously raise these themes. Often they examine different spheres of management: for example, Taylor has little to say on the issue of interviewing workers to ascertain how they feel about work, whereas Mayo quite precisely details how such interviews should be conducted (and claims to have led) on projects wherein thousands of workers were interviewed and encouraged to unburden themselves. Conversely, Mayo contributed little to debates on the technical division of labour, whereas one could safely say that Taylor was obsessed by the topic – so much so that today his name is synonymous with deskilling. Nevertheless, they overlap and complement each other. For example, in his talk to the Taylor Society in 1923, Mayo commented that he was continuing Taylor's project – he was in some respects doing a Taylor of the mind. To read the two as complementary enables the reader to see both of Federici's control mechanisms and to see that the concepts they developed have been germane to management ever since. In short (and very crudely), if you cannot confiscate the soul by seduction, you can try to force the body to submit to your control and will. This is management.

Frederick W. Taylor and Elton Mayo understood this. I will argue both are necessary to understanding the nature of management and its relationship to authoritarianism (see Chapter 1). Taylor insisted on using the division of labour to deskill the workforce. Mayo subsequently acknowledged that the new Taylorist nature of work had lost any inherent value to the workforce and hence he sought to persuade workers that they could find meaning through work groups that were formally organized and controlled by management. In essence, he sought to control the worker through his or her conscience and a hierarchical organizational culture. C. Wright Mills (1951: 225) argued that with the creation of the increasingly deskilled mass industrial worker and his or her reliance on their subjectivity in the 'personality market', the management of the division of labour had in some sense shifted from coercion to manipulation – from Taylor to Mayo (however, coercion was and remains important; see McKinlay and Wilson, 2013). Having been deskilled through the technical division of labour in the nineteenth and early twentieth centuries, workers were increasingly subjected to manipulation in an attempt to persuade them that work, the increased division of labour, the growing need to sell their subjectivity and the rise of the large corporations were all good for them. Indeed, for workers to reject such a proposition and its accompanying dependency was to exhibit irrationality (Mayo, 1923a, 1923b). Control necessarily becomes 'self-control' as Mills (1951: 183) expressed it.

Here the physical violence of Taylorism or scientific management becomes the mental violence of Mayo and the human relations school of management. Inherent in this transformation is a transition from the technical and specific skills of craft to the generic and individual skills of subjectivity that are developed in socialization, or what Marx called 'the general intellect' (Marx, 1973: 704–12; see Chapter 1). Having limited worker knowledge of the total production process through deskilling, management and capitalists created new forms of hierarchy, authority and personal dependency – the elite used the division of labour to establish new undemocratic forms of organization because they deemed workers' refusal of the rhythms and dependency of capitalism as irrational and 'pathological' (Michels, 1915: 23–40; Lippmann, 1935, 1938/1943; Röepke, 1948; Mayo, 1949: 3–51).

Dependency, knowledge and the division of labour

Paolo Virno (2004: 40–1) argues that the technical skill of craft, professionalism or expertise is hierarchical and that it enables a worker to stave off the excesses of management and the division of labour. As such, technical skill essentially creates alternative forms of authority to managerial hierarchy. It is for this reason that craft work was so decisively undermined in early industrial capitalism. This was done through deskilling and the replacing of expensive labour with cheaper workers or technology (Tronti, 1965). All of this was itself done through an assault on workers' skill and knowledge.

In the 'Fragment on Machines', Marx (1973: 704–12) notes a change in capitalism based on the prioritization of scientific knowledge. He argues that objectified knowledge in science and technology increased productivity so that labour was increasingly 'to the side of production' and an ever-decreasing direct element of it. He highlights the trend in capitalism for capital to replace workers through the use of science and technology (dead labour). As he puts it, 'Capital itself is a moving contradiction, [in] that it presses to reduce labour time to a minimum, while it posits labour time, on the other side, as a sole measure and source of wealth'. For Marx, this becomes increasingly unsustainable because the development of objectified human creativity in science and machines means the 'social individual' emerges as 'the foundation-stone of production and of wealth' (Marx, 1973: 706).

This 'social individual' is created collectively through spontaneous cooperation in and out of the workplace and is made up of persons within each of whom is a pre-individual (shared language, social cooperation, perception or culture) and the individuated elements of each individual that help to create his or her unique subjectivity (Virno, 2004: 80). When labour in the factory is replaced by machines it is this social individual, with its universal and individuated potential, that drives value capture in the personality market. This development highlights capitalism's prowess because societies have attained such a level of technological and science-led productivity that only a part of production time is necessary for immediate consumption. In turn, this means the social individual is increasingly developed outside the immediate production process, although not outside the circuit of capital, and hence management becomes ever more attentive to the outside of the production process as capitalism develops. One consequence of this transition is the creation of 'disposable time'. This comes about directly because of increases in productivity and capital's desire to reduce to a minimum necessary labour time through technology and management because of the necessity of 'escaping living labour' (Tronti, 1965: 4).

This is a pivotal moment for two reasons. First, 'disposable time' – free time, non-work time – enables labour to transform itself, to develop its potential and to reinsert itself in the production process as a different subject. Yet again, this development is not simply individualistic but is based on collective cooperation – the general intellect. That is, through communicating with living and dead labour, we are recreated as subjectivities in this process of individuation (Virno, 2004: 80). In this sense, the general intellect is 'a complex "social inheritance" – language and culture, but also "technical environment" and practical know-how – that functions as a means of humanisation' (Haug, 2010: 210). But, second, in so doing, the worker's subjectivity is further commoditized as a means of production that has to be managed. Marx's (1988: 85; emphasis in original) comment on this individuation is: 'The worker produces capital and capital produces him – hence he produces himself, and man as *worker*, as a *commodity* is the product of the entire cycle.' In this process our subjectivities and social relationships are transformed outside the immediate productive process and are then captured and harnessed into a capitalist form. That is, the general intellect is raided for its 'free gifts' and then privatized, commoditized and particularized, and thereby made available for capitalist valorization. One central example of this is Mills's (1951) managerial shift from skill or expertise to personality or subjectivity, and from coercion to manipulation wherein people willingly develop and offer up their subjectivities as capital to become persons or 'subjects of value' (Skeggs 2011, 2014) – what Becker (1962) would call 'human capital' but what I will develop as 'personal dependency'.

This is an important transition. As technology and science replace living labour in the factory (but by no means all factories; see Caffentis, 2011), value capture and potentially valuable activities emerge elsewhere – in sociality, communication, the social individual, the general intellect – because

> Free time – which is both idle time and time for higher activity – has naturally transformed its possessor into a different subject, and he then enters into the direct production process as this different subject. This process is then both discipline, as regards the human being in the process of becoming; and, at the same time, practice, experimental science, materially creative and objectifying science, as regards the human being who has become, in whose head exists the accumulated knowledge of society.
>
> *(Marx, 1973: 712)*

This transformed and ever-transforming subjectivity and sociality reshapes where potential wealth is created and value captured. Valuable activity is now captured outside and inside the factory and

> the measure of wealth is then not any longer, in any way, labour time but rather disposable time. If we continue to use labour time as the measure of

wealth we reduce this disposable time to labour time which means positing an individual's entire time as labour time, and his degradation therefore to mere worker, subsumption under labour. *The most developed machinery forces the worker to work longer than the savage does, or he himself did with the simplest, crudest tools.*

(Marx, 1973: 708; emphasis in original)

Thus, the rise of management, science and technology as part of capitalist planning and deskilling (Panzieri, 1961) changes value production and drives towards the total subsumption of society to capital as the outside of the productive process is ever more changed and managed (Tronti, 1965; see Chapter 6). Initially, this rise comes about from labour's refusal in the workplace (see Chapter 1): for example, the struggle of craft workers for whom "'plan and performance are one" and the craftsman is master of the activity and of himself in the process' (Mills, 1951: 222), and who therefore reject the new industrial work rhythms of capitalist valorization being imposed on them. It was in light of this rejection that their social position had to be undermined by deskilling, technology and the division of labour (see Chapter 2). But equally, the industrial worker refused these new work rhythms by simply walking off the job or demanding more consumption or more time off (see Chapters 2 and 3). In light of the refusal of these working conditions, management sought first to deskill and then to manipulate our subjectivities. This is the story of management's twentieth century and perhaps of today.

The decline of craft and the deskilling of labour under scientific management is a familiar story (see Braverman, 1974; see also Chapters 2 and 3). In the nineteenth century capitalist planning or management continually increased in size and scope so that it became even more ambitious: for example, it created new factories of dependent, unskilled (often female or child) labour; it developed new infrastructure projects to create new markets and new market forces; it engaged in race management techniques; and it deskilled craft work. In so doing, it responded to labour's resistance and to its trenchant retention of its own independence (see Chapters 2 and 3). Such resistance forced capital into ever more sophisticated planning that took it from the craft shop to the large-scale factory but, for most of the nineteenth century, left the outside of the work space unmanaged, except through the prioritizing of market forces and the promulgation of a new industrial work ethic (see Chapters 2 and 3, and Weeks, 2011). However, with the large-scale restructuring of US capital at the end of the nineteenth century, capitalist planning upped its game and increasingly looked to the outside of the workplace. The twentieth century took Taylor's interest in the worker–subject to new levels both inside and outside the factory, and in many respects this interest culminated in the neo-liberalism of President Herbert Hoover or Walter Lippmann or Elton Mayo.

The clearest sign of this transformation was the emergence of services in advanced economies and the development of the 'personality market' (Mills, 1951: 161–88), where subjectivity was increasingly raided as a source of value and hence as a thing to be managed and shaped – so that, as Kracauer (1998: 75) expressed it, capital could 'confiscate the soul'. As a source from the 'general intellect', the personality, the soul or the social individual is not developed by capital but rather created cooperatively 'as something exterior and collective, as a public good' (Virno, 2004: 37). In the emerging Fordist economy of the early twentieth century, capital increasingly sought to access this public good or this 'free gift' of sociality (Panzieri, 1961: 2; Smith, 2013; see Chapter 1). Just as labour's own political recomposition from the craft worker to the mass industrial subject demonstrated to capital the way to the next level of economic development and forced capital to push technology and planning to a new and higher level – the Keynesian state (see Tronti, 1965; Baldi, 1972; see Chapter 1) – so the emergence of disposable time, the potential of the social individual and the creation of wealth outside of the factory highlighted the future of value capture to management – namely, a future based in what the Ford manager John R. Lee termed 'the human element of our men' (Meyer, 1980: 69). This transition heralded new forms of management and new forms of dependency that are still with us.

It is labour, then, that shows capital the path to the future. Guido Baldi (1972) highlights the centrality of labour, not capital, in the creation of economic development. The political recomposition of the international working class is central to the change to Fordism. As we shall see, scientific management, the capture of labour's knowledge and the ever finer division of labour outlined in Chapters 2 and 3 are all responses to labour, to its knowledge, to its collectivity, to its soldiering and to its refusal. Thus, Baldi argues that capital's response to labour's refusal entailed early management encroachments into the workshop that were organizational and technological. In this sense, capital's plan necessarily grew in scale and shifted from the craft workshop to the mass-production factory. Such a growth was not simply about productivity, or an organizational or technological necessity; rather, it was about the necessity of capitalist control of knowledge in order to control production (see Chapters 2 and 3; Clawson, 1980). However, this control and reaction still left the factory and society divided: that is, capital had not included the state or society in its planning; indeed, it explicitly wanted the state to stay out of the factory (Montgomery, 1987). With the advent of the First World War and then the Depression, this altered. In particular, the Depression demonstrated the very instability of mass production and its dependence on working-class mass consumption. By demanding less work, more consumption and higher wages, working-class refusal of capitalist social relations drove society towards the future. It was the resistance of craft and other workers to early industrialism that led to capital's planned fix, which, in turn, left capital vulnerable to workers' demands for more free time, more consumption and higher wages – or a greater share of the social product – because of capital's very need to sell its mass product.

The response was to take capitalist planning out of the Taylorist factory and into the whole of society – what we call Keynesianism, social democracy or welfare state capitalism. The central tenet of this was a core political break with the past – namely, it made wages an independent variable no longer subject to downward pressure (although this was not true for the whole Fordist labour force, as the growth of secondary labour markets attests). The 'value of labour' is no longer determined by the market, hence the antagonisms of early neo-liberals to this 'false individualism' (Hayek, 1948; see Chapter 6). The class antagonism upon which wages are determined is now 'brought into the heart of production and is taken as the material given on which capital must rebuild its strategy' (Baldi, 1972: 14). Class antagonism shifts from risk and instability to become the platform for capital's next stage of development, the state becomes the key economic planner, and the collapse of the divide between the factory and society ensues. Rather than being made passive, the political recomposition of the working class enables it to be an active force that creates tomorrow. Furthermore, technology and planning are used, as Marx predicted, to drive labour from the factory. They push labour power or, better still, potentiality to other parts of the economy, such as education, health or retail, where affect, cognition, emotion or service becomes central. These other economic spheres, as we shall see, require yet another level of planning, so management moves from the body to the soul. Management thus makes a twofold move – a macro shift to planning the whole of society and a related micro shift to moulding worker subjectivity.[1]

This shift from the body to the soul in the early twentieth century was part of a broader capitalist planning which increasingly entailed the application of science to production and consumption via human resource management, technology, marketing and motivation theory (to name but a few). Hence, organization theory, human relations, management sciences, the regulation of communications and any form of increasing worker participation in the firm are all integral elements of the rational management and planning inherent within capitalism (Panzieri, 1961: 4; see Chapter 6). The state is central to this class mining of value; neo-liberals such as Lippmann (1922) and Mayo (1919) also knew this. Capitalists developed into a class as a result of labour's opposition to capitalist valorization and its impact on work and, as a class, they then required the state increasingly to plan economic development (Tronti, 1965, 1971; Baldi, 1972; Hanlon and Mandarini, 2015). As a response to labour's revolutionary potential in the early twentieth century, the state took over the planning of the economy by including labour in governance and turning the wage from a dependent variable fluctuating as the labour market dictated to an independent variable that became the bedrock of the new planned economy. Accompanying this increasing planning of society and the harvesting of the subject was a transition from submission to capital in the factory to the attempted subsumption of the whole of society to capital as Fordism developed both mass production and mass consumption (Tronti, 1965, 1971; Baldi 1972). In a manner that Braverman and labour process theorists underplay, capitalist planning also left the factory.

Organization, technology and the division of labour were used to undermine the resistance of the working class to capitalism in order to enable capital in its futile and perennial bid to escape labour (Tronti, 1965; see Chapter 1). As such, the factory became ever more Taylorized and mechanized. Accompanying this was the rise of the bureaucratic firm with its ever-lengthening lines of authority and hierarchy and its increasing desire to fracture labour through relatively meaningless grade differences and division (Stone, 1973; Edwards, 1979; see Chapters 2 and 3). This was paralleled by a growth in what we might call 'the salaried masses' (see Mills, 1951; Bendix, 1956; Kracauer, 1998), located in the rise of services that required both scientific management and a different set of management techniques and worker skills because, as one early management theorist noted, 'Business may be essentially impersonal but it is highly personal in services' (Bloomfield, 1915: 124).

These developments created much of what we call 'modern management'. As Mills (1951: 215–38) highlighted, workers were no longer anything like craft workers. Unlike craft workers, who saw life as an extension of craft, the mass industrial subjects of the factory and office separated work from life, did not understand (or care) how the whole production process was held together, increasingly worked in sales, marketing or an office rather than on the factory floor and were increasingly educated or certified even though such certification was unnecessary to the tasks they performed (Kracauer, 1998: 42; but see also Weber, 1948: 240–4; Mills, 1951: 161–89; Stone, 1973; see Chapters 3 and 4). Despite this growing certification, management was clear in its thinking – if worker knowledge about the production process was needed, this knowledge should be about a specific element of that process, rather than a general craft-type knowledge, because the latter would dangerously empower workers (Stone, 1973; see Chapter 3). Craft-like knowledge would give workers general technical skill and hence more autonomy, and as such it had to be limited.

However, for an economy ever more located in services, these developments gave rise to a problem of motivation and created the need for tame and benign personality traits. This meant that increasingly proper selection, hiring and training in service were needed to eliminate personal randomness. In the twentieth century a new form of rationalization was required – the rationalization of attitude (Mills, 1951: 180). Personality workers could not be left to chance because they represented the management and the organization. For example, in sales, 'Neglect of personal appearance on the part of the employee is a form of carelessness on the part of the business management. "Self-control" pays off' (Mills, 1951: 183). Management had to attend to the creation of the subject within the general intellect. Selection and training were made ever more paramount in the pursuit of the ideal worker-personality and a pseudo-science was used to invoke the objectivity of capitalist planning (Kracauer, 1998: 38–9; see Chapters 4 and 5). Just as respectability and 'knowing one's place' sold domestic service, human capital's subjectivity sold services so that 'From the standpoint of the direct production process it can be regarded as the production of *fixed capital*, this fixed capital being man himself' (Marx, 1973: 711; emphasis in original).

Accessing this fixed capital thus became one of management's central problems because it was here where value could be captured via 'good'-personality workers, it was where valuable activities were increasingly sourced and it was subjectivity that increasingly needed to be 'manipulated' (Mills, 1951: 110). This was the task human relations set itself from the 1920s onwards – it wanted to access the worker's 'total situation' so that it could acclimatize the worker to his or her new, degraded, but vital role (see Mayo, 1924a: 255; see Chapter 4). In no way could such a process be left to workers and to an unmanaged 'spontaneous co-operation' (Mayo,

1949: 120), because workers and their refusal were simply irrational – they had to be managed even beyond the workplace (see Chapters 4 and 5). What Mayo was seeking to achieve in this process was the alteration of the cognitive and affective maps of labour. He wished to reach into and shape the general intellect so that the social individual became the capitalist social individual whose sole purpose was the valorization of capital. If Taylor was the management theorist of the planned factory, Mayo was the management theorist who acknowledged that the divide between the factory and society had to be broken down. Whether he knew it or not, he understood the planned society – total subsumption.

As we shall see, the worker who is not reconciled to his or her role within capitalism is deemed to be irrational, a phantasist and even pathological in management thought. In this sense, management thought shares many of the same assumptions and ambitions as neo-liberalism. The job of management is to achieve a reconciliation between workers and their roles so that they willingly present the gift of 'spontaneous cooperation' to their co-workers and employers. To achieve such a goal, Mayo (1924b) echoed the first neo-liberals (Hoover, 1922; Lippmann, 1922, 1935; see also Chapter 6) by advocating the study of the whole worker inside and outside of work so as to mould the conscience and acclimatize the subject to their position in the division of labour and the work organization, and view themselves as completely embedded in market relations that would discipline them biopolitically (see Chapters 4 and 6). Through such study, the creation of a subject who identifies with the small work group (rather than the enormous bureaucratic firm) and seeks dialogue with management (without any real action resulting) could be created. In this manner the worker could be acclimatized to work, to their subservient role in society, and management could 'conquer the still vacant territory of the employees' souls' (Kracauer, 1998: 78). In so doing, Mayo attempted to achieve the collapse of the distinction workers had created between work and life – the very thing the Taylorist division of labour had led workers to establish by way of their refusal as they embraced consumption, pleasure and indiscipline (Weeks, 2011). Although Mayo is perhaps the most explicit in advocating this, he is by no means alone – selection, training and appraisal are still related to this today (see Townley, 1993). What he established was management as a neo-liberal project (see Chapter 6). In a deskilled world, management accesses the soul. Scientific management and human relations join forces.

Managing the free gift of the general intellect and creating dependency

Virno (2004) argues that, with the decline of craft or technical skill and the introduction of technology, workers are potentially made equal. He suggests that work is increasingly located in the communicative sphere and hence in a subjectivity that is developed outside of the immediate workplace. These twin processes also open up labour to a more capricious form of management wherein one develops a personality or subjectivity that is increasingly tailored to the marketplace. Indeed, this subjectivity is also increasingly transient and malleable as the whims of capital alter. Today, one reason why it is harder to resist management is because technical skill is embedded in machines. What seems clear is that under scientific management and Fordism leisure and the outside of 'work' were increasingly where the subject both wanted to be and was formed. As such, it became a place to be managed and from which to extract value. This is especially the case when 'personality' is being rationalized in the workplace in order to deliver a better, more predictable, constant 'coin of "fun"' (Mills, 1951: 237) for the worker–customer. An unmanaged outside, indeed a proper individuality, would lead to unpredictability in the 'factory of smiles and visions' (Mills, 1951: 167) and therefore threaten valorization, hence the concern with rationalizing the 'total situation' (see Chapters 2, 3, 4 and 5). Society needs to be totally subsumed to capital and managed at ever higher and ever deeper levels (Tronti, 1965; Hanlon and Mandarini, 2015).

This means the general intellect must be managed, shaped and raided for value (even if this shaping can never be complete; see Chapters 1, 5 and 6). The personality market requires the qualities of the general intellect, such as cognitive traits, linguistic abilities and affective skills like empathy or interpersonal smoothness, if it is to be profitable. But herein lies the rub. The personality market operates in skills learned in the general intellect and hence these skills come to capital as a 'free gift' (see Chapter 1). However, capital also aims to bend this free gift to its will by prioritizing only some of labour's different potentials – by creating activities and subjects of value (Skeggs, 2014). Management and selection indirectly feed back to the general intellect as the foregrounding of certain potentialities over others takes place. Capitalist hierarchy permeates the general intellect. After all, this is what selection is fundamentally about because 'it is not enough to feel the call, you must be chosen' (Kracauer, 1998: 33). In this sense, human relations and all the other 'soft' management techniques complement Taylor because they seek total control of the subject so that he or she adapts in order to be chosen (Mills, 1951: 233–5; see Chapter 6).

Furthermore, Virno (2004: 40–1) argues that within this economy the division of labour becomes arbitrary. It is not that workloads are not divided; rather, there are no objective technical criteria as to why Winston and not Maria should be on reception today, organizing the welcome for the international clients tomorrow and attending a training course next week. As such, professionalism, craftsmanship or skills are ever more redundant because in the contemporary work setting 'All workers enter into production in as much as they are speaking-thinking' (Virno, 2004: 41; see also Lazzarato, 1996). In an economy based on the sharing of the cognitive, affective, communicative and linguistic abilities of the general intellect, the division of labour located in technical skills crumbles as this technical knowledge is housed in technology, routines, procedures and regulations. However, with this sharing comes personal dependence and groundless hierarchy:

> The publicness of the intellect, that is to say the sharing of the intellect, in one sense causes every rigid division of labor to fall flat on its back; in another sense, however, it fosters *personal dependence*. *General Intellect*, the end

of the division of labor, personal dependency: the three facets are inter-related. The publicness of the intellect, when it does not take place in a public sphere, translates into an *unchecked proliferation of hierarchies* as groundless as they are thriving. The dependency is *personal* in two senses of the word: in the world of labor one depends on this person or on that person, not on rules endowed with anonymous coercive power; moreover, it is the whole person who is subdued, the person's basic communicative and cognitive habits.

(Virno, 2004: 41; emphasis in original)

This is the core of contemporary and past work. What becomes the vehicle for selection, promotion or redundancy is the subject's personality. When the product can no longer be separated from the actual producer, it takes on the appearance of 'servile labor' (Virno, 2004: 68). Think of eating out: the way you are served helps to determine the 'quality' of your dining experience, but the waiter or waitress appears to give you only rationalized affective servility, not technical skill (Dowling, 2007). If the affect is not satisfactory, we have a disappointing meal. This work may share many similarities with craft work: for example, the product and producer are inextricably linked, the craft worker – and, ideally for capital, the personality worker – expresses and develops him- or herself at and through work, and consumption and production are simultaneous in some sense (see Mills, 1951: 220–4). But there is one vital quality missing for the personality worker. The hoarding of knowledge in craft work by workers strengthens the division of labour and hence limits the personal dependency of the knowledge worker. The personality market allows no such protection, hence the arbitrariness of work and reward, of value generation and pay, and of hierarchy and authority.

This dependency was apparent in Weimar Germany. Kracauer (1998) highlights the growth in the importance of looks, of joining in, of appearances, of emotions, of affect and of employees seeking to project the right aura. Age, gender, sexuality, class, disability, accent, attractiveness, empathy and warmth are evaluated and put to work (or not). The workplace is individualized and made hierarchical on the basis of a seemingly capricious and authoritarian management in the pursuit of profit. It appears as caprice because any personality traits that are in vogue today may not be tomorrow, or management's assessment of what compliance and value look like today may not be the same tomorrow, or things may randomly change from one managerial regime to the next, thereby creating uncertainty, anxiety and compliance. Here capital can put to work or refuse the heterogeneity we create in the general intellect, depending upon its assessment of such heterogeneity's potential to valorize capital. McKenzie (2001) highlights how corporations have increasingly sought to access and profit from such differences via such techniques as equality and diversity management. Some subjects, activities and potentials are rejected and hence often subject to more aggressive management techniques.

This capriciousness is all supposedly achieved through objective tests, selection processes, promotion criteria and research from major universities, all of which are aimed at securing the 'Whole personality, right person and right place: the words drawn from the dictionary of a defunct idealist philosophy give the impression that what is involved in the test procedures currently being implemented is a genuine selection of persons' (Kracauer, 1998: 33–9; see Chapters 3 and 4). The spontaneous cooperation of the general intellect, combined with the unfree 'spontaneous coop-eration' of the firm, delivers to the individual personal dependency and to capital the free gift of the social individual. In a neo-liberal embrace, management and capital attempt to subsume society totally to their needs (see Chapter 6). As in the past, today we are tailoring our subjectivity to management's needs by acting as human capital, as investors in ourselves, as self-organizers, as self-managers and self-starters, as stores of data and information that are readily made available to capital – what some have called 'cognitive capitalism' (Vercellone, 2007), 'Empire' (Hardt and Negri, 2000) or 'immaterial labour' (Lazzarato, 1996).

The post-workerist cognitive capital thesis often suggests that this process is potentially liberating and that it roughly emerged out of post-Fordism or loosely in the post-1970s Western world. However, I will argue that this transformation is constraining and that it needs to be located much earlier – at least to the start of Fordism in the 1920s and 1930s and to management theory in the form of scien-tific management and human relations – if not to the birth of industrial capitalism itself. We are witnessing an extension of dependency and an intensification of the past rather than a radical break with them. As the technical division of labour was collapsed into technology, routines and procedures, management aimed to capture the modern soul and align individual subjectivity with the needs of capitalism so that labour would no longer be Smith's political problem, but would rather accept the new forms of authority that capitalism and management were establishing. Management is centrally about active intervention into institutional and organiza-tional life to recast subjectivity along competitive lines. In this sense it is essentially neo-liberal (see Chapter 6). Obedience is at the heart of this process. I hope that this examination of early management thought will enlighten our thinking about the nature of contemporary life – about knowledge economies, affective capitalism, cognitive capitalism or emotional labour and, most importantly, anti-democratic authoritarian hierarchy.

Structure of the book

What follows will link management to authoritarianism and the total subsumption of life to the needs of capital in the twenty-first century. It will do so via a close reading of early management thought and its relationship with the ongoing struggles for control in the factory, the office and beyond. It will argue that these struggles were waged from above and they were about controlling the physical and the mental life of labour. While today is not simply a replica of the past, the struggles over managed work in the first century of industrial capitalism contain much that is still pertinent. This is one of the purposes of what follows – to examine the poli-tical and neo-liberal nature of management thought and its reactionary attempt to shape life.

Chapter 1, 'Management's authoritarian heart', will map out the theoretical influences of the book and seek to demonstrate how capitalist cooperation in the workplace is inherently violent and how the division of labour and the creation of new forms of governance led to the emergence of what has been called the 'totalitarian organizational form'. Management seeks constant active intervention to foster competitive relations among labour and to re-engineer the subject and the society under elite leadership; hence, it is a fundamental part of the neo-liberal project. The division of labour and the rise of management and bureaucracy were absolutely central to this process of violence and the new hierarchies it unleashed. One other feature of this is the necessity of capital to capture the free gift of sociality in order to generate profit. Marx, Weber, Michels, Foucault, workerist, post-workerist and other material will be deployed in analysing these conflicts and changes.

Part II: The dark nature of management knowledge

Chapter 2, 'Class struggle without class?', examines the violent resistance to the enforcing of capitalist valorization on labour, and labour's desire to maintain its independence from capital and market forces. It does this especially through an examination of the nineteenth-century American experience, although it also refers to Great Britain. Central here is the formation of new forms of governance in the workplace, the home, the city and the state. The chapter stresses the importance of vulnerability and dependency: it was children, women, migrants and non-whites who were first compelled to accept the brutality of the factory and capitalism. In contrast to mainstream analyses, here violence and dependency are handmaidens to the ushering in of capitalism. In a manner akin to the use of colonies and subject peoples as testing grounds for violent expropriation, this brutality was then carried into the realm of skilled work as craft was systematically attacked and undermined so that its forms of authority, legitimacy and ways of being were downgraded and trammelled in order to eradicate craft or make it dependent on capital. These processes transformed the United States and turned it into an industrial powerhouse. Importantly, this was not a democratic process: the state supported the violence of capital and undermined forms of autonomy upon which labour had traditionally relied – 'free' soil and skill. The partisan state was a key feature of the transformation, as were the moral attack on labour, the increased division of labour, new forms of property rights and the rise of the factory.

Chapter 3, 'An almost equal division of the work and the responsibility', develops the nineteenth-century story through an examination of the division of labour and deskilling. In particular, it does this through labour histories of the factory and through a close reading of the work of management theory. This chapter outlines the violence of deskilling and the manner in which it created a new political subject – the mass industrial worker. This subject became a central figure in the rise of Fordism. Once again, intimidation, violence, new forms of governance and resistance are at the heart of the chapter. The move from the 'inside contract' to new forms of direct managerial control led to conflict, deskilling, the planned factory and, finally, to the rise of the modern corporation. This is a story of the expropriation of knowledge and the creation of organizational and managerial forms that left workers with a limited knowledge of the production process. Capital hoped that this would mean the workers would be easier to manage and mould. In Taylor we can see the contours of modern management thought in this process of violence. He has an image of the worker as lazy; he refers to science and neutrality as justifications for class expropriation; he seeks obedience to authority; and he highlights how his system will enable the worker to overcome his or her ignorance about what is in his or her best interest. Capitalism will be made safe through ongoing management–neo-liberal intervention. Within this, class, gender, race, migration and vulnerability were once again present, and from these struggles emerged the inherent class nature of the organizational form that dominated the twentieth century – the bureaucratic corporation where labour underwent a real subsumption to capital through expropriation and the management of the factory.

Chapter 4, '"Spontaneous cooperation": excavating the soul', examines the nature of the management transition from coercion to manipulation (Mills, 1951: 109–11). Importantly, violence or coercion were never obliterated in this process but always remained central to capitalist management – think of current struggles over land or student debt (Mezzadra and Neilson, 2013). Although I associate this with Elton Mayo, we must acknowledge that he was not alone: for example, Siegfried Kracauer (1998: 36) writes about management in Weimar Germany trying to gain control over the subject's 'total personality'. After the 'American Terror' (Jacques, 1996: 21), which restructured working relations, US capitalism saw the emergence of the planned organization and the planned society. Again, management thought and science were rolled out and put at the disposal of capitalism in ways very similar to Federici's analysis of their role in creating capitalism and the Enlightenment (Federici, 2004: 114–25). Here, management thought was used to marginalize other views of production and, indeed, other ways of life. Race, gender and class were again central to this process as labour was subjected to a moral and political attack, and deemed to be irrational and in need of leadership – all weapons in the armoury of early neo-liberals (Hoover, 1922; Lippmann, 1935, 1938/1943). Communication, cognition, emotion, affect, desire and the body were prioritized in this project and supposedly objective science was invoked to deliver explicitly political ends – namely, the establishment of the elite's right to lead not just in industry but throughout the whole of society. Resistance had to be de-legitimated and broken, subjectivity had to be reshaped and individual self-care had to be prioritized (on these neo-liberal tendencies today, see Brown, 2003, 2006).

Chapter 4 also examines the manner in which management sought to create new pliable subjectivities and to individualize labour so that the latter's desires could be shaped to meet the needs of capital. Public opinion in the workplace, the market and the home had to be reshaped so that it was made safe for capitalism (Lippmann, 1922; Bernays, 1928; Lears, 2000). The outside of the immediate production process increasingly became the focus of management. If the mid- to late nineteenth century was characterized by active resistance to the market and to paid employment, management's task in the early twentieth century was to make the market appear as the natural way for people to fulfil all their needs and for paid employment to appear as natural, meritocratic and rewarding. This was a new form of management. Rather than the coercion of Taylor, we witness the rise of the manager as someone who gets the best out of people, who listens to them, who improves workers rather than punishes them – this is management as progressive liberation. Central to this new form of management were cognitive and affective skills.

Attempting to control subjectivity became central to management; to create what Foucault might call norms of behaviour or governmentality. Populations that were deemed outside of these norms were subjected to severe governance. Technology, bureaucracy, planning, psychology, science and ongoing violence were central to the creation of these new ways of being and of disciplining. Furthermore, as routines, procedures and deskilling left labour without an understanding of the total production process, and as technology replaced labour in the factory, capitalist value and valorization were increasingly created in the subjectivity of the social individual. This transition combined with an emerging service economy so that personality and a compliant attitude (Kracauer, 1998: 38–9) became the drivers of value capture. Rather than being liberating, management had moved towards the real subsumption of labour within the factory and now, with the bureaucracy, the planning of capital and the psychological manipulation of human relations, it was inching towards what Edwards (1979) calls the totalitarian organization and the total subsumption of life to capital. The roots of 'cognitive capitalism' are not to be found in post-Fordism but at least around the time of the birth of Fordism itself. Management strategies were developed to gain control of the 'total personality' through the creation of new forms of community, cooperation, organization, hierarchy and anti-democratic authoritarianism – they aimed to collapse any liberal distinction between the economy and the polity, life and work, market and non-market, public and private. In this process, Taylorism, bureaucracy and human relations are complementary, rather than in opposition to one another.

Part III: Management, neo-liberalism and a history of violence

Chapter 5, 'Confiscate the soul', elaborates on this complementarity between coercion and manipulation. In particular, it highlights the similarities between the scientific management and human relations schools' projects. For example, both emphasized the moral and political nature of management and the necessity of ensuring capitalism's continuance; both made false claims to objectivity and used 'science' and 'expertise' to present management as a natural outcome of human change and the emerging social hierarchy as meritocratic; both stressed the desire to create a new subjectivity for the worker – a subordinate subjectivity that would align labour's interests to capital's interests; and both sought the reshaping of the organization and the creation of new lines of authority based on ownership, competition, organizational or bureaucratic position, and adherence to organizational goals. Indeed, these categories are central to management thought even today, despite much debate about flattening hierarchy, liberating workers and human capital as the source of value. Once again, in this rendition, management emerges as a neo-liberal project.

Chapter 5 also addresses Illouz's (2008) suggestion Mayo feminizes management by encouraging communication, openness and empathy. On the contrary, I will argue that Mayo and the human relations school 'feminized' labour, by which I mean that the rise of capitalism and the Enlightenment saw the expropriation of important forms of knowledge and economic activity that were concentrated in female and indigenous populations (Federici, 2004) and that following this violent expropriation – in which the factory and the plantation were central – women, colonized peoples and non-whites were made dependent and vulnerable to physical and psychological violence. One central characteristic of this violence was its desire to recast these populations and make them disciplined and controllable in the work sphere. Coming after the violence of Taylor, this was what the human relations school of management sought to achieve (as does its contemporary neo-liberal offspring – human resource management): disciplined and controllable populations within society.

The chapter also examines how this transformation led to new forms of resistance to management and how these new forms shifted where potential was formed, where knowledge was located, how subjectivity was created and recreated as the general intellect – those spaces outside of the factory or the office or paid employment – was increasingly placed at the heart of economic life. All of this led to further shifts in management, with its emerging emphasis on human resources and human capital. Indeed, labour's resistance to management led to the economic development of today, which is ever more located in capturing the wealth of the general intellect and its free gifts of socialized individuals who want to be – or have to be – 'subjects of value'.

Chapter 6, 'Management: the first neo-liberal "science"', outlines similarities between the past and the present and continuities that increase personal dependence. It argues that capital began to access personality or subjectivity to capture value quite early on. However, personality is not simply created by capital. It is also in the general intellect – in culture, communication, emotion, cognition and affect – and these are now absolutely central to the economy. However, in accessing them, management has sought to intervene continuously and actively to shape these free gifts to the needs of capital. The subject and his or her potential are to be moulded into the neo-liberal self-caring subject. This potential is created in the struggle (or not) with capital (Tronti, 1965, 1971; Mezzadra and Neilson, 2013). Today, this also means that the individual is exposed to the market and management without the protection of technical expertise. All we have to sell is our personality, so what should have been a moment of liberation – the death of hierarchy based in expertise – becomes a moment of dependency on the caprice of the market and management. Our 'morally pink complexion[s]' (Kracauer, 1998: 38) may be welcomed by the market today, but rejected by it tomorrow, thereby creating an ever more stressful and unstable relationship with work. Vulnerability, dependency and the capaciousness of management remain but the struggle continues – a struggle often conducted by groups deemed of no or little value.

However, the real work of the final chapter is to build on the previous chapters and the scholarship of early neo-liberal theorists such as Walter Lippmann, Herbert Hoover, Ludwig von Mises, Friedrich A. Hayek, Wilhelm Röepke and others to argue that management and neo-liberalism share the same foundations. It argues that management is fundamentally a tool for delivering neo-liberalism through the competition of the managed work organization. Both share the following: a belief in active intervention, the prioritization of competition, and the necessity of elite leadership. The purpose of all three of these features is the reshaping of subjectivity and social relations. The chapter depicts management as based on what Weber distinguished as an 'ethic of conviction' rather than an 'ethic of responsibility'. It thereby undermines the claims of management knowledge to objectivity to suggest that large swathes of management thought are anti-democratic, authoritarian and elite driven – or, again, neo-liberal.

Finally, there is a very brief discussion of the work of Durkheim because he is often seen as a significant influence on Mayo and human relations – a position I wish to dispute. As it is not central to the main argument of this book, this discussion is presented in an appendix.

Welcome to management's history of violence.

Note

1 Although not part of this book, one interesting examination of the personality market and the general intellect would be a critical engagement with the nature of the cognitive, affective and communicative skills of earlier important labour populations, such as domestic servants.

1

MANAGEMENT'S AUTHORITARIAN HEART

What follows has been influenced by a number of different theoretical approaches. As the Introduction indicated, it is particularly influenced by Marxism, with its emphasis on the extraction of surplus value, the conflictual nature of the employment relationship within capitalism, the role of compulsion within that relationship and the extraction of value from the free gift of sociality located in the general intellect. It is influenced by the tradition in Marxism known as workerism and subsequently post-workerism, which emphasize issues such as the refusal of work, the general intellect, optimism, pleasure, subjectivity and the reforming of class composition. Importantly, this tradition also de-emphasizes issues such as the dignity of work and its necessity, which are often found in other Marxist accounts of labour.

It also engages the work of theorists such as Max Weber and Michel Foucault. Most especially, this influence is centred on the issue of discipline within society – in the workplace, the marketplace and beyond. Weber's emphasis on forms of rationality, bureaucracy and regulatory structures is complemented by Foucault's interest in issues relating to attitudes, the body and behavioural discipline. Furthermore, emerging from these theorists is a concern with elements of the elite theory of Michels and Pareto and new lines of authority embedded within the bureaucratic organizational form that emerged in the nineteenth and twentieth centuries. I am also interested in the simultaneous emergence of neo-liberalism at this point. Later in the book – Chapter 6 – I examine the work of such people as Walter Lippmann, Herbert Hoover and others and the way this neo-liberal tradition resonates with management so that management is in its origins a neo-liberal project. Weber returns at that point as a reluctant neo-liberal. The use of these different perspectives enables us to see the core of management with its original and ongoing emphasis on violence, authority, discipline, subjectivity and biopolitics – all of which, as practices, are shaped by the need to extract surplus value and reproduce capitalist social relations.

Marx, cooperation and management

Marx (1976: 439–54) argues that cooperation within capitalism is a forced process. He recognizes the real benefits of human cooperation because it increases the productive capacity of the species. However, he goes on to outline how capitalism makes cooperation compulsory because the 'freely' entered-into contract between the worker and the employer is actually unfree and, because of this, the cooperation of the factory is not voluntarily entered into but driven by the valorization of capital. As such, within capitalism, the authority needed in cooperation is necessarily antagonistic. If we examine the employment contract first and then pursue the issue of cooperation, we will get to the nub of Marx's position vis-à-vis capital, labour and the employment relationship.

Marx (1976: 270–80) describes how the owner of money and the wage-labourer come to meet each other as equals within the marketplace, where they exchange cash for labour power. In typical fashion, he then highlights various elements that are hidden in this social exchange. First, he points out that the labourer must treat his or her labour as a commodity in the marketplace and hence that he or she is capable of both managing to alienate themselves from their labour power and of selling it in blocks of time so that ownership of it is never fully renounced. Second, society has to have evolved in such a way that this worker confronts it as a seller of the commodity labour power rather than as a seller of finished commodities within which his or her labour has been objectified.

> In reality, the worker belongs to capital before he has sold himself to the capitalist. His economic bondage is at once mediated through, and concealed by, the periodic renewal of the act by which he sells himself, his change of masters, and the oscillations in the market price of his labour.
>
> *(Marx, 1976: 723–4)*

Such a situation necessarily entails a historic separation of the worker from the means of production. This separation makes the worker free in the

> double sense that as a free individual he can dispose of his labour-power as his own commodity, and that, on the other hand, he has no other commodity for sale, i.e. he is rid of them, he is free of all the objects needed for the realization of his labour-power.
>
> *(Marx, 1976: 272)*

This double freedom is at the heart of capitalism.

However, for Marx, this double freedom hides the social creation of wage labour which actually entails a real loss on the part of workers because of their separation from the means of production. This separation comes about through violence, expropriation, privatization of previously common land and resources, 'bloody legislation', enslavement and persecution (Marx, 1976; Roediger and Esch,

2012: 71; Federici, 2004; Banaji, 2003). The turning of labour into a free agent to contract in the labour market conceals this separation and the fact that the worker is compelled to work. What is presented as the *potential* to labour in capitalism is in actuality the *necessity* to labour (Marx, 1976: 277). The freedom to exchange and to contract as an equal in the labour market is in reality an unequal freedom weighted against the worker. This weight is so great that it becomes compulsion. The idea that people equally pursue their individual self-interest and, through that self-interest, engage in a common endeavour of cooperation to enhance the property of both is simply untrue. On the contrary, workers and employers are set against each other because of this unequal exchange. But Marx goes further, arguing that on the basis of this unequal exchange the money owner emerges as a capitalist and the possessor of labour-power becomes a worker so that 'one smirks self-importantly and is intent on business; the other is timid and holds back, like someone who has brought his own hide to the market and now has nothing else to expect but – a tanning' (Marx, 1976: 280). As such, the defining characteristic of the employment relationship is one of antagonistic hierarchy within which the capitalist must control labour in order to extract value. Compulsion and discipline therefore have to be placed at the centre of capital as a social relation and, with this, so too have management and control (Banaji, 2003).

Thus, cooperation is not a cooperation of equals. Nor is it spontaneous – something to which we will return. When examining cooperation, Marx acknowledges the need for authority. However, he goes on to argue that, under capitalism, antagonism – rather than knowledge or know-how about production – is at the heart of the authority relationship. Within capitalism, cooperation is forced because it is driven first and foremost by the disciplining necessity of the valorization of capital: that is, people are brought together not to produce something of use – although that may occur – but to produce something that will enable capital to increase as capital. The search for profit, not use, drives cooperation. Furthermore, as the concentration of capital increases through this valorization and the number of workers involved in the cooperation process grows, so too does labour's resistance to capital, because the means of production face the worker as the property of another and cooperation increasingly confronts labour as exploitation. As such, workers' cooperation appears to them as something outside of their competence because it is organized by the capitalist. Cooperation appears as the management expertise of the capitalist. Marx (1976: 449–50) describes this situation as follows:

> These things are not their [workers'] own act, but the act of capital that brings them together and maintains them in that situation. Hence the interconnection between their various labours confronts them, in the realm of ideas, as a plan drawn up by the capitalist, and in practice as his authority, as the powerful will of a being outside of them, who subjects their activity to his purpose.

Central, then, to authority and discipline – that is, to transforming individual ability into labour-power – is the management of labour (Federici, 2004: 133). As the scale of capital grows, the capitalist is increasingly forced to plan, to manage, to hire managers, foremen and overseers, and, indeed, to accept a restructured state to organize production (Baldi, 1972; Tronti 1965, 1971). In so doing, capital contracts with the individual worker but it is only by bringing individual workers together in the actual labour process that cooperation is generated and surplus value achieved. Within this, the labourer is unfree – '[workers'] enslavement to capital is only concealed by the variety of individual capitalists to whom it sells itself' (Marx, 1976: 764).

It is also the fact that labour is at its most productive through cooperation because, 'When the worker cooperates in a planned way with others, he strips off the fetters of his individuality, and develops the capability of the species' (Marx, 1976: 447). But because labour is forced to prostrate itself before capital in this process, cooperation happens only through capital, such that 'capital develops into a require-ment for carrying on the labour process itself, into a real condition of production' (Marx, 1976: 448). With this, the capitalist becomes the centre of authority, com-mand and discipline. Importantly, then, the capitalist becomes the hub of authority in a productive system that is now both unknown and alien to the worker while this system is simultaneously exponentially productive. Cooperation and coordination thus 'appear to be a productive power inherent to capital' itself (Panzieri, 1961). However, the appearance that capital creates cooperation is itself something of a mystification. Cooperative labour is when labour is most productive, and it is also the very cooperative sociality of the worker that generates this productivity, *not capital* – 'the socially productive power of labour develops as a free gift to capital whenever the workers are placed under certain conditions and it is capital which places them under these conditions' (Panzieri, 1961). One aspect of capitalism that is often downplayed by management and indeed labour process theory is that coop-eration and hence value-creation are 'crucially dependent upon free gifts that capital claimed as its own' (Smith, 2013: 220). As feminists noted a long time ago, capitalism could not operate without the gift of cooperation. Skeggs (2011, 2014) recently highlighted the free 'gift of caring' from carers – mainly women – which is estimated at £119 billion in the United Kingdom alone. Such gifts originate in the general intellect – that is, they are formed more outside than inside the factory or the workplace. Hence capital's consistent and growing interest in the beyond of work – in the general intellect.

Located within the struggle to refuse, this gift of sociality to capital and the refusal to submit to capital as a social relation is always a part of capital's future. By this I mean that the struggle against capital holds the key to capitalism's development (as we saw in the Introduction). Despite the emergence of capital as the source of authority in the factory, it is the struggle against work that leads to economic development. Tronti (1965: 4; emphasis added) argues:

> Exploitation is born, historically, from *the necessity for capital to escape from its de facto subordination to the class of worker-producers.* It is in this very specific sense that capitalist exploitation in turn provokes workers' insubordination.

The increasing organization of exploitation, its continual representation at the highest levels of industry and society are, then, again responses by capital to workers' refusal to submit to this process. It is the directly political thrust of the working class that necessitates economic development on the part of capital which, starting from the point of production, reaches out to the whole of social relations.

Thus, in contrast to much Marxist theory, workers, not capitalists, are the driving force of change. Rather than merely experiencing or modifying change, workers *generate* it through their refusal of and insubordination at work. However, within this generation, and contrary to some post-workerist scholarship (Lazzarato, 1996; Hardt and Negri, 2000; Virno, 2004; Vercellone, 2007), I will argue that control of labour has not decreased as labour has left the factory, but rather that it is increasing and becoming more capricious as it aims for the total subsumption of society to capital (see also Smith, 2013). This control is growing in the increasing attempts to permeate the general intellect and control the social individual so that the individual becomes a subject of value totally engaged in activities that generate value or enable the capturing of value. As such, it attempts to collapse life into work.

As Marx highlighted, and as we shall see in Chapters 2, 3 and 4, with the expansion of the division of labour, the use of capitalist technology and more tightly integrated capitalist forms, the importance of capitalist control, authority and discipline grows. As we will see in Chapter 3, the recalcitrance of craft labour forced capital to divide the labour process further, which created the mass industrial subject whose recalcitrance then forced the creation of the New Deal and the Keynesian state's relationship to organized labour that was central to economic development (Baldi, 1972). Panzieri (1961) explains this need for ever greater planning as follows:

> The capitalist development of technology, as it passes through the various stages of rationalization, involves more and more sophisticated forms of integration, etc. – a continual growth of capitalist control. The basic factor in this process is the continual growth of constant capital with respect to variable capital. In contemporary capitalism, as is well known, capitalist planning expands enormously with the transition to monopolistic and oligopolistic forms, which involve the progressive extension of planning from the factory, to the market, to the external social sphere.

One sees elements of this in the non-linear transition from the formal to the real subsumption of labour. Simplistically speaking, within formal subsumption capital does not transform the labour process; rather, it takes hold of it through wage labour and forms of slavery and bondage (Banaji, 2003). It then uses this hold to force labour to produce for the market in order to generate profit and ensure the valorization of capital. As demonstrated in Chapter 3, the 'inside contract' reflects this formal subsumption. In real subsumption, capital constantly transforms the labour process in order to develop it intensely and to shift from an absolute to a relative extraction of surplus value. As we shall see in Chapters 2 and 3, scientific management is closely associated with this shift: first, through the initial subdividing of the labour process; and, second, through the use of constant capital to embed capitalist planning and control into the technology itself – with Henry Ford being most closely linked to this technological transition. Real subsumption entails the application of capitalist science to production and consumption via human resource management, technology, marketing and motivation theory, to name but a few (see Chapters 2, 3 and 4). Hence, it is important to bear in mind that organization theory, human relations, management sciences, regulation of communications or any form of increasing worker participation in the firm are integral elements in the rational management and planning inherent within capitalism (Panzieri, 1961). The state is also central to this because when capitalists developed into a class in response to labour's opposition to work, they increasingly required the state to plan economic development (Tronti, 1965, 1971). Business and management, sociology, psychology and economics all contribute to this subjugation. After this change came the transition of subsumption from the factory to society as Fordism developed both mass production and mass consumption (Tronti, 1971; Baldi, 1972; Hardt and Negri, 2000). Although it is hugely important, by stopping at the factory gate or the office door, early labour process theory (Braverman, 1974) underplays capital and management's desire for the total subsumption of society to capital.

Today, planning has moved out of the factory and into society as a whole because management is seeking to collapse the circuit of capital so that production and consumption occur almost simultaneously (Harvey, 1989: 101–200). This has been termed 'total subsumption' (Endnotes, 2010), wherein 'the whole society is placed at the disposal of profit' (Negri, 1989: 78). For example, one can see this planning in the advent of miniaturized, flexible, mobile technologies which ensure that we are always available for work and, through the re-targeting market (among other things), always available for consumption. Here, as with the labour market contract, capitalist planning is delivered to us as 'freedom': to consume; to work away from the factory, the office or the home; or to shop and organize as we travel and commute. However, rather than simply carrying a smartphone to freedom, we are carrying out capital's plan, because today this capitalist technology means our lives are ever more closely managed, tracked, calculated, assessed, modulated and recorded. In short, we are increasingly subject to management and planning or total subsumption (see Chapter 6).

We will see that, as planning and management have expanded, they have been constantly engaged in this struggle with labour, its composition and recomposition, with expropriating its knowledge and raiding sociality in all its forms for free gifts. The struggle to extract from and manage labour is the core element of class recomposition and hence of management, and, as such, it can never be simply left alone. Management needs to intervene constantly. One point of this book is to track management's growing interest in life outside of the factory and its – ultimately futile – attempts to subsume society totally to capital (Skeggs, 2014).

What follows is heavily influenced by these Marxist concepts. The free gift of sociality, antagonism, authority, hierarchy and discipline around work and cooperation is absolutely central to management thought and practice. In different ways, the first two management 'schools' of the twentieth century are deeply implicated in this compulsion, in the development of new lines of authority, in exploiting the gift of dissociated sociality, in subsuming labour to capital, in the desire to shape life within and, importantly, beyond the factory, and in their attempts to reconfigure the individual subject and hence to recompose the nature of labour and class, and ultimately to collapse society into the economy in a neo-liberal fashion. We cannot understand management without these Marxist insights.

Weber, Foucault and discipline

The second strand of influence comes from Weber's and Foucault's (different) emphases on discipline, practice, attitudes and the psycho-physical. In this section I wish to provide an account of how I will use Weber to examine management as an attack on labour through its overbearing emphasis on formal rationality and the centrality of discipline to capital. However, in relation to neo-liberalism and management, I will seek to emphasize an equally important and complementary strand to his work located in his ideas about leadership, bureaucracy and democracy (see Chapter 6).

For this chapter, the important insights of Weber come from his views on capitalist modernity and the growth of formal rationality, the rise of the bureaucratic form and the nature of discipline. These forms and practices were essentially about recasting social relations. As is well known, Weber (1978: I, 86–100) argues that formal rationality is typified by the growing importance of money, calculation, planning and double-entry book-keeping to achieve ever more control and profit. At the core of this change was the rise of goal-oriented rational calculation and the use of terms such as 'scientific', 'objective', 'ratio', 'percentage' and 'budgetary management'. Five aspects to this rationality are especially important for Weber:

1 valuation of all the means of achieving a productive purpose both in the present and in the future;
2 quantitative assessment of expected gains and actual results in order to compare every action;
3 periodic comparison of all goods controlled by the unit from the beginning of a particular period;
4 an *ex ante* and *ex post* verification of receipts and expenditures; and
5 an orientation to consumption based on needs that are defined through the principle of marginal utility.

Within this environment, money is the perfect calculating mechanism and double-entry book-keeping the ideal way of ensuring units within the enterprise compete. Thus, formal rationality is not a neutral concept because it 'presupposes the *battle of man with man*' (Weber, 1978: I, 93; emphasis in original) and it prioritizes new forms of producing and consuming, of organizing and of domination and authority (we will address these issues more fully in Chapter 6). Thus, for example, speaking of the factory, Weber (1978: I, 108) states: 'Strict capital accounting is further associated with the social phenomenon of "shop discipline"[1] and the appropriation of the means of production, and that means: with the existence of a "system of domination".' In examining this emerging system of domination, Weber rejects the argument that the (natural) market satisfied individual wants that were somehow out there and that the factory then dutifully provided. Rather, he argues that production is shaped by the twin processes of organizations creating new wants, desires and opinions, and of wealthy consumers who have the resources to consume and hence shape future production (and presumably taste).

One can see how these issues combine in the cultural transition that took place in the United States from 1880 to 1930. Lears (2000) argues that the growth of formal rationality and the bureaucratic organizational form led the professional and bourgeois classes to embrace a therapeutic and consumerist culture in order to achieve an authenticity and an experience that seemed to have been lost from (or was never achieved in) the previous pre-industrial era. This need for consumption was a push against the pricks of routinization in work and home life. Therapeutic culture encouraged people to view life as a project – a way of becoming rather than of being – or a never-ending, continuous improvement. Thus, domination, authority and power shaped work organization and the market and these then helped to shape the self so that the latter was never a neutral concept. As we shall see, managing subjectivity is a core capitalist battleground and Weber's insights on rationality and the bureaucratic form are important weapons on its terrain. I take these Weberian insights to suggest that the general intellect, the bureaucratic firm, consumption, public opinion, education and the outside of work all permeate and are central to work and subjectivity, and that this started early in capitalism, not with post-Fordism.

The growing importance and power of formal rationality meant that substantive rationality, or what we might call 'values', was altered. Substantive rationality organizes action and in many respects is based on clusters of values: for instance, friendship entails the cluster of loyalty, generosity and affinity, whereas beauty is based on a different set of qualities. These values act as a canon of belief as to how actions should be organized and oriented. As a self-confessed bourgeois, Weber argues that capitalist substantive rationality seems to be based on a belief that a minimum subsistence level for all citizens should be provided. Once this is achieved, it further appeared that the inequality emerging from the new (but not neutral) productive and organizational forms could be legitimated – wealth, power and authority could be redistributed in unequal ways. Therefore, although the formal and substantive rationalities of capitalism are separate, they appear to overlap or coincide enough to legitimate the emerging social order. As such, legitimation and the way it is formed (or not) is also a central element in his work on how humans exert power over themselves. Thus, in ways Weber, with his belief in methodological individualism, would not have accepted, I will argue the raiding of the collective free gift of the general intellect could be – and was – legitimated by the authority of capital so that the subject often saw this capturing of sociality and cooperation as a natural, legitimate and acceptable form of capitalist valorization. For Weber, many of these new forms and the manner in which they regulated life in practice were typified by that potential monster – the bureaucracy.

As we will see in Chapter 3, although he claims scientific objectivity in a way Weber does not, the engineer F. W. Taylor expresses much about the rise of instrumental rationality. Taylor's emphasis on the creation of a planning office for the entire production process is an early form of how Weber's 'files' organize 'the management of the modern office' (Weber, 1948: 197). The emphasis on bureaucracy and the organization of work via planned, written rules is central to scientific management. So, too, is Taylor's desire to make workers easily replaceable by other workers and to develop new lines of unequal authority and dependency. Weber's bureaucracy, with its focus on rational–legal rules, also takes us down this bureaucratic road. For example, Weber acknowledges that within a formal–legal rational system, judges (or any other skilled professionals whose job it is to interpret rules or procedures) would ideally be facsimiles of each other and hence replaceable (Weber 1948: 219). These links between Weber's bureaucracy and modern scientific management are obvious, and Clawson (1980) forcefully argues Weber's bureaucracy is not neutral but itself an outcome of class struggle. At the core of both, in different ways, is the issue of labour's substitutability and hence the (re-)emergence of individual dependency and subjugation to discipline.

However, for Weber, formal rationality and the bureaucratic form, with its planning and calculation, are both democratic in their initial intent, and in this they are similar to the market because both are 'Without regard for persons' (Weber, 1948: 215). Importantly, Weber highlights that this disregard for persons creates a tension between the democratic push which helps create bureaucracy and the anti-democratic nature of bureaucracy itself. He argues the desire to eradicate ascribed privilege, status and discretion generated the use of bureaucracy and the privileging of written rules and procedures, but, because bureaucracy relies on and foregrounds expert knowledge, those who are deemed 'expert' maintain, develop and expand their bureaucratic power to become a privileged group themselves – potentially a new type of aristocracy – while others are made dependent as individuals. As such, and unlike Taylor, Weber is fearful of claims to expertise and objectivity and of the bureaucratic organizational form, and he recognizes the powerful combination they make, with its capacity to create an unequal reshaping of social relations.

Essential to bureaucracy are the following: a clear-cut division of labour; specialization and an accompanying expertise; a hierarchical authority structure; a formal set of rules governing decisions and actions; an administrative group to record and maintain; an impersonal orientation to tasks; and a career path. Even today, in a world supposedly of flat structures, networks, entrepreneurship and intrapreneurship, these features pertain. Where would the 'new' economy be if it could not record, track, create rules for actions and decisions, enforce authority and divide tasks? All of these activities are central to contemporary work and social relations. For Weber, the office files or planning office have the potential to act like Hobbes's state – as an external force that could act as a power to guarantee the survival of the individual by punishing aberration (Federici, 2004: 150). The bureaucracy could stifle society and make us unfree; hence we required elite charismatic leadership to break us out of the routine (much of which overlaps with neo-liberalism; see Chapter 6).

Nevertheless, the anti-democratic bureaucracy – a form created by a democratic urge – goes on to reshape the world in such a way that it is increasingly necessary to the governed as they simultaneously lose their capacity to perform the tasks of governance without its assistance. In ways that resonate with Marx's analysis of capital and cooperation, Weber suggests that the bureaucracy that was generated to serve the citizen ends up confronting the individual as an alien productive authority to which he or she is potentially vulnerable. Thus, the bureaucracy has control over the populace, and the populace is both deskilled and confronted by an efficient, objective, rational, secretive, concentrated and powerful force that acts without regard to persons as people become means to an end. Bureaucracy becomes an external force. Famously, all of this means we are increasingly embroiled in the 'iron cage' of rationality (Weber, 1930/1985: 181). In this sense, Weber makes scientific management and the increasing division of labour problematic.

Central to bureaucracy's legitimacy is the rise of certification and education even when they are not functionally necessary (see Chapter 3). Within this, education and certification act as a new form of property (Weber, 1948: 240–4). The owning of this new property is based on economic resources and social position, and, as such, it further enables one economic group or class to dominate the rest of society. These newly emerging forms of property – located in an expertise that may not be very great – reinforce the anti-democratic nature of the dominant organizational form of the twentieth and twenty-first centuries. As we will see in Chapters 2 and 3, the expertise needed to organize these bureaucracies first had to be extracted from workers. Thus, in ways Weber only partially addresses, the extraction of knowledge is a moment of class expropriation. Furthermore, this emergent organizational form is itself characterized by discipline:

> The discipline of officialdom refers to the attitude-set of the official for precise obedience within his *habitual* activity, in public as well as in private organizations. This discipline increasingly becomes the basis of all order, however great the practical importance of administration on the basis of the filed documents may be.
>
> *(Weber, 1948: 229; emphasis in original)*

This is a crucial element of capitalism and management. Central to the bureaucratic organizational form, and indeed to management, is an emphasis on learning habits, obediently submitting to authority, the importance of written plans, and certification as a means of exclusion. Indeed, the bureaucrat as a form of subjectivity is created in these routines (Merton, 1940).[2] These 'habits' are used in an attempt to create the methodological individualism Weber places at the centre of his theory. Indeed, in today's dispersed economy, this rational, bureaucratic thread of control and logistics as habits, obedience, predictability and planning are used to coordinate activities across ever-increasing space. They have become more, not less, important. How else could Google track and mould your movements across time and space to generate advertising revenue? Information technology, the coordination of data and information within organizations and the use of the internet comprise a bureaucratic form – a new non-paper way of compiling Weber's 'files' or Panzieri's planning. Importantly, this process generates and shapes routines, is undemocratic and creates new power structures and systems of domination that largely leave the individual citizen or worker defenceless before impersonal bureaucracy, planning and management. They attempt to universalize and individualize simultaneously. As we shall see, the sciences of individuation – such as human resource management, economic utilitarianism, marketing, sociology and psychology – reinforce this domination because they seek to solve social and organizational pathologies in the private sphere through an emerging therapeutic culture (Mayo, 1933; Tronti, 1965; Lears, 2000; Illouz, 2008; Invisible Committee, 2009: 29–34).

Weber argues that bureaucracy goes beyond the state because it reproduces the state's relationship with the economy in very particular ways and, as such, is about the reproduction of socio-economic relations between individuals. In so doing, it constitutes human 'agency at the juridical level and hence helps to reproduce the social division of labour and its bureaucratic rationalisation independent of "individuals" and their particular attributes' (O'Neill, 1986: 46). The end point of this process arrives when individuals both self-discipline and are disciplined to fill particular roles (as we shall see shortly). As such, and to return to Marx, the independent subject is formally free to contract in the labour market because independence is achieved within the juridical sphere. Like many neo-liberals, Weber stresses the seemingly neutral role of law and regulation in shaping the relations of production. In his work, these regulatory and disciplinary forms, rather than valorization, determine economic activity.[3] Weber's analysis means the economy is seen as subject to the 'independent' laws of the market, which then discipline the whole of society – both capitalists and workers. The market is posited as free, even though it is not. Freedom is constituted in the juridical realm through the fair application of rules and regulations – that is, by the correct application of a rule (even if the rule itself is unjust), independence is seemingly maintained and hence social reproduction is facilitated. (Chapter 2 demonstrates some of the social relations of power inherent in the legal creation of US capitalism.) Importantly, the sphere outside of the state that seems most able to withstand the public bureaucracy (Weber's main target) is the private bureaucracy. Here, because private sector experts know their own field – the market – better than public sector experts, they can outmanoeuvre the state. Private bureaucracy and private expertise are thus both a higher form of bureaucracy and expertise and an even more undemocratic form of them (because they are private).

Importantly for Weber, the bureaucracy – be it private or public – as a rational, impersonal form is not ethical. Its form of domination is formally rational and without substantive values (Mommsen, 1974: 82). All rational impersonal institutions – the law, the market, the bureaucracy – are ethically neutral for Weber (Hennis, 1988: 90–103). For a relation to be ethical, it has to be personal. Weber (1978: I, 585) comments:

> every purely personal relationship of man to man, of whatever sort and even including complete enslavement, may be subjected to ethical requirements and ethically regulated … But this is not the situation in the realm of economically rationalised relationships, where personal control is exercised in inverse ratio to the degree of rational differentiation of the economic structure.

In this sense, Du Gay (2013a) is incorrect to argue that bureaucracy is necessarily more ethical than post-bureaucracy. Certainly, the bureaucrat conducts him- or herself in particular ways (Merton, 1940), but these need not be ethical. The instrumental rationality of bureaucracy means that they 'tend to submit everything to strict rational rules if only in order continuously to extend their own sphere of control' (Mommsen, 1974: 82). It was this tendency that, for Weber, killed off the 'personality' or that exemplary conduct and freedom which those who were dedicated to a task exhibited (Weber, 1948: 129–59; 1994: 309–69; Hennis, 1988). To suggest that bureaucracy – with its expansive, impersonal, formal rationality – might be a vocation ignores its lack of substantive rationality for Weber. In this sense, bureaucracy differs from politics or science.

The bureaucrat's task is to apply an impersonal rule even if he or she disagrees with it, 'as if it corresponded to his inner most conviction' (Weber, 1978: II, 1404). The bureaucracy and the bureaucrat can act in ways that are good or bad because the rules are impersonal and hence 'ethically neutral' (Hennis, 1988: 102). It was this potential to spread the impersonal, instrumentally rational form of domination that would undermine the personality and individual freedom, and push ethics to the private sphere (Hennis, 1988; 100), that led Weber to assert the necessity of charismatic authority, with its capacity to break routine and, as we shall see in Chapter 6, to dominate the mass while seemingly remaining answerable to them (Mommsen, 1974: 72–94; 1981). Indeed, by re-establishing the personal, this call for the charismatic had a better claim to being ethical because of its prioritization of the personal (as indeed might post-bureaucracy). As Weber (1978: I, 585) suggests, the patriarchal, the traditional or the charismatic is more ethical than the impersonal. For him (Weber, 1978: I, 582), rational methods of control enable the strong to become independent from the weak and hence less charitable or obliged to them. The depersonalized bureaucracy – like the market – is without ethics, and importantly both are like the market Mises (1944) describes, which seeks to push formal rationality into all corners of social life (Gane, 2013, 2014).

A further difficulty with the bureaucrat as ethical is that the link between him or her and the incorruptible nature of bureaucracy is built on such individuals' interest in status over profit (Weber, 1978: II, 1108–9). This status is intimately linked to education from which the bureaucrat derives position, but which was technically unnecessary (Weber, 1994: 83). Furthermore, democracy must oppose bureaucracy, even though it is increasingly dependent upon it (Weber, 1978: II, 991). Indeed, Weber praises US workers for rejecting the growing power of bureaucracy embedded in the civil service reforms in favour of being ruled by 'upstarts of dubious morality' (Weber, 1994: 69). Weber fears bureaucracy as a means to usher in a status-driven society of 'new aristocrats' (Titunik, 1997; see Chapter 6). Such views must question the idea that Weber saw bureaucracy as an ethical force and rather link it to theories by people such as Burnham, whom Orwell (1946) accused of an elite totalitarian managerialism.

Foucault takes many of these formal–legal rational themes of calculation, objectivity, expertise, planning, habits and procedures and folds them into his concept of normation and biopolitics. In this sense, he builds on Weber's work by extending the latter's rational legal framework to the body, the mind and the conduct of everyday life (Gordon, 2014). To quote John O'Neill (1986: 45; emphasis in original):

> his [Foucault's] studies of the prison, hospital and school go beyond Weber in grounding the legal-rational accounting techniques for the administration of corporeal, attitudinal, and behavioural discipline. Foucault thereby comple-ments Weber's formal-rational concept of bureaucracy and legal domination with a *physiology of bureaucracy and power* which is the definitive feature of the disciplinary society.

Here, Foucault's work on populations and biopolitics is central. He argues there are three elements to what he calls normation: the management of the population; the creation of desire; and the shaping of public opinion (Foucault, 2007: 71–6). As we shall see in Chapter 6, all three are important to neo-liberalism and to manage-ment. They are essentially about securing the population through the shaping, sifting, cordoning off, including or excluding elements of that targeted population.

Management of the population

Foucault views population as a dependent variable that has to be managed by calcu-lation, analysis, reflection, science, expertise, rationality and/or authority. This entails putting in place the correct systems, processes, flows and circulations, all of which become central to achieving security and exercising power. One way of thinking about this is Adam Smith's (1981: 524–42) claim that merchants generate the productive function of linking demand to supply by circulating goods, and thereby regulate the production and consumption of goods and encourage new positive forms of behaviour and habit – what Smith refers to as 'thrift and good management' among the 'inferior ranks'.

Smith argues that the merchant regulates consumption via market price and thereby lessens the possibility of famine. For example, during a bad harvest, if there is a set or just price, corn would simply be sold to the population at this usual price. However, the population would then consume it as in normal times without knowing, until it is too late, that these were abnormal times and that there was a shortage in annual production, thereby creating famine. However, if the price is regulated by the market and thus based on the merchant's self-interest and superior knowledge of supply and demand, it will fluctuate to reflect market conditions. What Smith outlines here is the 'new' way in which the market should operate. This is located in new and superior forms of knowledge, expertise and experts, and supposedly generates better population management techniques while creating new routines, new habits, new norms and new forms of calculation, analysis and accuracy. Thus, the market, like the factory or the prison, would and should discipline people to behave in new ways. However, this does not simply emerge. It entails struggle as different classes and groups respond to these changes in their ways of being (see Federici (2004) on the earlier – very gendered – nature of this struggle; or Thompson (1971) on the struggles during the emergence of this new moral economy in England). Smith (1981: 527) recognizes this struggle and seeks to recast the merchant as productive rather than as an object of 'hatred and indignation'. Within these processes, subjects are thus newly disciplined, entreated and forced to behave in new ways, and roles and behaviours are recategorized as progressive (or not).

A more recent corporate example of managing populations can be seen in the rise of modern organizations and human resource management. For example, in the United States this happened along race lines, wherein management explicitly sought to divide, and set against one another, the various 'races' within the labour force (Roediger and Esch, 2012).[4] Roediger and Esch (2012) forcefully demonstrate how, in the period before the Depression, race was used to divide the Anglo-Saxon workforce from the other 'races'. One can clearly see this in early human resource management. For example, Blackford and Newcomb (1915: 117) identify nine physical variables to the human capacity to labour. These are:

1 colour;
2 form;
3 size;
4 structure;
5 texture;
6 consistency;
7 proportion;
8 expression; and
9 condition.

In a manner that echoes the fine colour distinctions made by French colonists in the slave economy of Haiti (James, 2001), the US population is then divided into blonds and brunettes, wherein the latter with pink–white skin are deemed white and all others are deemed non-white (within which, again, there are important variations).

Unsurprisingly, as the population is divided, sifted, evaluated, analysed, calculated, measured and judged, white Anglo-Saxons emerge as best suited to lead. Each 'race' is disciplined and 'scientifically' slotted to its level. Within this, and provided it is managed correctly, each individual will harmoniously fulfil his or her allotted race role unless that individual is somehow pathological or exceptional. Thus, the population is 'scientifically' studied to develop roles, tasks and expectations (a practice that will re-emerge in this book). These studies are then used to place workers in the most suitable function, depending on their position within the population. Furthermore, deviation from the norm or the designated role is deemed a moment of individual rather than societal pathology. (A central issue to be examined in what follows is the individualizing of capitalism's pathology.)

Today, even if the crasser racism of this has been eradicated within human resource management, the basic tenets of population management remain (Townley, 1993). If we are tested enough, management believes it will get our measure and continue to assign us harmoniously to its tasks. Indeed, presently, one could only argue we are more sophisticated in our 'scientific' methods, because the principle has not altered. For example, Blackford and Newcomb (1915: 115) comment:

> If by elaborate tests, with special instruments, one could learn all about the aptitudes and character of a willing subject, the method would be almost valueless for practical use. We meet and deal with people under conditions which would make it impossible either to examine the palms of their hands or the bumps on their heads or to subject them to psychological tests.

Contemporary human resources may not examine palms or bumps, but it psychologically tests for aptitude and character via interviews, personality tests, IQ tests, attitudinal tests, appraisals, weekend test centres, outward-bounds programmes, references and leadership training. The modern subject may or may not be willing to engage in such population manipulation, but they are subjected to it regardless. Combine this with schooling, media or the family – what O'Neill (1986: 57) calls 'secondary socialisation' – and these practices appear to be more, not less, numerous as management continues to sift populations and discipline the individual, and indeed society, into accepting such power and control flow naturally from social organization. Planning the population is central to modern life.

The satisfaction of desire

The second element of security is the satisfaction of desire: that is, a problem of governance becomes the satisfying of individual desires even if they are not necessarily in the individual's interest. By so doing, governance delivers a collective interest – private desire and the public good become one and the same. Foucault uses Quesnay to describe this desire, but one can equally see it in the work of Adam Smith, who links the individual's self-interest directly to the public good. As we shall see in Chapters 2 and 3, the emergence of the factory is important here because inherent within it is the idea of a population that can survive only by selling its labour. As such, it is a population that needs to reproduce itself as a consumer in the (unequal) marketplace (Lippmann, 1914/1985, 1938/1943). Furthermore, the routinization of work encourages people to look for pleasure, release, meaning in consumption. As Mills (1951: 237) puts it: 'Everyday men sell little pieces of themselves in order to try to buy them back each night and weekend with the coin of "fun".' It is this doubly free population that is most subject to the persuasive machine of capitalism unleashed through propaganda, public opinion, advertising, marketing, schooling, corporate activity and the state (Lippmann, 1922; Bernays, 1928; Sellers, 1991; Lears, 2000). Although we should not see a monolithic or thought-out strategy regarding corporations and desire, corporations nevertheless used desire to manipulate and limit possibility. As Lears (2000: 10) puts it:

> The problem was that manipulative advertisers distorted this critique of bourgeois culture (a belief in positivism and rationality) beyond recognition. Emphasizing human irrationality, they used that emphasis to limit, rather than deepen, understanding of the human condition – to reject human freedom, rather than acknowledge its precariousness. Instead of transcending bourgeois culture, manipulative advertisers (like early therapists) helped revitalize it and transform it, creating new modes of hegemony for new managerial elites in the coming era of corporate capitalism.

Central here were managerial groups as both producers of this hegemony and as those who were also most subject to it as consumers. As those housed within the bureaucratic corporation, they managed the generation of many of the products and the desires of capitalism, yet they were also subject to anxiety about their usefulness, their roles, the nature of their work and the idea of life as a project. As such, they were also an essential target market for important and reshaping ideas about production, consumption, domesticity, gender roles and science and objectivity (see Chapters 2 and 3). Their compliance, their inability to refuse and their new desires were all central to capitalism. The cognitive and affective maps and potentialities of the general intellect were increasingly subject to persuasion and desire – they were simply too important to leave alone.

Thus, the population needed to be manipulated and persuaded to have certain types of desire in order to prioritize some potentialities over others and to create the market as the natural place to fulfil these desires and potentials (Lippmann, 1914/1985, 1922; Bernays, 1928; Bauman, 1998). By so doing, desire aims to discipline the property-less into developing a sense of commitment to the ownership of private property. A key element in the shift from competitive to monopoly capitalism was the rise of consumption and the creation and manipulation of desire and potential to generate new productive and consuming subjects of value (Bernays, 1928; Lippmann 1935, 1938/1943; Gramsci, 1971; Weber, 1994; Kracauer, 1998; Lears, 2000). As a result, wages replaced craft control of production as the key political issue in industrial relations (Panzieri, 1961; Tronti, 1971: 14; Baldi, 1972). Indeed, Harvey (1989) has argued that the contemporary world of post-Fordism has further developed and manipulated desire and potential in an attempt to shorten the circuit of capital and collapse production and consumption to enable the further extraction of value. However, importantly, desire and potential can also act as ways within which to reject the concept of work (Weeks, 2011). Thus, desire itself becomes a site of struggle.

Shaping public opinion

The third element of security is the turning of the population into a species or into the public. By this, Foucault means that the population becomes a series of regularities so that it has 'opinions, ways of doing things, forms of behaviour, customs, fears, prejudices and requirements' (Foucault, 2007: 75). Importantly, we develop routines and habits that are malleable and subject to influence via the experience of work, the market, education, media, propaganda, campaigns and religion – the general intellect is permeated by all of these influences. Today, attempts to access and shape the species in this regard have widened and deepened. However, even in 1825, Thomas Hodgskin was arguing that UK journeymen needed to attend to public opinion if they were to influence change. Similarly, Brown (1972: 222) notes the importance of public opinion in the United States of the nineteenth century. Indeed, much of the twentieth century is about the creation and structuring of public opinion by the elite. As Bernays (1928: 9–10) puts it:

> Whatever attitude one chooses to take toward this condition, it remains a fact that in almost every act of our daily lives, whether in the sphere of politics or business, in our social conduct or our ethical thinking, we are dominated by the relatively small number of persons – a trifling fraction of our hundred and twenty million – who understand the mental processes and social patterns of the masses. It is they who pull the wires which control the public mind, who harness old social forces and contrive new ways to bind and guide the world.

Pareto (1991: 93–4), when discussing the non-rational thinking of the mass, also suggests they are swayed by public opinion even though they are unaware of it. More savagely, the neo-liberal theorist Walter Lippmann (1922) suggests some simply need to be manipulated; they need to have their interiority managed. Through the manipulation of public opinion, the elite could shape the Cartesian conscience of the non-rational masses. The importance of public opinion and its manipulation is stressed by a wide variety of right-wing scholars. In different ways, Michels (1949: 152–4), Weber (1978: II: 1459–60), Burnham (1943: 113), Hayek (1944: 117), Mayo (1919) and Donham (1933) all argue that manipulating public opinion is a central elite management task if capitalism is to survive (see Chapters 3, 4 and 6).

For Foucault (2007, 2008), modern governance is the focal point of the struggle over the nature of the relations between groups and collectivities and their attempts to shape the three elements of normation and recast social organization – what he calls biopolitics. This struggle is a materialist conflict located in the daily practices of how people produce, consume and reproduce their existence. It is about routines, habits, rhythms, manipulation, legitimacy, affect, desire and potentialities. It is about what I call the general intellect, wherein sociality is disciplined and regulated. It is my contention Foucault's disciplinary power is important here. It is this production and reproduction that give rise to the discourse of how one should live. I will use these insights to examine management within this process but always against the backdrop of the Marxist emphasis on accumulation, social relations and class recomposition because it is here where one finds the origin of power.

All of this returns us to Weber, the conduct of life and management. In his discussion of discipline, Weber (1948: 253–64) mentions, albeit briefly, the factory, scientific management, power and the psycho-physical. He argues that discipline is essentially a moral, political and cultural exercise, the aim of which is to get people to eclipse their individual subjectivity and fuse it with a wider collectivity – the military, the monastery or, later, the factory. The more total subsumption, the more disciplined the group or society becomes. Ideally, then:

> The content of discipline is nothing but the consistently rationalized methodically trained and exact execution of the received order, in which all personal criticism is unconditionally suspended and the actor is unswervingly and exclusively set for carrying out the command. In addition this conduct under orders is uniform. Its quality as the communal action of a *mass* organization conditions the specific effects of such uniformity. Those who obey are not necessarily obedient or an especially large mass, nor are they necessarily united in a specific locality. What is decisive for discipline is that the obedience of a plurality of men is rationally uniform.
>
> *(Weber, 1948: 253; emphasis in original)*

At the core of discipline is the accommodation to 'routinized skill' aimed at the eradication of the 'irrational emotional factors' and the creation of a 'devotion to a common cause' (Weber, 1948: 254). As indicated in the extract above, the aim of discipline is to eradicate what was seen as the random, the non-rational or the irrational.[5] As we shall see, scientific management and human relations insist on this obedience. As such, the creation and management of discipline is a moral and political project aimed at achieving compliance in what we might think of as a Goffmanesque total institution. Discipline emerges initially in things such as the 'warrior communism' of early military forms. For example, in Sparta individual soldiers were socialized into communities, embraced the community goal as their goal and, by so doing, became ideal military (and later religious or worker) subjects. Discipline is thus central to management. Even when management says it seeks initiative and interpretation, it actually seeks the correct or the disciplined initiative and interpretation of management. When it seeks potentialities it seeks only *certain* potentialities. Management and discipline are interchangeable.

Central here is the military as it was the original disciplined institution. Importantly, the road to this military discipline entailed a loss of what Marx called ownership of the means of production. Before a soldier could be disciplined into the communal, he had to be disenfranchised in terms of ownership of the tools of his trade and of his ability to subsist without the military collective. Just as in Marx's analysis of employment, force and dependency create discipline.

> What has concerned us here has been to show that the separation of a warrior from the means of warfare, and the concentration of the means of warfare in the hands of the war lord have everywhere been one of the typical bases of mass discipline. And this has been the case whether the process of separation and of concentration was executed in the form of oikos, capitalist enterprise or bureaucracy.
>
> *(Weber, 1948: 261)*

This military discipline, Weber informs us, is the 'ideal model of the modern capitalist factory' (Weber, 1948: 261). The aim of the factory – and of management – is to rationalize work performance. However, Weber (1948: 262) also comments:

> The final consequences are drawn from the mechanization and discipline of the plant, and the psycho-physical apparatus of man is completely adjusted to the demands of the outer world, the tools, the machines – in short, to an individual 'function'. The individual is shorn of his natural rhythm as determined by the structure of his organism; his psycho-physical apparatus is attuned to a new rhythm through a methodical specialization of separately functioning muscles, and an optimal economy of forces is established corresponding to the conditions of work. The whole process of rationalization, in the factory, as elsewhere, and especially in the bureaucratic state machine, parallels the centralization of the material implements of organization in the discretionary power of the overlord.

Like Foucault, what Weber is indicating here is the way in which disciplining processes reshape the social, psychological and physical conditioning and potential of the subject. The factory is thus a space of capitalist production and of producing the new subject 'wherein the individual would function at once as both master and slave' (Federici, 2004: 150). Obviously, this reshaping is not neutral; rather, it is set in particular directions that are determined by 'the overlord'. Ideally, this dulls individuality through the prioritization of our 'devotion to the common cause'. But, to return to Marx (1976: 270–80), this common cause is one that is unequally created in the workplace and its relations of production because it occurs after the worker has been stripped of his or her ownership of the means of production. Thus, contrary to popular belief, capitalism, management and discipline are set against individuality.

O'Neill (1986) suggests that Weber, in his short commentary, underplays the role of a disciplinary society because he does not rigorously link the disciplining of the military to the disciplining of religious communities, the prison and the factory. In short, he does not join the dots in the capillary manner of Foucault. As such,

Weber is too cognitive in his approach to capitalism. While accepting this, Weber does emphasize the psycho-physical impact, the loss of individuality once disciplined, the development of new routines, and the lines of authority and power embedded within these transitions – aspects of which this reading of management will seek to develop. Through utilizing Weber and Foucault alongside Marxism, what follows will examine management's attempts to achieve this disciplining of the worker and how the worker resists, escapes and succumbs to this process to create tomorrow.

I will contend that the pursuit of profit, the shaping of the general intellect and the capture of its free gifts are central to this disciplining process. As we will see, discipline leads management to focus as much on the routines and attitudes of workers as on productivity, and as much on outside as on inside the factory, office or store. That is, it focuses on ensuring the reproduction of the social organization of capitalism and its profitability, thereby opening the way for various compromises, losses or setbacks to ensure reproducibility (which is important to neo-liberalism; see Chapter 6). Indeed, Mayo (1919: 40) explicitly chastises nineteenth-century managers for ignoring or downgrading the importance of the system's reproducibility in favour of short-term profit. As we will see, in this process, viewing scientific management and human relations as complementary becomes important. Crudely, Taylor seeks to discipline workers through deskilling to ensure that the production process, as a totality, confronts the labour force as an unknowable entity, while Mayo seeks to discipline workers' subjectivity and sociality so that they find meaning through new routines within or driven by the private enterprise and come to see it as the space where they can fulfil the human need for sociality, desire or potentiality and thereby devote themselves to the 'common cause'. Management thus simultaneously acts in a Cartesian and Hobbesian manner in Federici's (2004: 148–55) terms. By 1940, these management and disciplining processes had given us the routinized bureaucratic organizational form that, at least partly, encouraged the pursuit of meaning beyond its borders. Likening this control to 'a much more totalitarian system', Edwards suggests:

> [W]hat distinguishes bureaucratic control from other control systems is that it contains incentives aimed at evoking the behaviour necessary to make bureaucratic control succeed. It is this *indirect* path to the intensification of work, through the mechanism of rewarding behaviour relevant to the control system, rather than simply to the work itself, that imposes new behaviour requirements on workers.
>
> *(Edwards, 1979: 148 emphasis in original)*

Here Edwards is lighting on the need for workers to self-regulate, to display obedience and to acquiesce to management control; in short, to be disciplined, in Weber's sense. Manipulation becomes a key managerial battleground (see Mills, 1951: 110). The worker's refusal of work, his or her embrace of consumption, leisure, non-work and a rejection of the totalitarian form are at the heart of these struggles.

Management, authority and the return to status

A contemporary of Weber, Mayo and Taylor who examined the issue of the bureaucratic organizational form and authority was the elite theorist Robert Michels. When writing about political parties as organizations, Michels argued that societies were naturally made up of a mass of people and the elite. The elite were endowed to manage and to organize society because they were superior intellectually, economically and through their breeding and hereditary background (Michels, 1915: 80–92). It was not that the working class could not produce leaders; rather, the argument was that these leading working-class individuals were already naturally an element of the elite or, according to Pareto (1991: 72–89), the elite of the working-class movements were disproportionately bourgeois (see also Weber, 1994: 336). Michels further suggested that the masses were grateful to leaders and that they wanted to be led. Thus, he comments:

> The masses experience a profound need to prostrate themselves, not simply to great ideals, but also before the individuals who in their eyes incorporate such ideals ... This need to pay adoring worship is often the sole permanent element which survives all the changes in the ideas of the masses.
>
> *(Michels, 1915: 67)*

For Michels, the masses are malleable and need leadership, otherwise they will simply drift. In short, they need management (this theme is taken up in Chapter 6). Furthermore, because they have been accustomed to being ruled, they are obedient, indolent and 'need a considerable work of preparation before they can be set in motion' (Michels, 1915: 56). Obviously, it is leaders who put humans in motion. As with many thinkers today, Michels felt that the worker needed to be led. Here, capitalist authority emerges not from dissociated sociality but from natural leadership – a recurring theme in management (Bass and Steidlmeier, 1999).

In his analysis, Michels (1915: 23–40) argues that the masses are irresponsible and 'pathological', and that although organization may start out as a mass form, it quickly and necessarily ends up being controlled by the few because of the apathy and incompetence of the mass and the natural abilities of those who lead – thus 'organization implies a tendency to oligarchy' (Michels, 1915: 13). While acknowledging this, Michels finds it problematic because he is ultimately interested in democracy and why it is impossible as a result of the power of leadership and the weakness of the mass (Scaff, 1981). This is in contrast to Weber, who is more focused on how leaders can dominate the mass (Mommsen, 1981: 111; Scaff, 1981; see Chapter 6). The elite use organization to shore up their position, to manipulate and to lead the mass (see also Pareto, 1991: 55–7). Echoing Weber, Michels argues that political organization starts with a democratic impulse but ends up undermining democracy and replacing it with leadership, and that this tendency grows as the organization expands. At the heart of this process is the division of labour, which necessarily increases with more organization and hence enables leaders undemocratically to control the lengthening hierarchy as 'a mass which delegates its sovereignty to the hands of a few individuals, abdicates its sovereign function' (Michels, 1915: 28–9). As we shall see in Chapters 2 and 3, this increasing division of labour is neither natural nor neutral but is based on the violent expropriation of knowledge from the 'mass' and its transference to the elite.

Underpinning this view is a harsh analysis of the mass, which is deemed to be incompetent and apathetic when compared with the leadership (something neo-liberal management seeks to exploit; see Chapter 6). As with Weber, expertise, which might not be very profound (Michels, 1915: 83), enables leaders to act increasingly in an anti-democratic way. This 'expertise' is often simply about the day-to-day running of the organization and controlling its committees (although Michels also stresses communicative capability). Thus, organization is inherently anti-democratic and leaders come to lead because of the division of labour within the organization, leaders' expertise, their authority in committees, and the incompetence and acquiescence of the mass. It is the routine knowledge of day-to-day organizational processes, rather than some innate ability, that is central to this leadership, but the elite achieve this position in the first place because they have elite social backgrounds, education, authority and legitimacy. Organizational position and the desire to achieve it, not abstract expertise, are the essence of leadership.

Furthermore, this is at least partly achieved and legitimized through the new property form of certification. Michels argues that even democratic organizations, such as left-wing political parties or cooperative firms, tend towards oligarchy because this is a fundamental truth of all organizations. Central to this tendency is the 'right' of leaders to lead. They do so because they are rational, better educated, more competent and in control of the division of labour through which they both secure their position and seek to reduce the position of labour. As such, leaders can legitimately claim they should not be 'overruled by the majority which does not really possess any reasoned opinion of its own on the matters at issue' (Michels, 1915: 151). Yet again, the mass simply has irrational emotions and ill-thought-through opinions (also see Pareto, 1991). Organizational power and authority are about class, just as in Smith's analysis of the division of labour. Organization and the increasing division of labour become ever more important in a society that is increasingly planned. Controlling labour inside and outside of work is a necessity for this managerial aristocracy.

Building on Weber, Michels argues that bureaucracy is central to the elite maintaining their power. It is anti-democratic as a form of authority, and it enables authority to be exerted through control of the division of labour and technical expertise. The state bureaucracy also enables the capitalist elite to provide a place for the declining petite bourgeoisie with something akin to sinecures and thereby purchase their support (Gramsci, 1971: 277–320 makes a similar point). Thus, organization necessarily creates a world of rulers and ruled because of the 'technical indispensability of leadership' (Michels, 1915: 400). Within all of this, the mass and its sociality are predestined to be manipulated. While arguing that democracy and revolutionary movements have progressive qualities that open up society in certain ways, Michels concludes that these normally recede because of the weakness of the mass. He thus believes:

> The objective immaturity of the mass is not a mere transitory phenomenon which will disappear with the progress of democratization *au lendemain du socialisme*. On the contrary, it derives from the very nature of the mass as mass, for this, even when organized, suffers from incurable incompetence for the solution of the diverse problems which present themselves for solution. Because the mass *per se* is amorphous, and therefore needs the division of labour, specialization, and guidance.
>
> *(Michels, 1915: 404)*

Here Michels argues that new, undemocratic and seemingly legitimate forms of domination and authority are located within bureaucratic organizations. He chooses to focus on progressive left-wing organizational forms precisely to argue this point. For organizations with a fine division of labour, domination is inevitable. The division of labour that Smith made so central to his progressive capitalism is thus a tool of domination (something of which Smith was aware; see Chapter 2). Michels argues that this elitism is natural because some are destined to exert authority and dominate – usually, but not necessarily, the individuals at the top of the existing social hierarchy (see also Pareto, 1991). Central to this authority is the division of labour, natural ability, expertise, capacity to communicate, effort, position, the incompetence of the mass (which itself had to be created; see Chapters 2 and 3) and their desire to follow. That is, the mass is to be disciplined and to exhibit what Weber called 'devotion to the common cause'. A society of organizations is thus an undemocratic and elitist society.

However, as we saw in the Introduction, an analysis of capitalist history reveals not that the mass is incompetent but that it leads change in society and points the way to economic development. Nevertheless, one of the fundamental truths of management is that it actively seeks to use the division of labour to create a deskilled, malleable and obedient labour force – it uses fragmentation and deskilling in an unsuccessful attempt to manufacture incompetence. Although management scholarship is rarely connected to elite theory, this position peppers the work of classic management thought because management itself is elitist and undemocratic. As we will see, these views are implicitly, if not explicitly, endorsed by both scientific management and human relations. They emerge most obviously around the division of labour, the superiority of managers, the necessity of discipline and obedience, and the natural leadership qualities of the organizational elite. They also emerge in the corporate desire to manipulate consumers through marketing and advertising in the following manner:

> to some advertisers, the implication was clear that human minds were not only malleable but manipulable. And most potent manipulation was therapeutic: the promise that the product would contribute to the buyer's physical,

psychic, or social well-being; the threat that his well-being would be undermined if he failed to buy it.

(Lears, 2000: 9)

For management, the irrational mass needs to be soothed after the monotony of the new work regime – consumption acts as a salve to capitalism (Kracauer, 1998). But this also means our communicative, cognitive and affective skills are similarly subject to manipulation. Again, some producer and consumer potentialities are prioritized over others.

One can see elements of this elitism in Taylor's work on management. For example, he comments that management's key task is to shape workers' subjectivity: 'The most important and difficult task of the organizer will be that of selecting and training the various functional foremen who are to lead and instruct the workmen, and his success will be measured principally by his ability to mould and teach them' (Taylor, 1903: 1416). Equally, he argues that obedience to leadership is absolutely central to management:

> Perhaps the most important part of a gang boss's and foreman's education lies in teaching them to promptly obey orders and instructions received not only from the superintendent or some official higher up in the company, but from any member of the planning room whose function it is to direct the rest of the works in his particular line; and it may be accepted as an unquestioned fact that no gang boss is first to direct his men until after he has learned to promptly obey instructions received from any proper source, whether he likes his instructions or the instructor or not, and even although he may be convinced that he knows a much better way of doing the work. The first step for each man is to learn to obey the laws as they exist and next if the laws are wrong, to have them reformed in the proper way.

(Taylor, 1903: 1417)

Here Taylor anticipates Weber on the bureaucrat – a person who should obey. In all his writings, Taylor essentially dismisses the worker's right to organize production; he expropriates worker expertise and knowledge; he endorses management's right to manage and lead; he praises the rise of management's expertise; to manufacture incompetence, he simplifies work as far as possible through his extension of the division of labour; and he demands absolute obedience to leaders. Having extracted knowledge in an attempt to render workers dependent, he advocates the rise of the managerial expert elite with a right to lead. Taylor's planning room functions like Hobbes's state within which workers need to be led and disciplined. He perhaps differs from Michels in that he does not think the workers are incompetent. Indeed, in one sense he feels they are very competent, intelligent and capable of organizing, and that is a problem – hence his concern with the practice of soldiering (where workers attempt to control the pace of work) and his absolute desire to crush the competence of workers (see Chapters 3 and 5). He argues that workers need to be controlled and managed and to exhibit blind obedience to the authority of men of a 'higher calibre' (see Chapter 3). As we shall see, here Taylor is endorsing the need for acquiescence within the organizational division of labour. The elitist tendency of management 'science' is very much at the dark heart of modernity's project (Panzieri, 1961; Federici, 2004: 133–63).

Mayo, as the father of human relations, equally endorses authority and leadership in a manner that chimes with the elite theory of Michels and Pareto. He, too, was associated with the Pareto circle at Harvard. Central to this elite view of organization is the incompetence, irrationality and malleability of the mass. As we shall see in more depth in Chapters 4 and 6, these views very much coincide with those of Mayo. In his book *Democracy and Freedom*, he argues explicitly that workers are irrational and easily led by pathological politicized activists. Workers need to be disciplined back into the fold, and this is the moral duty of managers. Managers are charged with the leadership role of saving civilization because the state or labour are not only incapable of performing that function but are actually a direct threat to civilization. As Mayo puts it when discussing the evils of government regulation:

> With regard to its main purpose, moreover, this method [state regulation] entirely fails; proprietors and managers tend to become not more humane but less so. This is not merely because they resent 'interference', but also because the court deprives them of their social responsibility for the way in which they treat their employees. The court takes from the employer the right to make humane decisions.
>
> *(Mayo, 1919: 50–1)*

Following Weber, the law is rational and impersonal and, as such, incapable of ethics, unlike the direct personal relationship between employer and employee. Mayo is also sceptical about the benefits of democracy itself and supports a public choice understanding of the state. He equates modern democracy with the rise of state control. As he says:

> Modern democracies bear some resemblance to the historic tyrannies in their misconception of the art of government. All the objections which mankind discovered to the 'divine rights of kings' might be urged with equal force against the principle of State control of social activities. 'State control' implies a reversion to the very condition of things which democracy was designed to destroy; and especially so, when our political leaders altogether misconceive the nature of the social will.
>
> *(Mayo, 1919: 63)*

Thus he sees the state as an entity captured by the politicized mass because political parties and their leaders necessarily crave power, respond to electoral prejudice and stamp out diverging opinions with an iron law of conformity (Mayo, 1919: 14–30). He feels that such a proposition is to be feared because political leaders will respond to the irrationality of the workforce and their numerical superiority (as we shall see in Chapter 6, this is a neo-liberal view of democracy).

Mayo's work on the irrationality of workers enables him to propose reactionary and authoritarian views about leadership and elites. He argues that the working class was dislocated with the advent of capitalism, and its norms, rules and socialization practices were uprooted. This uprooting, which entailed privatization of the commons, bondage and slavery, the disciplining of workers (especially women) and the expropriation of knowledge in a variety of ways (Banaji, 2003; Federici, 2004), left the working class unable to adjust to its new role within the division of labour and the organization – that is, it could not or would not adapt to the role of the subservient, dependent, disciplined worker. Such a proposition left workers incapable of controlling their emotions; hence they were irrational.

Conversely, managers are much better adjusted to the new division of labour because they control their emotions, they have Cartesian self-control and they use the emerging bureaucratic form to develop their careers (see Bendix, 1956: 306 for an insightful critical analysis of Mayo). Managers can and do rationalize, control and understand their emotions, and this is why they have the right, the capability and the duty to assume leadership (Bendix, 1956: 313–17). The leadership elite understand both themselves and the non-logic of the mass, thereby making their work productive and, more importantly, morally and socially necessary. As such, the private sector, not the state, should take the lead within society because it is not subject to the electoral pressures of the irrational, prejudiced mass and it simultaneously disciplines workers.

Further than that, Mayo provided a legitimating rationale for management itself at a time when the bourgeoisie was undergoing a period of change, if not crisis. Lears (2000) highlights how the elite was concerned with its own role, its weakness, a loss of authenticity, its removal from more 'natural' agrarian and hardier work, the anonymity of urban life and its protection in the corporate form (this is also reflected in the elitist worries of Pareto (1991)). This concern with weakness also engendered fears about the bureaucracy as a less competitive space than the entrepreneurial form. Furthermore, it brought with it the attendant need to be communicative. By stressing leadership and the civilizing importance of corporate management, Mayo allayed these fears and helped to legitimate the emerging corporate order and its hierarchical forms (Bendix, 1956). He provided a rationale for the emerging managerial aristocracy.

Mayo explicitly rejects classical liberal individualism and liberal competition in favour of leadership, organization and cooperation. In doing so, he argues that society will disintegrate without this leadership. For example, he comments:

> *If there is no leadership and no social* organization to order the distribution of necessary commodities, the principles discovered by the logic of economics will apply. The disorganization of a specific society and the lack of organization between societies are thus indicated as exceedingly important human problems by the findings of the economists. These are problems that nowadays are thrust urgently upon our attention.
>
> *(Mayo, 1949: 37; emphasis in original)*

Given that liberal individualist economics could ask but not answer these questions, Mayo argues for leadership, organization, cooperation and obedience. His notions of leadership and authority function in ways similar to those of Weber and Michels with the proviso that Mayo has perhaps even less faith in the progressive role of democracy (Michels, 1915: 400–5; Mommsen, 1974). Here, leaders who control organizations in the private sphere will save society from disintegration. Like Taylor, Weber and Michels, Mayo (1919: 52–3) endorses an elite-managed, private-organization-dominated society. One reading of all this elitism holds out the possibility that all were in favour of at least elements of a fascist economy wherein corporate leadership is actively concentrated and supported through legislation, strong links with the state, the creation of cartels, the privatization of parts of the state through state sales, loans and contracts, and the curtailing of competition (see Merlin, 1943; Sohn-Rethel, 1978). However, although all (albeit Weber with some exceptions) would prefer the corporate elite to dominate the state elite because they are less subject to the irrational mass, and hence lines of authority, leadership, obedience and expertise are much clearer, this elitism is different from fascism (Mommsen (1981: 115) rightly rejects the idea that Weber was a fascist). Nevertheless, it is important for two reasons. First, it acts as a justification for anti-democratic hierarchies and forms of domination. Second, because elitism is a key aspect of neo-liberalism whose theorists use it to enforce the market. But an underplayed arena of elite neo-liberalism is the central aspect of elite use of the work organization as a major institutional force for the attempted creation of the neo-liberal subject. This directly implicates management and the work organization as one of the key vehicles for the neo-liberal project. In so doing, it also legitimates the entrenchment of a new caste and the decline of liberal democracy (see Chapter 6).

Compulsion and violence

To return to Marx, I see management and capitalism as located in physical violence, the violence used against subjectivity, the necessity of compulsion and labour's desire to refuse these. As Marx highlighted, this compulsion starts in the supposedly free contract made in the labour market. It is then exercised within the organization through forms of cooperation, divisions of labour, expropriation, expertise, technology and authority. The aim of this compulsion is to achieve discipline in Weber's sense: that is, it is attempting to mould labour so that it comes to see its interest as the interest of capital and hence willingly offers 'devotion to a common cause' that is the valorization of capital. In so doing, the individual worker-subject's creativity, discretion, judgement, interpretation and knowledge are manipulated and expropriated by management for capital and the individual is made replaceable. This is the unachievable goal of management and it entails permeating the factory, the office, the worker's soul and the sociality of the general intellect.

I use the term 'violence' in a manner similar to Benjamin in his 1992 essay 'On the Critique of Violence' (Benjamin, 2008). In that article, he suggests that law has two forms of violence – founding and reinforcing. Founding law is where one legal system is overthrown and a new one established. Reinforcing violence is the legal violence of the everyday – police, courts, contracts and so on. Interestingly, the German word Benjamin uses – *Gewalt* – does not simply mean violence; it also means authority, coercion, (executive) power and force. These other meanings are at play in this book. Equally at play is a broad interpretation of law to mean an appeal to expertise, to regulation, to rules and to science as well as to law. I will use this method of thinking to analyse management because this, too, is what it does – it whittles down judgement, discretion and potentialities in favour of a restricting authority aimed not at use but at surplus value. It prescribes, it regulates, it measures, it calculates and it limits interpretation in the interests of some anonymous thing called 'profitability', 'organizational need' or 'the market'. In short, it does violence.

One might think of founding violence as the 'bloody legislation' outlined by Marx (1976: 896–904). This legislation was used to usher in a whole new regime and method of regulating labour and the representation of labour (see Banaji, 2003; Federici, 2004; Roediger and Esch, 2012). One can see it in the violence of re-regulating social and economic life in eighteenth-century England as described by Thompson (1971) in his work on the riot and the moral economy, or in his earlier paper (Thompson, 1967) on time and discipline in the workplace. Indeed, he expressly uses the term 'discipline' to describe that new regime, commenting:

> If the transition to mature industrial society entailed a severe restructuring of working habits – new disciplines, new incentives, and a new human nature upon which these incentives could bite effectively – how far is this related to changes in the inward notation of time?
>
> *(Thompson, 1967: 57)*

As Thompson and Federici (2004) describe it, adapting to these new working habits was a violent and forceful affair aimed at expropriating worker knowledge and attempting to turn them into Michels's obedient mass. The work of the regulation school theorist Michel Aglietta (2000) also suggests that the transition from Fordism to post-Fordism was a similar moment of violence as new forms of social regulation were built out of the class recomposition that we are currently experiencing. But there is also the violence of conserving the new regime. This comprises the more prosaic violence of compulsion – the selections, the appraisals, the scientific application of technology, the shaping of incentives, the moulding of subjectivities, the planning, the everyday authority of the manager, the calculation and the discipline – as well as physical violence – the beating of children in the workplace, the slavery and bonded labour, the sexual abuse and the crushing of the vulnerable (Pollard, 1965; Banaji, 2003; Roediger and Esch, 2012).

Within all of this, one central tendency of management is to limit individuality. Discipline, and therefore management, is about merging the individual with the common cause and hence limiting individual creativity, interpretation or judgement. It is always about reshaping the subject, sociality and the general intellect. However, if management were actually to achieve this discipline, it would cease to be able to capture the free gift of sociality. It is this gift of sociality that emerges with human cooperation, and it is through this cooperation that we achieve our individuality. We are social before we are individuals. Thus, management is a contradictory process of seeking to capture and control the sociality of labour necessary to the production of value, yet it always needs labour to find ways to refuse this control in order to innovate. One merely has to think of the increased importance of open innovation as a strategic management tool just as the corporation stops innovating. Open innovation is itself built on a privatization model that is built on the ideas of sociality inherent in open-source software (Ettlinger, 2014) – a further reach into the general intellect.

What follows will attempt to use the theoretical insights provided by Marxism, by Weber and Foucault and by elite theory to understand and explain classic management knowledge and to highlight some of the fundamental tendencies within management thought more generally. In so doing, Marx, the general intellect and the pursuit of surplus value will be paramount. It is only with the backdrop of capitalist accumulation that one can make sense of the ways in which new forms of organization, of the expropriation of knowledge, of authority, of planning, of technology and of discipline come about. They are located in the logic of making the capitalist organization of social relations reproducible. In this pursuit, capital supports some potentialities over others. The need to reproduce these social relations ensures that capital has to concede, suffer loss, learn from labour and develop new ways of planning this reproducibility and surplus extraction. Ultimately, this reproducibility is what management and its violence are about.

In what comes next, it will appear that labour almost invariably loses – to deny a transition from, say, formal to real subsumption would be pointless – but this loss is never total and the future comes from within it. Resistance and struggle deliver tomorrow. If management's victory were total, capitalism would petrify because on its own it cannot invent tomorrow. That comes from labour, the class struggle and class recomposition. And yet, as we will see, management continually searches for ultimate, if futile, control.

Notes

1 As we will see, Taylor is at the forefront of this shop discipline.
2 As we will see, routine was an essential issue for Mayo (1937). He wished to create new routines with new emotional attachments in order to save capitalism.
3 Foucault (2008: 163) makes a similar point and argues that, *contra* Marx, the economy is shaped by, rather than shaping of, these regulatory and disciplinary forms in Weber (and indeed also in the ordo-liberals) – hence, the economy is not dominant. What follows rejects Foucault's summation and sees these disciplinary and regulatory forms emerging precisely from class recomposition within the relations of production (Clawson, 1980). As Federici (2004: 15–16) suggests, Foucault's analysis leaves him unable to discuss the origins of disciplinary power adequately.
4 One example of the manner in which race was deployed was the process of land grabbing in the building of US infrastructure (Roediger and Esch, 2012). For example, for every mile of track laid on the Transcontinental Railway from Iowa to San Francisco, an

astonishing 6,400 acres of mostly Native American land was handed to the railway companies. In this sense US capitalism resonates with the expropriation of wealth from peasants, women and indigenous populations that is synonymous with capitalism (Federici, 2004) and indeed land grabs today.

5 Irrationality is an important issue, as we will see in the next three chapters, because Mayo accuses the working class of irrational emotional activity and hence declares that they are not to be trusted.

PART II

The dark nature of
management knowledge

2

'CLASS STRUGGLE WITHOUT CLASS?'[1]

Attempting to manufacture incompetence

A parable of nineteenth-century America: the Amherst Carriage Company

Why, in the mid-1830s, did a group of workers, journeymen and citizens petition the Senate and House of Representatives of the Commonwealth of Massachusetts about the formation of the Amherst Carriage Company? Such a petition to state legislatures was not unique or indeed even uncommon in the early nineteenth century (*Harvard Law Review* 1989; Sellers, 1991; Perrow, 2002). Looking back, it may seem odd that the reason for the petition was the application by seven businessmen from the town of Amherst to incorporate a limited company. Two hundred and fifty-four others wrote in support of the application. At the time, creating a limited company required state approval and the demonstration of a public benefit in order for incorporation to be granted. Indeed, defining the public good emerges as a recurrent theme in the early nineteenth century (Brown, 1972: 219). By way of public benefit, the original seven businessmen rather weakly suggested that the 'business may be conducted with greater safety to themselves and to the community, and with more ease and economy' (Commonwealth of Massachusetts, 1938: 3). As we will see from this correspondence, the normation of the market was not accepted in the manner Adam Smith would have wanted. The market form, the extent of property rights, the types of organization and the purpose of production were all still debated and open to interpretation.

In follow-up correspondence in February 1837, supporters of the company proffered that the carriage company of L. Knowles and Co. had ceased trading and only a limited company could replace it (they never specified why the company had to be limited). They further suggested that incorporation would save jobs, capital and buildings, workmen's houses and working people's way of living. They then went on to state:

they have no doubt but the stock to a large amount will be readily taken and actually paid in, which will enable them to go on with the work in a safe and profitable manner, not only safe for themselves but vastly more so to the community; and we believe by incorporating said company the Legislature will be encouraging a branch of industry which will be very useful and creditable to the state.

(Commonwealth of Massachusetts, Senate Document, 1837a: 5)

In the remonstrance to the application put forward in January 1837, fifty-eight craft workers from Cambridge, Massachusetts – all of them involved in the carriage industry – argued incorporation should not proceed because it was not in the public interest. They maintained that, within the state, a high standard of carriage-making already existed without incorporation, and that incorporation would infringe upon the workers' 'just and equal rights' (Commonwealth of Massachusetts, Senate Document, 1837b: 12).

In March that year (Commonwealth of Massachusetts, House of Representatives Document, 1837b: 3), twenty-two individuals from East Bridgewater wrote to oppose the incorporation of the company, arguing that corporations are necessary only for very large, mainly state, endeavours and that 'in other cases where no such necessity exists, corporations are an evil, in as much as they tend to monopolies, and affect injuriously the less affluent portions of the community'. They then commented that corporations were less community spirited than other organizational forms because they had limited liability. In other organizational forms, individuals had more to lose due to their greater liability and hence they had a larger stake in seeing both the community and their business thrive.

Fifty-six craft workers from Salem further petitioned against the incorporation, arguing that corporations, again because they are privileged entities in terms of liability, damage the community, damage the workforce, damage those already in the business of carriage-making and, finally, damage the small entrepreneur because they are anti-competitive, tend towards monopoly and 'crush the small establishment' (Commonwealth of Massachusetts, 1837b: 5).

A second request for incorporation the following year was also accompanied by petitions and remonstrances (Commonwealth of Massachusetts, House of Representatives Document, 1838). Those in favour of incorporation argued that the investors had small sums of money and that incorporation would enable them to use that money wisely and secure their futures. They commented:

The petitioners for an incorporation are young, industrious and virtuous persons, of limited capital, no one of them having anything like a sufficient means to carry on a very limited business, and by uniting all their means they may be able to do a small, and, we think, profitable business, and should this be denied them they will be obliged to stop the business, sacrifice their property, and go to work for other capitalists, who have the means of carrying on the business, and if not of monopolizing it.

(Commonwealth of Massachusetts, House of Representatives Document, 1838: 4)

This particular petition represents an early form of the 'shareholder democracy' so beloved of neo-liberals ever since. What is presented in it is the new capitalist subject located in industriousness, thrift, investment and virtue. In the petition, supporters argue that incorporation would allow mutual help and frugal investment, and assist the workers' social mobility; or, as ex-President John Quincy Adams expressed it, incorporation allowed 'the poor ... Females and children ... the widow and the orphan' to prosper (see *Harvard Law Review*, 1989: 1892–5). The petition represents a small example of Foucault's normation as the emerging form of governance posits the private and the public good as one and the same. As we will see in a moment of founding violence, the legal profession established a new legal system to assert this new governance and the merging of the private and the public despite the opposition of the population (Sellers, 1991; Perrow, 2002).

However, yet again, craft workers wrote to oppose the application, suggesting that incorporation leads to monopoly and then to higher prices. Furthermore, they argued corporations are anti-entrepreneurial and deny the young social mobility. They continued to argue that 'acts of incorporation do not add to the safety of the community from *fraud, deception* and *loss* and should not be granted except there is a large capital required' (Commonwealth of Massachusetts, House of Representatives Document, 1838: 8; emphasis in original). In this rendition, the corporation was a privatizing sectional interest set against the community – here, the private and the public goods are different and in conflict.

Finally, in a telling petition, from 6 February 1838, journeymen craft workers argued that, as journeymen, they looked forward to being their own masters when they would not have to relinquish to others the value they created (perhaps these workers were acknowledging the increasing gap between masters and journeymen in the early nineteenth century – see Thompson, 1978; Sellers, 1991: 285–8; Wilentz, 2004: 237–48). These journeymen argued, 'we believe that incorporated bodies tend to crush all feeble enterprise, and compel us to wear out our days in the service of others'. They went on to dispute the right of capitalists to earn money from a business in which they had no skill and of which they had no knowledge. They commented: 'incorporations put means into the hands of inexperienced capitalists, to take from us the profits of our art, which has cost us years of labour to obtain, and which we consider ought to be our exclusive privilege to enjoy' (Commonwealth of Massachusetts, House of Representatives Document, 1838: 10). For these craft workers, the incorporated capitalist organization represented both increased personal dependence and the direct capture of value created by them by an unknowledgeable class – a group often referred to simply as 'speculators'. In this correspondence knowledge, not capital, should be paramount in production. Here, the workers are disputing capitalists' right not only to manage but to have any involvement in what the workers saw as 'their' (the workers') craft – capitalists should not own their (the workers') means of production, which was theirs by right through their craft training. They did not desire the cooperation the capitalists would force on them and, just as importantly, they rejected the idea that capitalists had valuable knowledge or expertise – at this stage, the capitalist was not the organizing authority described by Marx. For these workers, value was created not by capital but by the art of their craft, by cooperation and authority located in skill and knowledge, and it was only this art that made capital or the physical means of production of any use, because capital would lie idle without labour and its energy and knowledge (Hodgskin, 1825). Here, craft itself was viewed as the inalienable property of the craft worker. It could not simply be sold as other commodities were because it was bodily attached to its owner and gave him or her independence. As Virno (2004) describes, and as we saw in the Introduction, the hierarchical nature of skill within the division of labour offered these workers personal independence and with this, as we shall see, a central role in the shaping of the social order. As F. W. Taylor put it in his testimony before the Special House Committee on Scientific Management, craft was the capital of the craftsman; and Gary Becker (1962) would make precisely the same argument fifty years later. But these nineteenth-century workers disagreed with such a proposition. For them, knowledge, skill and craft were not capital in any straightforward sense. Rather, they were the escape route to an independent way of life. Knowledge and capital were in conflict.

These workers were defending a way of thinking about work and life and a regime of production located in craft wherein the worker, after years of training, was entered into a guild as a master with political rights and duties to the community. In this way of thinking, craft workers may be partly capitalist but they could not act simply as capitalists – although it could be argued that such terms are problematic for explaining their contradictory class position (Clawson, 1980). As with their craft skill, their money capital was restricted or tied – it was not a 'normal' capital. They had not the freedom to move it or invest it anywhere – to invest in carriage-making, one had to be a master craftsman oneself or subordinate one's capital to a master craftsman in the field. First and foremost, authority and social mobility came from skill and know-how, not from capital. Speculation as a means to a livelihood was left to unknowledgeable people with wealth who sought to thrive on the labour of others. Craft workers were socialized into work and life as apprentices and journeymen, they shared knowledge, built robust social organizations, imbibed ways of living, had firm beliefs about how work should be organized and managed, and had strong views about the role of work within life (Mills, 1951; Montgomery, 1987; Wilentz, 2004). The distinction that emerged later between work and life did not exist for these workers. A cooperative and shared sociality was the foundation stone of craft work.[2] This era is emblematic of a production process Marx called 'the formal subsumption of labour to capital' (Marx, 1976: 1023–34; see also Wilentz, 2004: 23–61). But in America at the time this craft regime was under threat and was subject to a set of violent processes that left it declining as an innovative political force by the middle of the century (Gordon et al., 1982: 18–47).

Reflecting the fact that in 1838 the craft workers' 'Artisan Republic' (Wilentz, 2004) was in the midst of terminal decline, the Amherst Carriage Company was (of course) incorporated by the Commonwealth of Massachusetts. This small defeat for labour acts as a parable of the times. Through a variety of practices and struggles, capital slowly established hegemony over American society and its ways of living – so much so that within a century Bernays (1928: 75) could comment:

> Public opinion is no longer unfavourable to the large business merger. It resents the censorship of business by the Federal Trade Commission. It has broken down the anti-trust laws where they think it hinders economic development. It backs the great trusts and mergers it excoriated a decade ago.

However, before capital and its corporate organizational form were accepted, a series of struggles needed to occur. These included: the decline of a rural subsistence economy; the expansion of the state and infrastructure (the two were closely related); the rise of the factory; the destruction of a craft regime of accumulation; mass immigration; a repositioning of gender relations; an elite-led reconfiguration of property rights and economic life; and the end of individual autonomy as a worthy or realistic life goal.

The key outcome of these struggles was the unintended emergence of a new political subject. This political subject – the mass industrial worker (see Chapters 3 and 4) – dominated the twentieth century, although it has been suggested that it is in decline today (Hardt and Negri, 2000; Gill and Pratt, 2008). Within approximately fifty years of the Amherst Company's incorporation, F. W. Taylor would demonstrate how capitalists could best exert authority and manage and control workers via the piece-rate and the division of labour (see Chapter 3); within seventy-five years, corporations were attempting to harvest not only the individual's labour but his or her subjectivity (see Chapter 4); and within a hundred years, workers were simply expected to accept new forms of authority as unquestionably legitimate (see Chapter 5). Thus, it reads as though the founding violence of the first half of the nineteenth century was achieved and capitalism could run merely on reinforcing laws, regularities, routines and practices. However, needless to say, normation never ran so smooth and the discipline discussed in Chapter 1 was never fully achieved. Each of these encounters with the nascent and then formed working class pressurized capitalism and reshaped the basis on which capital as a social relation operated because labour changed the terms of its own reproduction through various forms of refusal (see Hardt and Negri, 2000: 204). But first and foremost, this refusal created the capitalist class, shifting it from an economic interest of the *individual* capitalist to a *class* interest seeking to use the state to dominate labour politically and subsume the whole of society to capitalist interests (Tronti, 1965: 5; Negri, 1989: 79).

It is easy to forget this early hostility to the corporation or label it as an understandable but unjustified fear of the future. However, this was not merely suspicion, mild fear, wariness of corporate excesses or a general tiredness and disappointment – although it was perhaps all of these, too. Rather, it was active hostility. The corporation was seen as elitist, anti-community, a vehicle with which to promote those *without* knowledge or skill, expropriating the value created by those *with* knowledge or skill (see Montgomery, 1987: 42–6), tending towards monopoly, and concentrating economic and political power – all of the things Michels (1915) suggested. It was based on a belief that the corporation was pathological. And, of course, it is (Bakan, 2004). This antagonism was not anti-market per se (Perrow, 2002). Indeed, Brown (1972) argues that the US citizen at the time embraced modernism/capitalism and was adept at calculating risk, time, the market and the importance of political changes and ideologies. Equally, Negri (1999: 152–4) argues that the United States was a bourgeois state in the nineteenth century. Nevertheless, wariness remained. It was located, at least initially, in a belief that capital and the corporation would create or cement the elite, and hence the populace implicitly feared Weber's dark premonition and Michels's desire – they feared it would destroy a better society located in individual independence.

Within fifty years of Smith's *Inquiry into the Nature and Causes of the Wealth of Nations*, his benign capitalism was in crisis, and it has remained there ever since. This crisis has always been rooted in living labour and who controls production, where and how production takes place, the origins of the knowledge central to its taking place, how it is to be managed or regulated, and who reaps the rewards and why. In the first half of the nineteenth century, America fought a violent battle for its own soul, and the world has, if only partially, been shaped by the aftermath of this conflict. One of the central issues of pre-Civil War America was how to manage the questions and crises embodied in the Amherst Carriage Company's petitions and remonstrances.

Demise of a limited political subject?

Jacksonian or antebellum America was a fraught space with a number of sides pitted against one another. At the heart of this struggle was the fate of perhaps the primary political subject of the 1800s – the autonomous craftsman and the small farming families who lay at the heart of Jeffersonian and then Jacksonian politics. These were the majority of the population, although because of the undemocratic and elitist nature of many of the states, much of the population was denied a voice and thus they were not always the majority of the electorate (see Sellers, 1991: 107–8; see also Brown, 1972, who presents a different view of this economic and political participation). Out of this struggle would emerge a new class consciousness wherein allegiance would shift from being a member of a trade to being a member of the working class (London experienced a similar shift in the late nineteenth century; see Stedman-Jones (1974)). In the 1820s, the United States started to witness struggles between masters and journeymen as the latter attempted to enforce a decaying moral economy based on agreed book prices; mobility in the form of apprenticeship followed by journeyman status followed by the equality of masters, authority and cooperation in the workplace located in skill, knowledge and craft (even if it was more unequal than this idealized image; see Marx, 1976: 1023–9); the importance of non-market relations between labour and small artisan bosses; craft control in the workplace; and a rejection of incorporation (Montgomery, 1968; Clawson, 1980; Sellers, 1991: 285–9; Wilentz, 2004: 145–72). However, by 1825, the Artisan Republic was dying. Of course, the United States was not alone in this – as E. P. Thompson (1967, 1968) observed, the UK experienced a similar set of struggles with a similar set of outcomes.

All of these struggles over production concerned the very future of America. At the time this was common knowledge, hence the widespread nature of political participation and discourse (Brown, 1972; Foner, 1995). People realized that they were involved in the founding violence of a new society, hence the intensity and creativity of their struggles. The coming of the corporation would help shape this future, but it was often reacting to other forces. In a real sense, the corporation symbolizes the changes taking place in the antebellum period. These changes deeply impacted upon working life, gender relations, religious belief, nativism, the fate of Native Americans, slavery, the colonization of parts of what was then Mexico, immigration, consumption, family life, inequality and ideas about unemployment. However, at this stage the corporation's importance was also largely symbolic – it was a portent of the future. Hostility to incorporation and to the tripartite expansion of the market, the state and the corporation was the central political characteristic of the craft worker and the small farmer, and this characteristic shaped political and legal struggles in pre-Civil War America (the troika of state, market and organization are similarly central to the neo-liberal management project today; see Chapter 6).

In time the Artisan Republic would be coerced into submission and the craft worker and farmer would be replaced by the mass industrial worker. This struggle gave rise to new ways of being, new ways of managing production, new desires and potentialities, new ways of shaping public opinion, and new beliefs about the relationship between knowledge and capital. However, in creating the mass industrial worker, it also developed different, broader concepts of equality to those of the craft worker, even if racism, sexism and discrimination around sexuality remained (Roediger and Esch, 2012). Within the late nineteenth- and early twentieth-century mass industrial subject, there was awareness among working people of what bound them. This binding was located in opposition, and it was this solidarity and opposition that helped to create the twentieth century. In contrast, the craft worker was hierarchical and had long resisted solidarity with unskilled labour. Indeed, Federici (2004: 92–7) directly implicates craft workers and the state in the first onslaught of primitive accumulation that was directed against women. For instance, she argues that craft workers sought to downgrade female labour and expropriate female knowledge about the body and reproduction. Following Foucault, she claims that the state sought control of the body because it was the producer of labour. It most especially sought control of the female body and the knowledge relating to reproduction because women, their bodies and the knowledge they held were all central to the reproduction of labour. The body was a body to be disciplined as labour power. Craft workers, fearing female competition, engaged in this campaign of expropriation and facilitated the turning of women and their labour into a 'new commons': that is, as a free gift to be used by capital and the male worker in the reproduction of social relations. Hence, the equality of craft was always limited.

Virtuous labour as independence

Sellers (1991) argues that the defining traits of early nineteenth-century US life were: a belief in the virtue of working people; the centrality of individual/familial independence or autonomy; the embrace of market forces alongside a belief that they needed to be checked to halt their corrosive nature; and a suspicion of elites, the corporate form and an expanding state. All of these concerns shaped Jacksonian America. What they symbolized was a desire for economic independence to ensure that the political subject was free from undue influence at the ballot box and in political life more generally (Brown, 1972). For working people, this autonomy was found in land and craft skill, and it allowed them to resist those who would put 'self-interest' before the 'public good'. Success was not simply measured by wealth but also by not being beholden to others, by being independent.[3] By avoiding the travails of the working people of Europe or the slaves of the South (Foner, 1995), a working (white) person could be virtuous and autonomous rather than a mere obliged servant to a parasitic and aristocratic elite (Perrow, 2002: 22–47). Foner (1995: xii) suggests, 'Not only personal dependence, as in the case of a domestic servant, but working for wages itself were widely seen as disreputable.' Indeed, as late as 1861, in his State of the Union address, Abraham Lincoln commented on the primacy of labour before capital:

> Labor is prior to and independent of capital. Capital is only the fruit of labor, and could never have existed if labor had not first existed. Labor is the superior of capital, and deserves much the higher consideration. Capital has its rights, which are as worthy of protection as any other rights. Nor is it denied that there is, and probably always will be, a relation between labor and capital producing mutual benefits. The error is in assuming that the whole labor of community exists within that relation. A few men own capital, and that few avoid labor themselves, and with their capital hire or buy another few to labor for them. A large majority belong to neither class – neither work for others nor have others working for them. In most of the Southern States a majority of the whole people of all colors are neither slaves nor masters, while in the Northern a large majority are neither hirers nor hired. Men, with their families – wives, sons, and daughters – work for themselves on their farms, in their houses, and in their shops, taking the whole product to themselves, and asking no favors of capital on the one hand nor of hired laborers or slaves on the other. It is not forgotten that a considerable number of persons mingle their own labor with capital; that is, they labor with their own hands and also buy or hire others to labor for them; but this is only a mixed and not a distinct class. No principle stated is disturbed by the existence of this mixed class.
>
> *(Lincoln, 1861)*

To return to the Introduction, to Chapter 1 and to Marx, labour rejected the free contract capital offered because capital was merely the fruit of labour and the contract was viewed as subjugation, not freedom. As we shall see, capitalist coop-eration and authority would have to be forced on to the worker, who, heretofore, had used the division of labour and scarcity within the labour market to accumulate not (only) wealth or capital but independence.

The nineteenth century is the story of the eradication of this independence and way of thinking and its replacement with a seeming acceptance of wage dependency. But before this way of thinking collapsed the material conditions upon which it was based needed to be violently destroyed and the class structure recomposed. Importantly, this recomposition was twofold – it created both the mass industrial worker and the capitalist class, which was transformed from a collection of individuals into a class in the crucible of labour's refusal. As the century progressed there was a growth in wage dependency – by 1850, wage earners outnumbered slaves and by 1860 they outnumbered the self-employed (Foner, 1995: xv–xvi). The US labour force had been degraded into accepting wages for a living – they had been made wage dependent within the division of labour (see also Foner, 1995: 32).[4] In the 1890s, the American Federation of Labour (AFL), under Samuel Gompers, accepted the elite ideology of free labour and argued that free labour was wage labour (see later) and that labour should organize around favourable wages and security of employment rather than independence. The ideal of autonomy, at least temporarily, had been buried in the emerging biopolitics (Foner, 1995: xxxviii).

However, it would be wrong to see this as purely negative, because wage labour also entailed making capital dependent; it destroyed the patriarchal and racist society of the Old Republic; it led to a vociferous and less deferential working class who, 'driven by feelings of insecurity' (Sellers, 1991: 32), demanded democracy and political entitlements that might not otherwise have been forthcoming; and, despite all the gender, ethnic and racial tensions, it forged the working class that created the twentieth century (Montgomery, 1974; Sellers, 1991; Wilentz, 2004; Roediger and Esch, 2012). Hence, we should view these struggles with sympathy while embracing the creativity of what was unleashed because it left capitalists following the creation of the new world that emerged out of working-class struggles over their own reproduction (Tronti, 1965).

Prior to this transition, rather than being wage labour, free labour had embodied being an independent artisan or an independent farmer. As we saw above, Lincoln argued that wage labour was a temporary situation experienced by the young and/or the journeyman before they moved on to autonomy (in reality, at this point wage labour was also experienced in the factory by women and children and on the infrastructure projects built largely by landless migrants and immigrants; see Gumus-Dawes, 2000; Perrow, 2002; and Roediger and Esch, 2012). Lincoln suggested that advancement and social mobility were ingrained in US society and they entailed the achieving of autonomy – by implication, then, to be permanently dependent was to be a slave, a woman or childlike (Federici, 2004: 200). Lincoln argued that advancement and autonomy were 'the order of things in an equal society' (quoted in Foner, 1995: 16), notwithstanding the fact that by 1861 the growth in US inequality had been staggering: between 1774 and 1860, the richest

10 per cent of the US population saw their share of the country's total wealth increase from 49.6 per cent to 73 per cent; the top 1 per cent saw their share rising from 12.6 per cent to 29 per cent, with most of this increase occurring after 1820 (Sellers, 1991: 238). So Lincoln was wrong about working life, but workers already knew that equality was a myth and that the reality was one of people forced into wage dependency with its new forms of authority and planning (Marx, 1976: 439–54). What had crushed equality was capital (and increasingly, as the century wore on, capital in the shape of the corporation). Michels's organizational elite were in full swing. The rise of the large firm and the corporation would ensure that capital as a social relation dominated society and that worker knowledge was either expropriated or downgraded to new lines of authority; that is, 'capital is productive of value only as a *relation*, in so far as it is a coercive force on wage-labour, compelling it to perform surplus-labour, or spurring on the productive power of labour to produce relative surplus-value' (Marx, 2000: 93; emphasis in original). The nineteenth century is the story of this compunction. As we shall see, unsurprisingly, labour resisted the compunction of this violence, this 'coercive force'.

An encroaching capital: an encroaching market and the decline of independence

As stated above, at the centre of early nineteenth-century autonomy and free labour were the issues of craft and land. The vastness of the US landmass was important even at the time of the American Revolution. Indeed, these 'open' spaces led Edmund Burke to propose a peaceful solution to the tensions between Britain and the United States (Negri, 1999: 139–41). In terms of land, autonomy was bought through the expropriation of Native Americans and the destruction of their way of life because land was used as a moment of individualizing property acquisition. As we shall see, as space is closed off, the expropriation upon which it is based (Negri, 1999: 143) turns on the 'local' or the Yankee population in the form of capitalist social relations, and becomes imperialist and expansionist by starting to mine its 'own' citizenry and population for profit. In areas that were long planted – especially the North East – land became increasingly limited as the population settled and expanded (Gordon et al., 1982: 48–99). In other words, as land became more difficult to command, capital accessed the white population – Weber (1994: 68) too laments the ending of 'free' US land as one factor in ensuring the increasing serfdom of the American worker. Brown (1972) argues that the doubling of population every generation from 1730 onwards put pressure on this system until the early nineteenth century, when land further west was 'reopened' by new communications designed to enhance expansion.

The predominant early nineteenth-century subsistence lifestyle of independent farmers required large families, a strict gendered division of labour, limited inter-action with the market economy, and communities where mutual help was taken for granted; that is, the economy reached into and was built upon a set of free gifts (Sellers, 1991: 3–34). Key to this economy was not the large farm but the large family. Having large families to work the land of a small farm intensively provided for most of the family's needs in terms of food, clothing, shelter and warmth. This was how the economy reproduced itself. It was facilitated by the fact that, for the first half of the nineteenth century, much of the United States' rural space was a 'great forested commons' (Sellers, 1991: 10) where people could hunt, fish and gather berries as part of their own reproduction. At this point, it had not been completely subject to the enclosures and primitive accumulation that were familiar in Europe (Marx, 1976; Federici, 2004). The goal of this independent family was simply to reproduce itself. This shaped its economic activities. It entailed a strict patriarchy, six to eight children, late marriage, marriage as a practical endeavour rather than a love affair, extended lactation, considerable sexual freedom for the young and a notable lack of interest in organized religion. Farmers had a variety of skills and occupations so that they could adapt to changing economic circumstance or changing family stages: for example, acting as a local carpenter in the winter months to generate income (Sellers, 1991: 9–15). Multi-tasking was also central to the craft worker (see Montgomery, 1968).

Debt and taxes were anathema to this subsistence economy because both pulled the farmer into a cash nexus (Sellers, 1991: 15).[5] Hence, there was considerable fear of an expanding state with its attendant taxes and of the creeping market economy. Much of the first half of the nineteenth century embroiled these subsistence farmers in a struggle over the role of state and federal government and the desire to facilitate or reject a capitalist economy. Jacksonian America wanted to curtail the state and the market. In so doing, it was in a constant fight with capitalist interests, state elites and the judiciary as it tried to hold back or limit large infrastructure projects, new corporate forms, new forms of property, new ways of living, new ways of calculating, new norms and new forms of authority and discipline.

One example of this state–market relationship was the pro-business Republican New York legislature financing of the Erie canal at a cost of $7 million between 1817 and 1825. This money was raised via taxes and had the effect of cutting freight costs from $100 to $9 a tonne so that by the early 1830s the canal was shipping twice as many goods to New York as the Mississippi did to New Orleans; by mid-century, it was carrying over $200 million in freight annually. Such investments had the twin effects of raising taxes and rapidly expanding the market. As New York did, so too did other states in a bid to stay ahead in the capitalist race (Sellers, 1991: 81–90). What today we could call 'economic development' exacerbated a fault line between a minority who sought state–market expansion (and saw these as largely one and the same) and a majority of citizens who were at best ambivalent, if not downright hostile. In this struggle over and resistance to these changes, the capitalist class was cemented. This fault line emerges most especially in the workplace, in the new forms of organization with their new lines of authority, planning and cooperation, and in the increasing division of labour. As Tronti (1965) suggests, the capitalist class was forged in reaction to worker resistance to the changing division of labour, and to overcome this resistance it turned to the state to plan the economy and society.

In this form of development, transportation cost money, opened up subsistence communities to markets, and forced these communities into a cash economy (Perrow, 2002). Indeed, President Monroe explicitly linked transportation to the delivery of a capitalist society. He argued that each area of the United States had its particular market advantage in the country's division of labour and only through massive infrastructure projects could such a bounty be delivered to US citizens. However, in delivering such a bounty, he felt the Republican Party would have to alter the Constitution and break with the Jeffersonian notion of the Union as a compact between equal states in favour of one wherein the federal state was paramount. (As we shall see, a powerful judiciary was decisively in favour of this vision, despite the opposition of the people.) In so doing, he abandoned the ideals of his colleague Jefferson and moved towards the doctrine of his old enemies, the federalists – capitalist class formation in action (Sellers, 1991: 82–5).[6] This was an important step. For example, there were numerous local rebellions against centralizing colonial governments and the compromise between the federalists and the regions was a key factor in the evolution of the United States as a modernist state (see Brown, 1972; Negri, 1999). But before such a transition could take place, the population had to be managed, sifted, placed in hierarchies and encouraged to have new desires, potentialities and opinions – in short, regulated externally and internally disciplined.

Thus, the state, transportation and infrastructure were important factors in the undermining of the moral economy of the early nineteenth century in ways similar to those outlined by Thompson (1971) for Britain in the eighteenth century. With communications came a shift away from a use to an exchange economy, and from a just to a market price. As highlighted in Chapter 1, Smith (1981: 524–42) notes the central role of communications in creating a capitalist economy when he asserts that merchants are the pivotal nodal points in the corn trade and help to regulate production and consumption by encouraging profit and thrift. However, such state, market and communications expansion was often resisted by local populations. In 1819, a pro-capitalist generation of politicians was driven out of office after allocating themselves a large salary increase, creating an activist federal state, trebling federal peacetime spending and raising taxes. In the election of that year, two-thirds of the House and half of the Senate were replaced in what was seen as a deliberate rejection of these pro-capitalist developments. Yet 1819 was also a key year in the judiciary's violent pushing forward of the capitalist agenda (see Sellers, 1991). Indeed, Monroe's two-term presidency oversaw major pro-market legal reforms and state expansion to facilitate the market to which the majority of the population were hostile. Through the 'corrupt bargain' election of 1824, the pro-capitalist John Quincy Adams defeated the conservative, anti-market Andrew Jackson to become president and push for further pro-capitalist reforms. Having seen the popular-vote-winner Jackson lose that election, the electorate gave him a clear majority in 1828 and 1832, but this failed to stem the pro-capitalist tide. Thus, the market agenda was driven forward by the constituted power of the state that had been designed precisely to limit, structure and domesticate constituent power (Negri, 1999). (As we shall see in Chapter 6, this anti-democratic agenda is vital to neo-liberal management.) The people were overruled.

A mix of corruption (Perrow, 2002: 141–59), a blatantly politicized judiciary (see below) and an emerging and violent economic reality on the ground continued to usher in capitalism and destroy a subsistence rural life (*Harvard Law Review*, 1989; Sellers, 1991: 47–51. (In the UK, Scotland experienced a similar fate (see Ferguson, 1995), as did the Celtic fringe more generally (see Hechter, 1999).)[7] It was a loss of a way of living that had a variety of repercussions. The 1820s saw a generational and a gender shift in interests. If the older generation (especially men) valued a use economy, their children (especially women) embraced the market with a degree of enthusiasm because they desired a new way of life. Given the patriarchal nature of rural existence, this is perhaps unsurprising. However, it pulled farms into a cash economy and with this came pressure to change routines, practices and rhythms to facilitate production for the market (Thompson, 1971; Sellers, 1991: 3–33). The farmer was encouraged to become a new type of farmer–subject geared towards an exchange economy – one who calculates, rationalizes, anticipates and analyses (see Brown, 1972: 219, who argues that this happened earlier and was widespread by the 1820s). He was encouraged to embody the new, emerging norms of a market society based in consumption, material prosperity and capital rather than the idea of autonomy located in knowledge and self-sufficiency (Sellers, 1991: 155–6; Foucault, 2007, 2008). This is normation in action.

The construction of infrastructure made this exchange economy easier and pulled rural America ever further into the world of cash. Infrastructure was central to the creation of the railway company that Chandler (1977) makes the seminal organizational form (although see Perrow, 2002, who suggests the seminal form is the textile mill). However, Chandler underplays the centrality of primitive accumulation and theft in this emergence. For example, the transcontinental railroad from Iowa to San Francisco received a state subsidy in money and 6,400 acres of largely Native American land for every mile of track it laid (Roediger and Esch, 2012: 71). It laid this track by paying a pittance to its (mainly Chinese) labour force, who were often 'in the position of a slave – like a "coolie" imported in bondage' (Roediger and Esch, 2012: 78).

Equally, the early history of the Lowell Mills demonstrates some of these changes (Gitelman, 1967; Perrow, 2002). In its initial 'benign' phase, the Lowell Mills were worked by young rural women who took some years away from country life to earn cash for their dowries, a brother's education, other family needs and extras (Sellers, 1991; Gordon et al., 1982).[8] The company provided room and board and policed the women's morality while they earned the cash wages that were increasingly part and parcel of rural life and which they increasingly desired. And, of course, the company used the state-fostered infrastructure to bring its products to the market. Here, managing the population, desire and potentiality, and the shaping of public opinion dovetailed to establish new subjects and new forms of discipline. As we shall see in Chapter 3, the gendered nature of the emerging cash economy was important to the emergence of the mass industrial worker of the twentieth century.

The other emerging factor that hastened the demise of a rural subsistence economy concerned free soil. This rural model was built on the assumption that nearby free land was available for the farmers' large families to use when their children grew up and had families of their own (Foner, 1995). As white North East America became longer established, individuals and families had to move ever further away to access free soil, and this put increasing pressure on their subsistence because the family's desire to reproduce itself meant a major uprooting needed to occur after years of settlement. Alternatively, as the nineteenth century went on, the family could embrace the market via cash crops and/or break up elements of the family so some seek employment in the labour market. They could embrace the new, emerging forms of capitalist cooperation and authority. These developments, coupled with a growing consumer desire, and an increasing female chafing with patriarchy, reshaped the family and the rural economy – all of which meant change. This, however, is not to say that free soil became unimportant. For example, in the late 1820s, the United States expropriated approximately 100 million acres from the Creeks and the Cherokees. At the time, alongside his attacks on banking and internal infrastructural developments, President Jackson hoped that such expropriation could be used to create new subsistence farmers who would act as a bulwark against the growing capitalist hegemony (Sellers, 1991: 90–102, 308–13) – on another's expropriation a sectional independence could be achieved. However, Jackson failed in his attempt to use free soil to maintain the dying ideals of his vision of individual autonomy, and his policies were rightly rejected as theft by radical thinkers such as Cornelius Blachly.

This annexation of free soil was also bound up with slavery in that it relieved pressure from poor whites in the Northern states for autonomy. But it was actively supported by the Southern elite, who wished to use it to spread slave-owning to the new states – a major bone of contention between the antebellum North and South. Slavery was used ideologically by the Northern elite to expound on the virtue of free labour, which supposedly gave rise to industriousness and innovation, in contrast to slave labour, which supposedly created indolence and economic retardation (Sellers, 1991; Foner, 1995). Obviously, such claims (and their rejection) had an ideological role. However, what seems certain (and is largely understated) is that many modern management techniques were developed on the slave plantation, because, as Marx (1973: 513) points out, 'we now not only call the plantation owners in America capitalists … they are capitalists'. In what I can only presume is an ideological move, the relationship between slavery and management is a seriously neglected field in business and management (see James, 1970; Banaji, 2003; Cooke, 2003; Roediger and Esch, 2012: 20–66; Crane, 2013). A free labour market may or may not give rise to a more industrious and innovative labour force, but arguably slavery gave rise to modern management. The contention over whether slave owning would be expanded into the new states was only temporarily resolved during the 'Missouri Crisis', when it was agreed that Missouri could be admitted to the United States as a state with legal slave owning and Maine was admitted as a state without slave owning in a bid to keep the balance between slave-owning and free states equal.

Nevertheless, as land became increasingly scarce or distant, the subsistence economy of the rural North East succumbed to market pressures that served up a population for manufacturing. For example, in Massachusetts between 1820 and 1870, the agricultural workforce dropped from 60 per cent of the population to just 13 per cent due to a combination of rural flight and massive immigration from Ireland (Keyssar, 1986: 15). Between the years 1830 and 1890, some 3.325 million people passed through Boston to produce a net population growth of only 387,000 (Sellers, 1991: 239). People were moving both into and within America as never before and this movement was increasingly tied to the search for work in the cities. People were transporting themselves into wage dependency.

This transition also broke the link between manufacturing and agriculture. Previously, farms had been part of the industrial production process and provided materials and products for, say, textiles or shoemaking – often as part of the putting-out system. Montgomery (1968: 4) comments that in the early 1800s, 'Most manufacturing, in other words, was carried on outside the major cities,' and he suggests that in New Hampshire every second farm had a loom that wove 100–600 yards each year at a time when journeymen averaged 829 yards and a factory loom 1,111 yards. Even then, within the city, factory production was dwarfed by home production. For example, in Philadelphia city and county, factories produced 65,326 yards of cloth, compared with 233,232 yards produced by handlooms in family homes (Montgomery, 1968: 19). But this agricultural–manufacturing nexus was declining and the rise of a new supply of dependent labour from rural migration and immigration enabled the development of the factory system as the flight to free local soil dried up. Even so, rural families went into the factories only out of absolute necessity – quite simply, the free contract and dependency were unattractive. The Slater Mills system of the early 1800s, for example, realized that the firm could get women and children into the newly emerging factory only if it provided the men of the household with outside work, because those men refused factory life (Gumus-Dawes, 2000: 28–9). A combination of massive immigration, rural exodus, rapid urbanization and the increasing semi-skilled and unskilled nature of work within the division of labour further pulled the rural and industrial workforce into the Massachusetts market economy and created the need for workers to buy goods and services they had previously self-provisioned (Keyssar, 1986: 9–36; Perrow, 2002). The new technologies of control, dependence and normation were establishing themselves.

Killing the Artisan Republic: new technologies of control

The craft worker was one of the key political subjects in the United States in 1800 (Wilentz, 2004). Craft workers were reasonably prosperous and had an occupational sense of community wherein one's trade defined one's identity (Stedman-Jones, 1974; Wilentz, 2004: 92–5). They were at the pinnacle of a labour market that was historically characterized by scarcity of labour, which was therefore expensive. As such, 'every man controlled his own labour', thereby creating social relations that made workers independent, if still somewhat deferential, to hierarchy (Brown,

1972: 207). Journeymen expected upward mobility and to attain the status of master; and apprenticeship had non-pecuniary obligations for both master and apprentice, with the former expected to educate, clothe and socialize the latter into the world of work and adulthood (Montgomery, 1968: 6–7). There was skill, but little distinction between work and life. Crafts had moral obligations to the community that were often reflected in their banners: for example, New York's carpenters displayed on their banners the slogan 'we shelter the homeless' (Wilentz, 2004: 246). Similarly, during the food riots that occurred regularly in eighteenth-century England, bakers were spared because of their adherence to the old ways and to something like a just price (Thompson, 1971: 106). It was Smith's middlemen and merchants who experienced the wrath of the crowd, and particularly of women. Women were also prominent in urban US riots (see Montgomery, 1987: 140–5).[9] Even though they were growing, the new routines, habits, practices and beliefs of the work organization and the marketplace were still disputed.

However, by the 1860s, this craft world was collapsing and increasingly coming to be viewed as unnatural and outdated. One outcome of this disintegration was the emerging class consciousness that was ever more evident among journeymen (Montgomery, 1968: 6–8). This shift was tied to the development of radical politics, such as the Working Men's movement calling for education for all and an equal distribution of property (Carlton, 1907); increasing labour unrest among both male and female unskilled workers (Perrow, 2002: 58–60; Wilentz, 2004: 168–71); the emerging links between journeymen and unskilled workers – often immigrants – in, for example, New York's General Trades Union during the 1830s (Wilentz, 2004: 251–4); and the rise of the large factory owner who, through subcontracted networks, the inside contract and/or the subdivision of shop labour, slowly but relentlessly tried to drive down wages. For example, Wilentz (2004: 123), speaking of cutters in the tailoring trade, comments: 'all pretensions to craft vanished in the outwork system; with the availability of so much cheap wage labour formal apprenticing and a regular price book had disappeared'. Although this trajectory was not uniform, with some trades surviving and even prospering as crafts – including carpentry, shipbuilding and food preparation (Wilentz, 2004: 132–42) – most went the way of the cutters and experienced degradation, increasing inequality and the end of a way of life. This end was brought about by an increasing division of labour, the rise of the factory or large firm, the moral crusade against the emerging working class and the traditional way of viewing working life, and new forms of private property.

The increasing division of labour

Adam Smith (1981: 13–24), in his discussion of the division of labour, touches on some of the essential contradictions of capitalism – its massive productive capacity, the rise of machines to replace labour, the emergence of time as a central issue, the problem of the worker's 'habit of sauntering and of indolent careless application' (Smith, 1981: 19) and the manner in which the market creates more, not less, interdependence. In his description of the pin factory, Smith (1981: 15) comments on the transition from an industry wherein one man did all the tasks to one wherein

> One man draws out the wire, another straights it, a third cuts it, a fourth points it, a fifth grinds it at the top for receiving the head, to make the head requires two or three distinct operations, to put it on is a peculiar business, to whiten the pins is another, it is even a trade by itself to put them into the paper, and the important business of making a pin, is in this manner, divided into about eighteen distinct operations, which in some manufactories, are all performed by distinct hands, though in others the same man will sometimes perform two or three of them.

As we saw in the Introduction, such division gives rise to staggering productivity increases, so much so that Smith calculates a single worker could move from producing a maximum of 20 pins a day to producing 4,800.

What Smith describes had started to emerge around the middle of the eighteenth century: in 1755, the Birmingham button-maker John Taylor had divided making a button into seventy different tasks to be carried out by seventy different workers (Pollard, 1965: 265). Thomas Jefferson, who credited Smith with writing the 'best work' on political economy (Negri, 1999: 158), used slave labour to start a nail factory wherein slaves were 'arranged along an assembly line of hammers and anvils' (Ellis quoted in Cooke, 2003: 1906). Jefferson weighed the nails and raw materials given daily to each individual slave in order to assess their efficiency and calculate waste – a form of 'proto-Taylorism' (Cooke, 2003: 1906–7). Calculation, measurement and efficiency combined to deliver Weber's formal rationality, and the increasing division of labour enabled the capitalist and capital to appear as the organizing force, as a 'real condition of production' and as the source of authority in the factory (Marx, 1976: 448).

The division of labour generates three main capitalist advantages: increased dexterity of the worker because he or she now concentrates solely on one small, unskilled task; a saving of time because the individual worker does not have to move from one task to another (and even more time can be saved if the workers are all corralled in a single location – the factory); and, finally, it enables the application of technology and the replacing of labour with fixed capital. So the division of labour gave capitalists greater control over workers through a reorientation of time and space, it generated productivity increases, it allowed the replacement of labour with technology and – although Smith is less forthcoming on this point – it massively redistributed wealth and power from workers to capitalists through the down-grading or expropriating of knowledge to capital. Is it any wonder capitalists and managers embraced it with gusto?

However, as Smith adroitly points out, the increasing division of labour has other effects, too: it creates the worker as a new sort of political problem that hence requires a new form of governance (Foucault, 2004, 2007); it deskills; it creates unnatural, permanent hierarchies and lines of authority that are ideologically passed off as natural; and, if left unchecked, it is never-ending. Smith (1981: 782), worrying about the division of labour, advocates the use of education and an expanded state to ameliorate these damaging effects. Otherwise, he forecasts the emergence of a group within society that would be uneducated, never mentally stimulated, uncivilized by monotonous work[10] and therefore a social and political problem.[11]

As we shall see, part of the moral crusade against the workforce and the elite's attempt to ensure the population accepted the unfolding division of labour as 'natural' meant that state intervention, schooling and instruction would sometimes play the sort of role Smith hoped they would. Furthermore, Smith predicted that social mobility would decrease because of the division of labour, and society would become permanently and unjustifiably unequal. However, he also suggests that the reasons for this will be mystified and workers, as victims of this process, will be blamed for their own predicament:

> The difference of natural talents in different men is, in reality, much less than we are aware of; and the very different genius which appears to distinguish men of different professions, when grown up to maturity, is not upon many occasions so much the cause, as the effect of the division of labour. The difference between the most dissimilar characters, between a philosopher and a common street porter, for example, seems to arise not so much from nature, as from habit, custom, and education. When they came into the world, and for the first six or eight years of their existence, they were perhaps, very much alike, and neither their parents nor playfellows could perceive any remarkable difference. About that age, or soon after, they come to be employed in very different occupations. The difference of talents comes then to be taken notice of, and widens by degrees, till at last the vanity of the philosopher is willing to acknowledge scarce any resemblance.
>
> *(Smith, 1981: 28)*

The division of labour gave workers new forms of subjugation, dependence and authority; deskilling; the expropriation of their knowledge; a working life full of boredom and repetition; made them replaceable by machines and cheaper workers; made unnatural hierarchies permanent; turned them into a political and social problem; and generated the modern organizational form that confronted them as a mystified entity. Is it any wonder they opposed it and viewed it as class struggle forced on them from above?

Capitalism is about this struggle and refusal – about turning labour power into actual labour, controlling the means of production, the organization of the production process, and the value derived from it (Marx, 1976). The experience of the craft workers in the nineteenth century was also about this – about shifting them from a task-oriented labour process that they controlled to a clock-oriented one that – if they were involved in it at all – they did not. Moreover, within this new labour process, they were often deskilled, subject to new managerial forms of discipline and increasingly degraded (Thompson, 1967). However, task-oriented work and craft were to decline only slowly and through conflict.

In the United Kingdom and the United States, workers observed older non-capitalist traditions, such as working intensely for part of the week in order to take other days or time off, observing St Monday after a weekend of entertainment, simply not showing up for work, drinking on the job or leaving the factory as they pleased without telling the foreman (Pollard, 1965; Thompson, 1967; Gutman, 1973; and, presenting a different view of the relationship of the US worker to time, see Brown, 1972). Gutman (1973: 557–8) demonstrates how many of these ways of working, despite the enormous pressure from capital, were maintained. For example, cigar workers struck for the right to leave the shop without telling the foreman and to uphold privileges such as the right to keep and sell damaged cigars. Until the twentieth century, they also tried to maintain the privilege of being read to by a fellow worker while at work (in Cuba, they still have that right). Nevertheless, although it was an uneven process, as we will see in Chapter 3, craft workers eventually lost much of this type of control over their working conditions. Central to the craft worker's demise was the increasing division of labour (Englander, 1987). Firms gradually began to use this to weaken craft traditions and power, and to force an ever-wider gap between masters and journeymen.

Marx describes how the division of labour starts with spontaneous cooperation in the labour process, which then becomes a regular, conscious pattern that remains more or less unchanged in the guilds. This changes in manufacturing as it further subdivides the labour process either by forcing craftsmen to specialize in one role or by subdividing the labour process to enable the replacement of craft workers with labour that is 'ready to hand and only waiting to be collected together' (Marx, 1976: 482). This, in turn, 'mutilates the worker, turning him into a fragment of himself' (Marx, 1976: 482). As we saw in the Introduction, this process is finally completed with expertise and technology, wherein science confronts the worker as capital. Capitalism is about the expansion of this planning and control through science, technology, human resource management, marketing, modulating the subject and consumption (Panzieri, 1961). Furthermore, it generates Weber's bureaucratic form, which stands before the worker as an unknown entity and, from the worker's fragmented position, seems to be organized by the authority of the capitalist, the manager and the elite (Clawson, 1980).

We can see these processes at work in the tailoring crafts of New York. The tasks were divided into coats, pants, vests and trimmings and the emphasis was placed on the speed of the production process – quality was unimportant because much of the product was intended for slaves in the Southern states. Distinct tasks with measures of accountability were allocated to individual workers who were then subject to a pace of work and a piece rate established by the management (Wilentz, 2004: 122–4). The piece rate was vital to this new economy (see Chapter 3). The product was often subcontracted out to tailoring outworkers, who made up 46.3 per cent of New York's tailoring craft workers (Wilentz, 2004: 115). This extremely sweated labour was often done by dependent women and children. In such a world, the traditional craft worker's control over the production process, the expectation of mobility from apprentice to journeyman to master, a life of relative prosperity and a significant role within the polity all disintegrated. Not all crafts, and indeed not all craft workers in the same craft, experienced this: those in emerging mass markets, such as the clothing trade for slaves, were most likely to experience this increased dependence and degradation. But, in essence, the days of craft were ending by 1860.

Taylorism is often credited with the decline of craft in management theory. However, Taylor came at the end of a process that had been unfolding during the first half of the nineteenth century. Although craft workers did not decline immediately and were militant later in that century (Montgomery, 1987: 130), as one of the major political subjects of the economy they were finished perhaps as early as 1860 or 1870. From thereon, they were fighting to preserve a decaying world. As we shall see in Chapter 3, they were subject to, and destroyed by, the material processes of normation – subdivision, piece rates, set tasks, calculation and time control. Furthermore, in the emerging biopolitics, their view of knowledge as the essence of authority, their belief in labour as the source of value, and their desires for autonomy and control within the labour process were viewed as increasingly anachronistic, against economic progress and outside the norm of industrial life (Wilentz, 2004: 302–5). They were externally regulated and internally disciplined.

However, before their final demise, craft workers challenged the new regime. Perhaps their most significant challenge concerned what created value, where it was created and who had the natural right to it. Craft workers strongly endorsed Ricardo's labour theory of value. Ricardo (1996: 19–20) criticises Smith for holding inconsistent views on value. Smith suggested value was formed by the quantity of labour expended on a good but he then asserted that value is also the price the good could obtain in the market. Ricardo argues this confuses matters because it means that the wage that labour can command in the market is equal to the value of the product that labour produces – and this ignores both profit and rent. Ricardo (1996: 19) categorically states that labour is the source of value:

> That this [the quantity of labour embodied in a product] is really the foundation of the exchangeable value of all things, excepting those which cannot be increased by human industry, is a doctrine of the utmost importance in political economy; for from no source do so many errors, and so much difference of opinion in that science proceed, as from the vague ideas which are attached to the word value.

As such, some of the value workers create is expropriated by capitalists, and if wages rise, profits must fall (Ricardo, 1996: 34). Here, there is an inherent conflict between workers and capital. For early nineteenth-century craft workers, this seemed obvious and natural (Buttrick, 1952; Williamson, 1952; Clawson, 1980; Englander, 1987). They had traditionally produced goods on demand in small groups or on their own for which they charged a book price based on the labour time involved. As apprentices and journeymen, they expected to pay a surplus to the master by way of learning their craft but, as the Amherst Carriage debates attest, upon achieving master status, they expected to reap the full and just reward for their labour. The authority for paying this subsidy was located in the master's superior knowledge, experience and role as a trainer of the next generation of his or her craft. This authority was necessarily social rather than individualistic: master craftspeople used their knowledge of the social individual – that is, knowledge handed down to and then developed by them – to assert their authority. Thus, for these workers, market and value were increasingly in opposition. In 1830s New York (Wilentz, 2004: 240–5), craft workers argued that their craft was a property, not an alienable commodity. As with today's artist, programmer or intellectual (see Graw, 2010; Lucas, 2010), it was inalienably part of the worker – indeed the occupational community – and, as such, should not be subject to expropriation by capitalists/managers because the craftsperson should retain its full value rather than earn mere wages. Craft knowledge and the limited collective trumped capital.[12]

Needless to say, capitalists/managers rejected such claims and asserted that wages – be they high or low – were rightly set by that independent arbiter of value: the market. As the nineteenth century unfolded, Ricardo's theory of value was replaced by marginalist economics located in the marketplace, and this set the tone for the debate around wages which were increasingly detached from value in Ricardo's sense. This shift coincided with the decline of craft and the rise of the factory, wherein only a part of the product was put together by the individual worker, thereby weakening any sense of the proper value of the product. Here, work had no inherent labour value, only a market wage, and it was confronted by capital and the capitalist as the organizer, planner and necessary requirement of the labour process itself (see Chapters 3 and 4). The worker did not produce a commodity but was guided to produce just a part of a commodity by the planning of the capitalist or manager. The commodity had become a product of all specialized workers, thereby mystifying the relationship between labour time and value (Hodgskin, 1825; Marx, 1976: 475–6). Simultaneously, the production process became more social under capitalism, while the individual worker became more isolated, replaceable, dependent and unimportant, such that capital and then management, as the planner of production, are themselves rendered productive.

The rise of the factory

Developing in parallel with these changes in the craft division of labour was the factory. This was a horrendous space in the eyes of working people (Pollard, 1965: 160–74; Thompson, 1967, 1968: 207–32; Sellers, 1991: 280–5; Gumus-Dawes, 2000; Perrow, 2002: 48–64). In both the United Kingdom and the United States the factory was initially linked to the workhouse. In Philadelphia, the Guardians of the Poor established a workhouse and textile factory with local taxes in 1812 (Perrow, 2002: 50). In the UK, after legislation in 1723, 60 workhouses were built in the provinces and 50 in London (Pollard, 1965: 163). The factory was closely associated with these and other workhouses, and indeed it had to be because free labour did not want to enter it. If working people had a choice – if they had independence – they stayed away. Given this, employers turned to *unfree* labour, especially pauper children

(Pollard, 1965: 160–74). To fill their factories, capital and the state needed to coerce labour.[13] This is unsurprising as working people wanted to maintain their existing lifestyles, independence (or at least semi-independence), rhythms and routines, all of which had to be broken down if labour were to be made profitable. Left to itself, the new economy would have failed in light of this refusal, so capitalists increasingly acted as a class and increasingly looked to a disciplinary state to force acquiescence (Tronti, 1965). As Pollard (1965: 162; emphasis in original) comments, when discussing the anti-factory views of working people in Yorkshire: 'This resolution [against factory work], it should be stressed, and many others like it passed in Yorkshire represents not the harking back to a mythical golden age, but the defence of *existing* social relationships.' These existing social relationships and the culture that maintained them had to be systematically traduced if capitalism were to survive its birth pangs, otherwise labour would have rejected capitalist cooperation. For example, Britain simultaneously experienced both labour shortages in the factories and a labour surplus as families were removed from the land during the Highland clearances and the enclosure movement in England. Although there was labour, it simply refused to enter factories unless compelled to do so. The workhouse, the prison and the school facilitated this founding violence.

The United States experienced similar issues. Echoing Pollard's comments above, Sellers (1991: 123) observes how existing social relations were threatened to ensure that labour was unable to refuse: 'But now, as working people began to see, an expansive capitalism threatened the traditional moral economy, that promised them a decent competence, ultimate independence, and the civic equality and respect of republican citizenship.' One way in which working people tried to maintain this 'decent competence' was by availing themselves of free soil and craft knowledge. Indeed, free soil and the exodus of families to the West kept labourers' wages high in comparison with those of Europe – although the gap between skilled and unskilled workers was also higher in the United States (Montgomery, 1987: 58–111; Wilentz, 2004: 303). As in the UK, the factories were first filled by the most vulnerable and the most dependent: that is, by women, children and especially migrants (Gutman, 1973: 544; Montgomery, 1987; Gumus-Dawes, 2000; Perrow, 2002).[14] This happened in the mills of Rhode Island, Manayunk and the famed Waltham system. Perrow (2002: 54) suggests that by 1840 between two-thirds and three-quarters of the workforce in US textile mills were women or children working twelve to thirteen hours a day, six days a week. Wage dependency was central here, but so was gender. Women were seen by employers as more vulnerable, compliant, better suited to the factory, and easier to remould as subjects in an employer-dominated space. Even in industries dominated by craft workers women made up 25 per cent of the workforce and were based in those sectors of the factory that were most unskilled, flexible, temporary or automated (see Williamson, 1952: 85 for a description of the Winchester Arms factory). But the subject is also (re) made in the factory (Burawoy, 1979; Weeks, 2011), so importantly, regardless of the sex of the worker, capital actively sought to 'feminize' the workforce because of this dependency and vulnerability (see Chapter 5).

Where workers were not dependent they avoided the factory altogether or stayed there for only a short while before moving on: for example, the first phase of the Lowell Mills in Massachusetts employed Yankee farm girls who stayed for a few years to accumulate some cash in the increasing cash economy of the state (Sellers, 1991: 280–5). In the more exploitative second phase of the Lowell Mills (Gitelman, 1967; Gumus-Dawes, 2000; Perrow, 2002: 70–5), wage labour was based increasingly, but not exclusively, on mass immigration from Ireland as a result of the Great Famine. Here wage dependency was near total, just as it was in the mines, large infrastructural projects and, increasingly, in the cities (Gutman, 1973; Roediger and Esch, 2012). Vulnerability, expendability and not a little hate drove the management of capitalism. Immigration on a huge scale turned a labour shortage into a glut, enabling employers to reduce wages and increase exploitation. Furthermore, technological innovation was designed to ensure the Lowell Mills could make more use of children. And once they were on the workforce in large numbers, employers were able to reduce adult wages by up to 90 per cent for certain jobs. In this environment, the social bonds of caring were stretched so that families were forced to send their children to work in the factories because they could not survive on adult wages alone. (Oddly, Gitelman (1967: 244–5) suggests that the Irish did this voluntarily.) By 1865, children made up just under half of the total Lowell Mills workforce. As Marx observed, compulsion, not free exchange, creates cooperation in the factory.

In many respects, then, management and planning originated in the alleged free choice of vulnerable women and small children. Here, families and immigrant communities would (unwillingly) stress certain potentialities to their children, friends and relatives, and hence soften or prepare them for the drudgery and discipline of the factory – another free gift to capital. Violence, as Benjamin (2008) understands it, is the foundation upon which the factory is constructed.

New York tells a different story (it did not have Lowell-type factories prior to the 1850s), yet it shares similarities. From 1800 to 1850, the city's population grew by 750 per cent – at the time the highest growth rate in the world. By mid-century, half the population were immigrants and 80 per cent of those were wage-dependent Irish and German workers. Half of all the Irish male adults worked as day labourers, and 25 per cent of all Irish females were domestic servants – perhaps the ultimate badge of servile wage dependency (Foner, 1995: xxii). Thus, unskilled work and dependency flourished. Moreover, Wilentz (2004: 107–44) suggests that there was also a degradation of work and that craft apprenticeships were almost completely abolished in the 'sweated trades' of clothing, shoes and furniture: skilled workers were either sweated or replaced by the less skilled through an increasing division of labour.

Originally, then, the factory was a place of unfree labour, or 'forced labour', as Marx (1988) called it. Entry to the factory came from poverty, vulnerability and extreme wage dependency, which made it a highly gendered and racialized space and ensured the widespread use of children. It also made the factory exceptionally profitable. As such, immigration to the United States was a central bulwark against labour's desire for independence. Immigrants and slaves hastened the country's capitalist development by providing compelled labour. Traditional norms were also harder for the immigrants to keep, making their communities more susceptible to 'normation'. One might think of Ford's grotesque 'graduation' ceremonies, during which immigrant workers walked down a gang plank in 'shabby rags' before emerging from the symbolic melting pot in neat suits: a transition from 'hunkie to American' (see Esch and Roediger, 2009: 30–1; Roediger and Esch, 2012). Vulnerability, desire, a lack of options, the need to embrace a cash economy, and the disparaging of immigrant communities and ways of living through public opinion all facilitated this normation, even though the communities themselves resisted (Montgomery, 1987: 139–50). While very different to slavery, such processes give the lie to the argument that labour was free to choose, as promulgated by the North's commercial elite (Foner, 1995).

The rise of the factory had other impacts, too (Marx, 1976: 455–91). First, labour was confronted by the factory as an external weight. As we saw in the Introduction, the manufacturing division of labour presupposes a labour force without any means of reproducing itself except as labour-power, the concentration of the means of production in the hands of capitalists and the emergence of an organizational form that stands before labour as – at least partly – mystical or unknowable. Added to this, there is a ready-made pool of vulnerable labour waiting to be scooped into the factory – several workers sell their labour to one capitalist who 'applies it as combined labour-power' in the workshop. In the United States, this pool of labour was often made up of immigrants, rural migrants and African Americans (Gordon et al., 1982: 48–99). This labour force was created through violence, famine, expropriation, migration, indentured and indebted labour and slavery – common themes in the origins and continuance of capitalism. (For valuable insights on the relationship between wage labour, other forms of labour and the rise of capitalism, see Banaji, 2003.)

The worker exists only because of the workshop, rather than vice versa. Because labour has lost its means of production and reproduction, it can function only in the workshop. As Marx (1976: 482) writes:

> It will continue to function only in an environment which comes into existence after its sale, namely the capitalist's workshop. Unfitted by nature to making anything independently, the manufacturing worker develops his productive activity only as an appendage to that workshop. As the chosen people bore in their features the sign that they were the property of Jehovah, so the division of labour brands the manufacturing worker as the property of capital.

However, in its resistance to its own expropriation in the capitalist workshop, labour forces the individual capitalist to seek out other capitalists and hence creates the capitalist class and the capitalist state (Tronti, 1965). Wage labour becomes naturalized and reified, and organizations appear to operate to an elite-controlled, mystified logic. Hence, people find the notion that this is based on coercion or domination rather abstract (Weeks, 2011: 1–37).

Second, capital is increasingly where knowledge of production is located. Knowledge of the production process becomes ever more hardwired into technology and procedures (Panzieri, 1961; Braverman, 1974). Science becomes a handmaiden of capital as knowledge is expropriated from workers via the division of labour, deskilling, technology, routines and work scripts, so that science confronts the worker as capital. As we saw earlier, here the collective worker's productive capacity grows as the individual worker's capacity is impoverished in the factory through forced cooperation (see also Chapters 3 and 4). Within this, Michels (1915) and Mayo (1933) see control of the organization and its division of labour not as an act of class violence (even though it is), but rather as an act of natural elitism. They view this is a positive development – something not located in theft.

Finally, as we saw above, the factory worker produces only one element of the commodity, which increases the necessity for cooperation, giving rise to new struggles and forms of organization among workers (see Chapters 3 and 4) as well as new forms of hierarchy located within organizational control. Production is mystified through scale so that the capitalist and management both become necessary.

Law, violence and new property rights

Legal changes in the nineteenth century solidified capitalism in America. These changes were often enacted against the wishes of the people, and it seems clear that lawyers had a very partisan and politicized class agenda. Here the juridical level that Weber and neo-liberalism (Davies, 2014) suggest makes us formally free as individuals (see Chapter 1) is itself created by elite interests in a moment of class violence. As the craft workers remonstrating with the Senate of Massachusetts about the Amherst Carriage Company argued, this 'freedom' means that labour is compelled to work as a dependent wage earner. Lawyers acted as the 'shock troops of capitalism' (Sellers, 1991: 47). In this sense, they were intimately involved in creating management and the modern US economy.

During the first half of the nineteenth century prosecutions shifted from an emphasis on morality crime to property crime; lawyers increasingly came from the same families; they were recruited from the same elite colleges; they were intimately linked to commercial elites; and they systematically targeted political power. For example, from comprising less than one-third of the members of the first Congress, they were a majority from 1813 onwards. Obviously, they also dominated the courts and the interpretation of law (Sellers, 1991: 47–8). Lawyers engaged in class struggle from above. Very quickly in the first half of the nineteenth century lawyers created a whole new legal world – a founding law (Benjamin, 2008) – so that by the 1830s and 1840s a new system was already in place based on property and the (redefined) public interest, property and anti-combination, property and personal injury, and property and incorporation (*Harvard Law Review*, 1989; Sellers, 1991: 45–55; Perrow, 2002; Banaji, 2003).

In his thesis that the Declaration of Independence was an open, democratic moment of constituent power that was later shut down by the framing of the Constitution of the United States, Negri (1999: 170–4) touches on the role of the judiciary. Using the *Federalist Papers* (especially pages 78–83), he argues that by strengthening judiciary power and the independence of the judges, by enabling them to interpret the Constitution and by insisting that the Constitution 'be preferred to the statute, to the intention of the people, to the intention of their agents' in any dispute among states, between individuals and states, or between a state and the federal government, all constituted power – and especially the judiciary – was enhanced. Furthermore, this legal work and knowledge accumulated over time so that it became central to deciding constitutional norms and conflicts. This gave the judiciary power over what Negri calls 'the implied powers' of the Constitution. The judiciary has been given the role of 'constituent power' within government in the sense that it sanctions innovation via its near monopoly on interpretation of the Constitution. For Negri (1999: 174), this is 'a deceit and a fiction', but nevertheless real in its consequences.[15]

One example of these consequences can be seen in the judiciary's use of its role in the early nineteenth century. In 1819, Dartmouth College and New Hampshire went to court over the state legislature's desire to put political appointees on the Board of Trustees. Although endowed with public land, Dartmouth resisted the Act and took the case to court, wherein the college's legal representative, the judge hearing the case and the future Chief Justice of the Supreme Court, John Marshall, all appeared determined to offer corporate bodies 'immortality and individuality' and to empower them against the state. In essence, they gave the corporation private rights and limited the state's ability to interfere with any corporate charter. In all of this, Sellers (1991: 86) suggests that 'Justice Story, in his zeal for his friend Webster's cause, considerably overstepped the bounds of judicial propriety.' Furthermore, as 1819 rolled on, the federal courts became more aggressive in limiting state legislatures' ability to encroach on federal power, to relieve existing debts among citizens, and, as suggested, to interfere with the chartered privileges of corporations. In what we would today call a neo-liberal tactic, the state was recreated as an actor with rights that 'are in no sense superior' to those of the corporation (Lippmann, 1938/1943: 299). Moreover, the corporation was empowered at the expense of the democratic state and the citizen. In spite of the wishes of the Jacksonian population and the idea of public interest as a moral or political interest, the private and the public were increasingly seen as one and the same thing and the rights of private profit were enhanced.

None of this was functionally necessary in the manner that Chandler (1977) suggests when he discusses the emergence of corporate America (which came at least three decades later). Rather than Chandler's 'organizational imperatives' (see Gordon, 1984: 83–4), we seem to have material interests and political ideology (see Sellers, 1991; Perrow, 2002). During the first half of the nineteenth century there was a political struggle over whether private property was compatible with the public good and whether the state or federal government and legislature should be more powerful (*Harvard Law Review*, 1989). Emerging capitalist forces – in which the lawyers and judiciary were a fundamental bloc – sided with the federal government and capital against the anti-market orientation of the majority of voters and the states that were accountable to those voters (Sellers, 1991). In this struggle, the judiciary and the lawyers acted as a bulwark against democracy by 'adapting law to meet the needs of entrepreneurs' and 'making property "inherent in the human breast"' (Sellers, 1991: 51; see Chapter 6). In so doing, and through decisions such as *Dartmouth* v. *New Hampshire*, they redefined the public interest role of the corporation to mean its own private interest – the private and the public interest were now one and the same thing, and with this came pro-market ways of managing the population (*Harvard Law Review*, 1989). A new normation was created through foundational violence, and the burying of the Artisan Republic proceeded.

Lawyers simplified the transferral of ownership; they conferred rights on owners to use their property however they wished (as long as it was for business purposes) and in so doing weakened the claims of adjacent property owners; and they enshrined the 'free contract' of labour so that personal injury claims at work became harder to pursue against corporations. By the 1830s, corporations were being granted 'eminent domain' (or 'compulsory purchase', as it is known in the UK) over natural resources so that they 'were empowered to buy these resources at the expense of others. The lawyers intensified anti-debtor legislation; increasingly introduced anti-worker rules as workers slipped into wage dependency; and introduced the concept of contributory negligence and fellow-worker negligence in personal injury to increase employers' protection from claims (Sellers, 1991: 45–55). In reality, the directly democratically unaccountable courts allowed capital to externalize costs in areas such as health and safety, labour law, environment and consumer rights (Perrow, 2002: 44–5). This was a foundational process as one set of legal structures was reinterpreted or set aside to make way for new legal forms and constituted power triumphed over constituent power. With it came Foucault's biopolitics as new routines, habits, norms and practices were established.

Central to all of this was the free labour movement – or the belief that all US citizens were working citizens and therefore equally free to ply any trade and succeed. In terms of labour, this emphasis on the free contract was a rejection of the General Trades Union's 1830s campaign which stressed that working people's labour was their property, rather than an alienable commodity, and that, following the labour theory of value, it should not be stolen by employers and masters. That is, knowledge, skill and labour, not capital, should be paramount. Workers wanted the full value of what they created (Wilentz, 2004: 242–5).

Of course, in 1844, Marx was describing the very alienation of labour that these workers were attempting to reject through their struggle. In a moment of class struggle, the judiciary rejected such a vision and sided explicitly with capital and with the myth that the new republic was based on free labour and freedom of contract wherein every citizen was equal to succeed and no element of the community held 'sway over the rest' (Wilentz, 2004: 275). In short, it strengthened the concept that labour was a pure commodity – as an alienable property form – and in so doing sided with the authority of compelled cooperation and the elitism of the capitalist organizational form. However, this notion was not readily accepted, so a moral crusade was a necessary accompaniment to the very real material changes that were taking place on the ground.

The moral crusade against the working class

Destroying a way of life is not easy. However, it was necessary if the population was to be directed towards certain potentialities and made to comply with (and even desire) the norms of the emerging economy. As described, this recasting required coercion but it also demanded a legitimating ideology that praised the new and disparaged the old. (See Hodgskin, 1825 on the importance of public opinion in the struggle between masters and journeymen in the UK, and Brown, 1972 and Bernays, 1928 for its importance in the United States. Also see Chapter 6.) The emerging industrial order desired compliance, efficiency, certainty and stability above all else (Jacques, 1996: 114–24). As we saw above, this led to new property rights legislation to ensure more capital-friendly certainty (although this was not guaranteed; see Gordon, 1984), and it required a newly disciplined labour force. Consequently, the nineteenth century witnessed a moral crusade against the older traditions of the working class. This was a fundamentally anti-democratic endeavour led by commercial, religious, political and educational elites, including Harvard, Princeton and Yale (Sellers, 1991: 364; Roediger and Esch, 2012: 98–138).[16]

Central to this moral crusade were the concepts of free labour and social mobility. Unlike the slave-owning South, the North supposedly embodied free labour: that is, people were free to choose a job they enjoyed, at which they were skilled, which they wanted to do and, through their individual desire and the labour market, in which they were free to succeed.[17] There was some truth in this: for example, female labour often wanted to leave the patriarchal rural economy (Sellers, 1991; Foner, 1995: xxiv). However, as we have seen, behind this freedom lay substantial compulsion. 'Freedom' supposedly facilitated industriousness, innovation and prosperity and it was turning the United States into the most dynamic economy in the world. However, in reality, social mobility was declining. Needless to say, Southern elites rejected the whole notion of 'free labour' and argued that the Northern poor were no more than 'wage slaves' (Sellers, 1991; Foner, 1995: 66).

Accompanying the myth of free labour was the belief that social mobility was possible as long as workers were disciplined, industrious and gave up their previous dissolute practices in order to develop a better work ethic: that is, they were obliged to willingly subject themselves to the new norms (see Weeks, 2011: 37–78). This followed the familiar path of condemning absenteeism, worker control of the labour process and drinking alcohol (all of which could be viewed as forms of refusal) while extolling the benefits of thrift and ambition – Weber's 'Protestant work ethic'. But then the focus shifted as the century wore on: the work ethic was no longer linked so much to asceticism or religious belief; instead, it was increasingly related to the capacity to consume as a way of forging an identity (Lears, 2000;

Weeks, 2011). Although religion's influence waned overall, a parallel phenomenon was an increase in the intensity and type of belief for those who remained religious as US and British capitalists became increasingly active in spreading religion. The capitalists participated in this partly to persuade themselves that the factory system they were creating was moral, but they were also driven by a desire to 'rescue' those who had failed to adapt to the new society – the drunkards, the prostitutes and the criminals.[18] These same businessmen were deeply involved in the temperance and abolitionist movements and some of them went on to form welfare management systems (Sellers, 1991: 202–36; Barley and Kunda, 1992). Similar processes occurred in the creation of the new worker subjectivity evident in the UK (Bendix, 1956: 22–116; Thompson, 1968: 385–41; Stedman-Jones, 1974).[19]

Another element in this crusade to instil the new characteristics that were required of workers was schooling. Increasingly, capitalists and statesmen saw the advantage of education because it would discipline children into regularity and teach them to concentrate, obey, appreciate effort and industry, and compete against each other for individual achievement (Sellers, 1991: 394–5; Perrow, 2002: 55–8). School and teachers were deemed to be cheaper than jails and jailers, and as such they would help to discipline and create the new workforce while also encouraging individualism and civic responsibility (see Brown, 1972: 219; Gutman, 1973: 585). Education also promoted literacy, which was a driver in breaking down collectivist thinking. When combined, schooling and literacy would enable children to negotiate and compete in the free labour market. Capitalism-friendly, state-regulated education and literacy would replace the outdated craft/parental apprenticeships of the previous system, thereby helping to make capitalism appear 'natural' (Sellers, 1991). Here, education is 'the essential ordering of the relationship between the generations – in other words if one wishes to speak of control, control of generational relations, not of children?' (Benjamin, 2008: 114). In this world, children, like the earlier generation of rural females, could school their parents into the ways, desires and potentialities of the new world as much as their parents could school them. Ideally, such cross-generational schooling would create a compliant workforce (see Chapters 3 and 4). But education was not alone in performing this role: the prison system, social welfare and medical services all served up people for work, too (Weeks, 2011: 7).

In short, the moral crusade was part of a process that tried to reconfigure workers' subjectivities so that they would self-discipline (this is an ongoing and central management issue). Capitalism attempted to reshape the general intellect and the cognitive and affective maps of labour. Of course, it could never achieve this completely, but importantly, the outside of the factory has always a place of capitalist conflict. Education, for example, worked to discipline children into future work roles *and* acted as a source of knowledge to resist some of the impositions of capital as a social relation, as Marx acknowledged (see Vercellone, 2007). Nevertheless, the argument was that if workers would only adopt the new practices and beliefs and see capitalism as a natural and benign system of production, they would prosper under it. Free labour meant anyone could succeed, provided they developed particular potentialities and accepted particular norms. Failure to do so was deemed an individual – not a systemic – failure (Foner, 1995: 23–4).

Capitalism required a new subjectivity if it was to secure the population and it changed our relationship to a great many things within the general intellect. For example, families became smaller due to economic expense and the desire for, and need of, consumer goods. US birth rates amongst the white population declined from 55 per 1,000 in 1800 to 43.3 in 1850, and children per female declined from 6.4 in 1800 to 4.9 in 1850 (Sellers, 1991: 240). The UK experienced similar declines in the same period (see Pollard, 1965: 160–208). Gender relations altered as women entered the factory and the marketplace both out of necessity and through a desire to avoid patriarchal structures (Sellers, 1991; Foner, 1995; Jacques, 1996). People migrated more. Individuals related to themselves differently and were encouraged to self-manage, produce more labour from themselves and internalize new moral precepts that valued ambition, industriousness, time consciousness, self-improvement, consumption, sexual abstinence outside marriage and material success over economic independence. Descartes's conscience was being put to work and the general intellect was being permeated with capitalist social relations.

All of this fundamentally altered how people reproduced life. Increasingly, as Weber notes, the worker confronted capital as labour-power without access to the means of production. Increasingly, the worker was an 'operative' or a 'hand' rather than a craft worker and he or she confronted the organizational form as the creation of capitalist planning. The new industrial culture that was emerging was epitomized by the mass industrial subject. As we saw in the Introduction and Chapter 1, in this new world discipline, industriousness, the capacity to obey and the willingness to accept authority were supposedly the keys to success. However, as we will see, the population was never so secured for capitalism. It continued to resist all of these pressures and to develop new and creative political subjectivities.

An emerging class consciousness

These developments gave rise to refusal and to an emerging political and radical consciousness. For example, having been influenced by the utopian socialism of Robert Owen, the physician Cornelius Blachly (1839) vigorously rejected this new world in his paper 'Some Causes of Popular Poverty'. He argued that the world belonged to everyone equally and that, rather than have a concentration of property in a few hands, the United States should redistribute land, abolish inheritance rights, accept humanity's interdependent and communal nature, reject individualism and give the workers the value they had created. This was a direct attack on the unfolding capitalism and its emerging elite concentration of private property and organizational power. For Blachly (1839: 111), only labour created wealth and hence only labour was entitled to it.

Similarly, writing in 1826, Langton Byllesby (1961: 11), 'a mechanic of some repute', fundamentally rejects Smith's market order. Using Jefferson's rallying call for constituent power in the Declaration of Independence and its claim that 'All men are created free and equal with an unalienable right to life, liberty and the pursuit of happiness', he argues:

> the present social economy is not capable of diffusing it [happiness] further, but on the contrary, gives intimation, should it continue, of restricting its benefits to a still smaller portion of the human family, who have adopted the existing manners and habits of civilization, through their irresistible tendency to generate an excessive *inequality of wealth*, and the oppressions incident thereto.
>
> *(Byllesby, 1961: 28; emphasis in original)*

Like Blachly, Byllesby was influenced by Robert Owen. He accuses capitalists of laziness and vice, and asserts that the knowledge and activity of labour are the only sources of wealth. *Contra* Hobbes, he suggests that the state of nature is an idyllic space ruined by plunder, and argues that plunder, property rights, money and what he calls 'trafficking' (a market beyond simple exchange) are central to the assault on the communal and craft way of life. As such, they must be eradicated.

One of the leaders of the Working Men's movement, Thomas Skidmore, is even more forthright:

> One thing must be obvious to the plainest understanding; that as long as property is unequal; or rather, as long as it is so enormously unequal, as we see it at present, that those who possess it, *will* live on the labour of others, and themselves perform none, or if any, a very disproportionate share, of that toil which attends them as a condition of their existence, and without the performance of which, they have *no* just right to preserve or retain that existence, even for a single hour.
>
> *(Skidmore, 1829: 4; emphasis in original)*

In addition, the early nineteenth century witnessed the activities of Robert Dale Owen, Frances Wright and others involved in socialist agitation; the rise of radical political movements; increasing industrial unrest among both the skilled and the unskilled; the growth of new alliances and solidarities among those who historically had been very different and separate groups (Perrow, 2002: 58–64; Wilentz, 2004: 168–72, 219–54); and the emergence of the General Trades Union as well as the less radical, more reformist/conservative movement into which Andrew Jackson tapped (see Braverman, 1974; Sellers, 1991; Perrow, 2002; Wilentz, 2004). By the 1830s, parts of the United States had a nascent class consciousness and it was moving from working *classes* to a working *class* (Sellers, 1991: 305). In this sense, it shared some similarities with eighteenth-century England (Thompson, 1978). In the run-up to the 1828 presidential election, the Workingman's Party in New York demanded equal property, food, clothing and education for all (Wilentz, 2004: 194). A few years later, in 1836, 20 per cent of New York's population turned out to hear radical speakers protest against a legal judgement of foundational violence that had made union combinations illegal. At the time, it was the largest meeting in the young republic's history (Wilentz, 2004: 290–2).

All of this demonstrates the unease with which nineteenth-century America welcomed the development of capitalism and its new routines, rhythms, norms, categories and forms of authority and hierarchy. The unfolding society, its insecurity, its increasing wage dependency and its greater productive capacity seemed contrived, unnatural and in need of change. Byllesby, Blachly and their cohorts, like craft workers more generally, asserted Ricardo's labour theory of value as the basis for a redistribution of wealth (Sellers, 1991: 285–90; Wilentz, 2004: 242–5). There was deep-rooted fear of the increasing concentration of property and of an emerging power elite of speculators (Sellers, 1991: 301–31). This was linked to a fear of money capital, which was perhaps most obvious during the so-called 'Bank Wars', wherein 'the farmer/worker majority', along with President Jackson, sought to rein in the banks, which were accused of 'extortionate enterprise' and economic disruption (see Sellers, 1991: 321). As we have seen, large numbers of farmers and craft workers were suspicious of the market, too – Byllesby's 'trafficking'.

The emerging society was viewed as hostile and its struggles led to class consciousness and a rejection of the four propositions of capital: namely, that capitalism and the United States were classless and free; that they provided equal opportunity for each and every industrious citizen; that US wage earners were prosperous; and, finally, that the interests of capitalists and workers were identical (Wilentz, 2004: 303–4). As we shall see in Chapter 3, the development of management in the second half of the nineteenth century was strenuously resisted by workers. When employers and managers succeeded in overcoming that resistance, they did so only through coercion and the limiting of democracy and, indeed, possibility (Negri, 1999: 1–36).

Notes

1 The title of this chapter is taken from the essay by Thompson (1978).
2 This should not be read as suggesting that crafts were not hierarchical, gendered or race-based spaces.
3 Obviously there are enormous injustices here about who is and who is not a citizen or 'worthy' of being free (Federici, 2004; Roediger and Esch, 2012).
4 Jacques (1996: 25) provides different figures, arguing that 90 per cent of white male workers were self-employed as farmers, merchants or craft workers. His figures include only white males, however.
5 The 1786 Shays Rebellion in Massachusetts was largely fought over these issues and it is widely thought to have influenced the US elite into drafting the Constitution in the way that they did – that is, to give more centralized power to the federal state (see Negri, 1999: 141–91).
6 This tension between the federal and local states would eventually lead to the 'South Carolina Doctrine', which declared limits to federal expansion by arguing that local states had more power than the federal state and could choose to opt in or out of legislation and development programmes (Sellers, 1991). For example, see Senator Daniel Webster (1830: paragraphs 7–11) for a summary of the doctrine as it emerged in the Nullification

Crisis. Eventually, what was embodied in these tensions exploded into the violence of the Civil War.

7 In this sense, although we should be fearful of a simplistic linear narrative, we must reject Jacques's assertion 'that it is *not* useful to study this time with reference to linear progressive history. Rather we must attempt to see this as a world within which social relations were configured along lines unsuspected, barely imaginable today' (Jacques, 1996: 40–1; emphasis in original). However, simply to accept this is to risk depoliticizing the changes involved and how they helped to shape today.

8 Although, see Gutman (1973: 551–3), who argues that even in this 'benign' period, many of the women were unhappy and unable to adjust fully to industrial life.

9 The United States experienced female-led food riots into the twentieth century: for example, in 1902 Jewish women in New York led a food riot against the unjust price of kosher meat and the failure of retail butchers to maintain a boycott of the Meat Trust, with which they were in dispute. The riots quickly spread to other cities, and a rabbi in New York's Lower East Side was asked to set the price of meat for the Jewish community in a manner akin to the European *shtetl*. Again, as in eighteenth-century Britain, there was no looting on a large scale and the state (never homogeneous) was not completely on the side of either the business elite or the press in these matters (Gutman, 1973: 574–6, 567–8).

10 Elton Mayo felt that the monotony of work allowed workers to slip into a reverie wherein they thought too much. After witnessing the actual rise of the mass worker (a phenomenon that Smith had only imagined in the *Wealth of Nations*), Mayo held monotony and reverie as at least partly responsible for the workers' adherence to socialism, an ideology from which he believed they needed to be weaned by human relations.

11 Marx, as would be expected, favours Adam Ferguson, who is much more sceptical about the changing division of labour (and, indeed, capitalism more generally). Ferguson (1995) feared it would divide work in terms of head and hand (as it did) and that it would fracture the individual (as it did). Marx rightly criticizes Smith for downplaying the negative aspects of the division of labour and suggests his schooling remedy is meted out in 'prudently homoeopathic doses' (Marx, 1976: 484).

12 In the UK, journeymen were making similar arguments in their rejection of any positive role whatsoever for capital (Hodgskin, 1825).

13 An earlier version of this can be seen in the Spanish corralling of the rural indigenous peoples from the conquered lands of Latin America into designated labour camps or villages to ensure a steady supply of recalcitrant labour for the mines, wherein most would perish through exhaustion, disease or accidents (Federici, 2004: 227). Yet again, the practices of the periphery return to the metropole.

14 Although, importantly, women and children were not mere victims; they struck and resisted the factory (Gutman, 1973; 546; Perrow, 2002).

15 Although not developed here, neo-liberals and Weber have argued that common law and the strengthening of the executive and the judiciary over the legislative branch of government are beneficial because they weaken democracy and parliament's answerability to citizens. This is important because democracy enables people to avoid the 'spontaneous market' of neo-liberalism (Chapter 6). As this chapter highlights, this use of democracy was exactly what the US population attempted – and failed – to do in the nineteenth century.

16 Moral crusades against the working class, women, immigrants and other subjects of no value have, of course, continued up to the present day.

17 Lincoln's State of the Union Address reflects elements of this thinking.

18 This was not a traditional form of religious belief. Benjamin (2008: 112) notes that 'all religions have held the beggar in high esteem', yet the religious fervour of the nineteenth century held the beggar responsible for his or her own plight.

19 Importantly, religion was not simply a pro-market variable. Perrow (2002: 61) suggests that religious revivals may also have brought workers together and hence enabled them

to organize, while Sellers (1991: 220–5) argues that the rapid growth of the male-dominated Mormon Church was a reaction against the market as men experienced social decline. Furthermore, the religious practices and traditions of immigrants were often seen as hindrances to capitalism because they operated on a pre-industrial timescale (see Gutman, 1973). In 1914, Ford went so far as to sack 900 workers for staying away from work to celebrate the Eastern Orthodox Christmas (Montgomery, 1987: 236).

3

'AN ALMOST EQUAL DIVISION OF THE WORK AND THE RESPONSIBILITY'[1]

Driving towards the mass industrial subject

The changing division of labour

The story of work and early capitalism is sometimes a story told as loss, a shift from an egalitarian craft world to a less egalitarian industrial one. It is a story of deskilling. We reduced the craft worker to elevate the society is the positive gloss; or we deskilled the worker to impose a new – unequal – economic order. There is perhaps truth in both renditions of the story. Capitalism, and US capitalism more than most, largely thrived on the non-craft worker – the immigrant, the woman, the child, the non-white subject, those in debt. As we have seen, the most vulnerable delivered our contemporary world. First and foremost, capitalism abuses the vulnerable and the dependent, and it is upon their experience that capitalist social relations thrive. One consequence of such a position is that radical critiques of this transition must reject the notion of a return to some form of craft experience or a return to concrete labour producing goods for use value in small-scale communities (on these tendencies in Marxism, see Weeks, 2011: 79–92). Rather, capitalism pulled into its orbit millions who had no craft experience, who went straight from the land to the factory, who were skilled in ways that craft workers would never have recognized, whose experience was a mass, semi-skilled one. Thus, there is no authentic concept of work to fall back on or to restore (Negri, 1991: 10). The emerging mass industrial subject recognized this (Mills, 1951).

In the second half of the nineteenth century the United States experienced an enormous change that radically transformed the society, recomposed its class system and altered production and employment. Bendix (1956: 255) suggests that between 1870 and 1910 the primary sector of the economy declined as an employer by 75 per cent – down from 53.5 per cent in 1870 to 31.6 per cent in 1910. In the same period, the US population more than doubled – increasing from 39.8 million to 91.1 million – much of it wage-dependent migrants. Montgomery (1987: 59–60) further argues that the nature of employment in the non-primary sector changed. The poorly defined category of 'labourer' increased from 8 per cent of the employed population to 12 per cent. However, he also notes that the head of the US census of 1910 suggested that one-third of all male employees should be classified as 'labourers'. Capitalism did not destroy the labourer as a worker; as a way to make a living, unskilled physical exertion grew in the second half of the nineteenth century. From 1870 to 1910, the number of labourers grew by 408 per cent – twice as fast as, for example, the construction sector as a whole – because prefabrication reduced the need for skilled labour. Generally, the labourer was a male immigrant or Afro-American farm worker leaving the land. Craft workers took to labouring only in very hard times, and if a white American worker became a labourer he was assumed to be a 'drunkard' or trying to avoid the police or his family. He was considered undisciplined (Montgomery, 1987: 64–5).

Reflecting on this 'non-standard' employment structure, Montgomery (1987: 112) suggests that in an innovative industry such as electric light bulbs, by 1910 60 per cent of factory production workers were between sixteen and twenty years of age, 35 per cent of them were daughters of US parents, 40 per cent were daughters of immigrant parents and 25 per cent were immigrants themselves. He argues that the 'typical' industrial worker was a 17-year-old unmarried woman of German immigrant parents and that she was at the cutting edge of industrial innovation, consolidated capital and the formation of a new working class. Often these workers were located in corporations that were 'tireless promoters of standardized methods, systematic accounting and control of costs, they changed work processes and materials incessantly' (Montgomery, 1987: 112–13) – Marx's constant revolutionizing of the production process. However, they were also often managed via piece rates and the foreman's empire – wherein the foreman assigned tasks, hired and fired, and set the pace of work (see Nelson, 1995) – rather than Taylor's scientific method. Their employers were usually the major bureaucratic firms that consolidated US capital in the late nineteenth century and were geared towards both the domestic and the international markets in a range of industries, from consumer to capital goods: the likes of Heinz, Campbell, American Tobacco, International Harvester and Remington Typewriter. These were the firms that went on to dominate corporate America for much of the twentieth century and gave us the modern capitalist behemoth (Chandler, 1977; Edwards, 1979: 42–7; Montgomery, 1987: 173). For their workers, capital and management were the organizing authorities at work.

In short, the working world was undergoing a period of radical change. Farming was in steep decline, wage dependency was the norm, females, immigrants and non-whites were key elements of the industrial workforce and craft workers were in decline, although they retained their militancy (see Braverman, 1974; Edwards, 1979; Montgomery, 1987). In contrast to earlier in the century (see Chapter 2), there was a much greater ideological belief in leadership and the legitimacy of bureaucratic corporate capitalism, while the concept of self-help and a work ethic based on mobility and consumption were taking hold. But this ideological shift and the increasingly widespread belief in the legitimacy of the corporation and the meritocracy of the market, although real, were by no means universal. Middle-class reformers rejected the emerging or existing and consolidating elite based on the concentration of capital in the late 1890s: some 30 per cent of manufacturing capital was consolidated at the turn of the century (Edwards, 1979: 65–71; Gordon et al., 1982: 107). And, as we shall see later, labour continuously protested (Gutman, 1973). Weber's (1994) new aristocracy was not yet legitimate. Finally, immigrants and children continued to act as the wellspring for the industrial firm's labour force (Montgomery, 1987: 48). Indeed, immigration is central to understanding the US experience. Gutman (1973: 561) suggests that whereas only 6 per cent of those living in London came from outside Great Britain in 1880, the figures for immigrants and the children of immigrants as percentages of the total populations of San Francisco, St Louis, Cleveland, New York, Detroit, Milwaukee and Chicago were: 78, 78, 80, 80, 84, 84 and 87, respectively. If, as we saw in Chapter 2, manufacturing was leaving the farm and the urban home to become more metropolitan, then it was the immigrants and their children who were the foundation of this shift.

Although it was a very different place from the first half of the nineteenth century, there was still strife in post-Civil War America well into the twentieth century.[2] For example, the 1870–90 period was one of industrial unrest and the tentative start of industrial unions via organizations such as the 'Knights of Labor' (Brody, 1965; Montgomery, 1987). Bendix (1956: 265) notes union membership grew fivefold between 1897 and 1905, and that this was accompanied by 'considerable violence' on both sides. Gitelman (1973: 3–6) suggests that somewhat later, from 1915 to 1935, the United States had twice as many strikes as France and that the US strikes were generally more violent. Across a range of industries – coal (Gitelman, 1988), steel (Brody, 1965), the docks (Montgomery, 1987), transport (Edwards, 1979) and electrical goods (Montgomery, 1987) – there were industrial strikes and unrest, and it has been suggested that the labour problem was the most intractable issue in the United States up to and after the First World War (Gitelman, 1988: xi). Brown (1972: 222) describes the USA as a fragmented society before and after the Civil War in terms of economics but also in terms of personal and social goods, and public and religious life. Jacques (1996: 59–61) calls the imposition of the new social contract between 1875 and 1910 'the American "Reign of Terror"'.

One can get a sense of this ferment from the establishment of the Pennsylvania State Police. This was founded along the lines of the Royal Irish Constabulary, which operated as a quasi-military force under state of emergency legislation for almost the entire period from 1830 to 1890. This form was deemed necessary to defend the realm against a campaign aimed at repealing the Act of Union between Ireland and Britain; the dislocation that came with the Great Famine; resistance to land clearances; two armed rebellions; democratic demands for Home Rule under first Daniel O'Connell and then Charles Stewart Parnell; and an almost continuous 'land war' led by left-leaning leaders such as Michael Davitt (Lyons, 1971). The Pennsylvania State Police were modelled on this quasi-military force because of the scale of civil and industrial unrest in the region. Perhaps another indication of the level of ferment is the scale of industrial injury. For example, in the Carnegie steel plant in Pennsylvania – the world's first billion-dollar corporation and a technological achievement – 25 per cent of the workforce died or were injured between 1907 and 1910. As we saw in Chapter 2, the courts increasingly put the onus on the worker in cases of personal injury. Gordon et al. (1982: 100–64) argue that industrial unrest grew between 1880 and 1900, generated increasing links between skilled and unskilled workers and started to focus on issues relating to the control of the production process rather than purely individualistic economic concerns.

Amid all this turbulence, the United States was on its way to becoming the world's industrial power house. In the 1860s it was the fourth-largest industrial nation after Britain, Germany and France. By 1894, the 'American system' had generated the world's largest industrial machine, and the country was producing almost as much manufactured product as the other three combined (see Gutman, 1973). The latter half of the nineteenth century and the opening of the twentieth were a time of vicious, often violent, industrial conflict. As such, for the craft worker and the employer, 'Between 1843 and 1893 compromise between such conflicting interests was hardly possible' (Gutman, 1973: 559). And the mainly immigrant unskilled labourers in the mines, the steel industry, textiles, glass, transportation and construction joined unions in disproportionate numbers from the mid-1880s onwards (Gutman, 1973: 566). When people did not join unions they refused in other ways and often moved jobs and/or location, thereby creating a sense of unsettledness. In short, the late nineteenth and early twentieth centuries were a time of industrial warfare. Major strikes took place on the railways in 1877, at McCormick's International Harvester in 1886, at Carnegie's steelworks in 1892, at Pullman in 1894, in the Colorado mines in 1903, 1904 and 1914 (the last of which resulted in the 'Ludlow massacre'), at McKees Rock in 1909, and at Bethleham Steel in 1910 and 1919, when a quarter of a million steelworkers downed tools (see Brody, 1965; Gutman, 1973; Hessen, 1974; Edwards 1979: 48–71; Gitelman, 1988). Many of these strikes were accompanied by bloodshed. Brody (1965: 15), when discussing the steel industry, explains what lay at the heart of this conflict:

> The spirit of economy determined the industry's labor policy. Steel men saw labor as an item of cost that, like any other, had to be narrowed to the irreducible minimum. This was indeed the main effect of technological innovation. Mechanized handling of materials, integration of the smelting, refining and rolling stages, and continuous rolling techniques all multiplied labor productivity by eliminating men or increasing operational speed. Steelmakers sought to increase productivity further through close supervision and rational disposition of work and scheduling. Theirs was essentially the outlook of scientific management (although not necessarily the actual prescriptions of the movement's founder, Frederick W. Taylor).

Although he is talking only about steel-making, many of the issues Brody highlights can be rolled out to other industries because they encapsulate factors common to industrial relations generally: work pace, driving down wages, use of technology, piece rates and ever-closer supervision – essentially who controlled the labour process. While there were welfare programmes at the likes of Rockefeller's firms, McCormick International Harvester and US Steel in the early twentieth century – what Jacques (1996: 109) refers to as a shift to management as a form of stewardship[3] – these ameliorating tendencies were often subordinate to Taylor-like cost-controlling strategies (see Brody, 1965; Gitelman, 1988; Barley and Kunda, 1992). The struggle to answer the question of who controlled the production process made labour an intractable problem and it also redefined worker subjectivity by reshaping work and non-work life and thereby giving rise to the mass industrial worker.

In some respects, the union was at the centre of economic life at this time – although, as the 'new labour history' scholars have taught us, it is important not to overemphasize its role in labour's refusal of capitalism because many people never joined a union. Instead, they resisted in other ways: for example, workers might change localities or jobs, while immigrants might return to their home countries (although this largely ended as a route out with the First World War) or fall back on their ethnic groups and families for support (see Gutman, 1973; Brody, 1979; Bodnar, 1980). Unions were not given any legal protection until the First World War. However, if workers were strong enough to form a union against an employer's will, they were allowed to combine from 1842 onwards (although there were still legal challenges to them doing so in the 1890s). Legal challenges enabled employers to enforce 'yellow dog' contracts, wherein workers had to agree not to join a union; if the workers subsequently reneged on these contracts, they might be sacked. For example, in 1918, Western Union Telegraphy sacked 800 workers because they had joined a union (Gitelman, 1988: 244) and Bethlehem Steel sacked the three men who had brought forward the grievances of 700 workers (a key factor in precipitating the 1910 strike; see Hessen, 1974). These were typical management responses to the refusal of workers. But so too was the collusion embedded in the regular meetings of leading capitalists, such as J. P. Morgan, John D. Rockefeller, Henry Frick, Charles Schwab and Elbert Gary (Gitelman, 1988: 305–30) and the establishment of information-gathering organizations, such as the Employers Association of Detroit, which had 1,600 files on 'militants' in 1904 and an amazing 180,000 by 1912 (Nelson, 1995: 129). The capitalist class did not emerge organically; it was formed through the refusal of workers. But this capitalist class formation meant labour's capacity to combine was never straightforward.

In this period labour relations were dominated by the issue of the 'open shop' (Bendix, 1956: 267–74): that is, by management's insistence that workers must meet capital as individuals in a free and open contract and that management be allowed to use the property it controlled – plant, buildings and hired labour – however it saw fit, without interference. Employers sought the full legal use of 'their' property and labour resisted this full legal use. Because it was supposedly like any other property, management insisted labour was freely hired by capital and, having entered the contract, had given up any right to object. Without labouring the point too much, in this regard free and slave labour shared some similarities. Slave owners were also confronted with the problem of recalcitrant labour that needed to be persuaded, managed and, when necessary, violently punished so that they obeyed and accepted the unfree ownership contract to which they were subject (Roediger and Esch, 2012: 40–66). Labour took a different view and saw itself as a unique, value-adding entity that did not merely obey. In the sphere of free labour, this gave rise both to industrial action and to new forms of management, such as the greater use of welfarism (Brody, 1965), company unions (Rockefeller, 1916), an embracing of aspects of scientific management (Montgomery, 1987), greater use of industrial psychology (Mills, 1951; Bendix, 1956), sponsoring chairs at universities and the growth of business schools (Gitelman, 1988),[4] the blacklisting of union organizers (Bendix, 1956: 270), the use of police to intimidate workers and their families (Gitelman, 1967, 1988), the demonization of unions as 'unAmerican' through the press (Brody, 1965: 135–45), and vitriolic attacks suggesting workers were ungrateful and irrational when they rejected company unions and/or company welfare in favour of worker control or independence (see Brody, 1965: 176). Such attacks were a particular trait of Elbert Gary (Gitelman, 1988: 310) and J. D. Rockefeller, Jr.

In short, these tactics of manipulation, violence and intimidation demonstrate how intractable the labour question was, because they belie capital's underlying weakness. Capital needed labour, and by conceding its need for the police, for the university chairs, for the press campaigns and for the new regulating and disciplining management techniques, it tacitly acknowledged that labour was a unique 'property' to which it had to respond. It could not treat labour as it would a machine. Work would increasingly require new forms of organization on the parts of both labour and capital.

As was suggested in Chapter 2, by the 1860s the craft worker as a dominant political subject was in retreat. However, although damaged by the changes of the first half of the nineteenth century, craft workers were to experience yet more rapid change, to which they reacted by forming closer alliances with operatives and labourers. This created a new subject – the mass industrial worker. Central to this process were the factory, the division of labour and the real subsumption of labour to capital. This transformation of production was so complete by the 1890s that the craft-led American Federation of Labor had accepted management's right to manage and now advocated better working conditions and pay rather than the right to control the production process in the way that craft workers had done historically (Foner, 1995: xxxviii). Indeed, in 1895, during a question-and-answer session after Frederick W. Taylor had delivered 'A Piece Rate System: Being a Step towards the Partial Solution to the Labour Problem', a former president of the Brotherhood of Machine Molders congratulated him on his paper, saying it was a 'landmark in the field of political economy' (Taylor, 1895: 889).[5] Work, the division of labour and management were changing.

At the heart of this change were an expansion in the processes leading to the division of labour, the continued expropriation of workers' knowledge, the further growth of the factory, more immigration, crusades against working-class life that emphasized the moral importance of being 'productive' and the introduction of new factors, such as the concentration of capital on an unprecedented scale, the emergence of the large bureaucratic private firm, the use of technology and science to subsume labour to capital, the rise of many current management techniques, the expansion of 'new' classes of work – semi-skilled hands, labourers, white-collar workers with class, gender and racial implications – and, finally, alterations in consumption and the emergence of new cultural forms. But first and foremost, this era was one of 'industrial war'. This conflict often went unobserved, but it was war nevertheless because 'men were contending for power' (Brody, 1965: 9).

The changing nature of organization: skill and the workshop

In his masterful study of labour history *The Fall of the House of Labor*, the historian David Montgomery starts with an analysis of the undermining of worker control in the workshop. He opens by examining the level of autonomy craft workers exhibited and the role of workers and craft unions in setting pay rates, controlling the speed of work, how workers were trained and socialized, and the nature of hierarchy and authority. One might say the workers owned the work even if the capitalist owned the product of that work: that is, the workers were subject to the laws of capitalism and the market but they were not directly managed in the production sphere. They experienced what Marx called a 'formal subsumption of labour to capital' (Marx, 1976: 1023–35; Clawson, 1980: 111–25). Often the work was subcontracted to the craft workers and they then allocated tasks, work rates, training systems and pay rates from the original price they had obtained from the capitalist. However, as we saw in Chapter 2, this world came under threat from the capitalist deployment of hired wage labour in the factory, the increasing subdivision of labour and mechanization with the emergence of 'systematic management' (Litterer, 1963; Nelson, 1995: 35–64). Nevertheless, these workers continued to have a large amount of autonomy and control, and

> They exercised this control because they fought for it and their position in that struggle drew strength from the workers' functional autonomy on the job, from the group ethical code they developed around their work relations and from the organizations they created for themselves in order to protect their interests and values.
>
> *(Montgomery, 1987: 13)*

Workers enjoyed independence because of their control of knowledge, organization, collectivism and sociality. Autonomy in organizational life was never granted; it was defended and attacked (Clawson, 1980; Nelson, 1995).

As Montgomery goes on to show in the rest of his book, capital set about replacing workers' functional autonomy with Taylor's (1903: 1387–95) 'functional management'. This entailed the destruction of collective work life, the self-organized worker production process and the ethical code of craftwork – the shared cognitive and affective maps of craft labour. At the centre of this struggle were socialization, subjectivity, knowledge and what we might now call 'organizational culture'. Before management could manage or leaders could lead, workers' knowledge had to be expropriated and the division of labour made ever finer (Litterer, 1963; Nelson, 1995: 38–40). Managerial knowledge or expertise had to be violently stolen. Workers needed to be convinced that it was in their best interests to allow management the right to manage, to hand over knowledge to management so it could manage and to derive fulfilment from working hard to earn wages that would allow them to express themselves via consumption (Mills, 1951). (On the link between the work ethic and consumption, see also Weeks, 2011 and Lears, 2000.) And if convincing them proved impossible, then they had to be coerced (Pollard, 1965: 258). Violence was used to break the craft workers' independence, and it was also employed against the already dependent migrants, women, children and the unskilled. Descartes and Hobbes could be combined through the new bureaucracies that became mechanisms of class war where 'social control of the system is such that irresponsibility is organized into it' (Mills, 1951: 111). However, during this struggle for control of production (as we will see), workers created a new, more inclusive and more powerful industrial class despite all of management's efforts to individualize, divide and limit such potentiality.

One way much work within leading technical industries of the second half of the nineteenth century was managed was through the inside contract system. In its purest form, this system meant that the owner/management of a firm was responsible for the provision of space, machinery, raw materials and working capital, and for organizing the sale of the product (Buttrick, 1952; Williamson, 1952; Clawson, 1980; Englander, 1987; Nelson, 1995; Perrow, 2002). However, within such ownership, the raw material itself was turned into the finished product by a contractor and a team of workers. The contractor hired the employees, allocated tasks, supervised the work process and received a contract rate from the company – the gap between what the contractor received and what they paid to the workers represented the contractor's profit. This was similar to the 'putting-out' system but it was not identical to it, as it did not precede the factory but rather was a central element of the factory system itself (Perrow, 2002). At the base of this regime was a capitalist–speculator who often lacked knowledge of the production process. (As we saw in Chapter 2, this lack of knowledge was something craft workers resented about the emerging corporate form.) Williamson (1952: 21; emphasis in original) comments about Oliver F. Winchester: 'he represents a new breed of *entrepreneur* in the firearms industry' because he had no technical knowledge about the production process. Equally, in the steel industry (Montgomery, 1987: 9–57), at Singer Sewing Machines (Nelson, 1995: 38) and in the government arsenals (Buttrick, 1952), the lack of capitalist knowledge about the production process forced capitalists to use this system, especially when technological advances, interchangeable parts and competition led to an ever-increasing necessity for greater concentrations of capital (Brown, 1972: 221).

This system was most apparent in the cutting-edge, virtually mass-producing, knowledge industries of the time. Here, knowledge, skill and/or craft were central to authority in the factory. Ownership without knowledge had no real authority in the factory. Capital confronted the worker as speculation, not authority. In these technologically progressive industries planning was not capitalist planning but knowledge worker/craft worker planning. An *almost* equal division of work and responsibility was achieved. However, the division was weighted too much on the side of labour, leaving the workforce with too much knowledge and therefore too much power.[6] This meant the situation was not quite the worker stripped of the means of production that Marx discussed under the free contract; workers still retained a monopoly over knowledge, which enabled them to exert authority.

As we shall see, although the two systems were often in opposition, the inside contract system operated somewhat like the 'foreman's empire' of the Pullman works, because labour controlled knowledge in both systems. In the foreman's empire, a foreman was given a piece rate for a job, set wages, tasks and times, and was accordingly rewarded on the basis of savings, although the foreman himself (it usually was a man) was paid a salary/wage. This system persisted into the twentieth century (Mills, 1951: 77–112; Edwards, 1979: 32; Nelson, 1995; Esch and Roediger, 2009). In the inside contract system, a contractor was given a contract price to then organize the production process. But the two systems were hostile to each other because of their respective relationships to knowledge. For example, Singer Sewing Machines and the Winchester Repeating Arms Company both hired and learned from contractors before getting rid of them and hiring foremen as salaried employees and 'managers' in their place (Williamson, 1952: 131–8; Clawson, 1980: 111–25; Nelson, 1995: 35–55).

One of the outcomes of the expanding market society was the development of ever-greater demand for capital and consumer goods. With this expansion came the growth of larger factories and an increasing demand for labour; both led to a greater need to maintain the inside contract system until knowledge of production had been expropriated (something today's knowledge workers should note). This did not occur until the late nineteenth/early twentieth century in most industries, including arms, steel, transport, coal, textiles, watchmaking and wood and leather manufacture (see Braverman, 1974: 61). However, these developments altered the inside contract relationship because new problems of coordination and logistics emerged with the growth of larger factories – especially between different contractors and foremen (Litterer, 1963: 375; Chandler, 1977). For example, work flow had to be managed because contract group A would not be interested in making contract group B's work flow easier if this had the effect of hampering their own; quality had to be controlled because group A would happily pass shoddy work on to group B if its own remuneration were not impacted by doing so; increasingly different large contractors had to be coordinated; plant and equipment had to be maintained, even though it was not necessarily in the interests of any single group to do so; and costs and expenses for the whole operation demanded coordination (Buttrick, 1952: 207–8; Pollard, 1965: 38–47; Braverman, 1974: 59–69). Supposedly, all of this pulled capital ever further into management and centralized the issue of knowledge.

But this functionalist account – something of which Englander (1987: 430) accuses Chandler – ignores other aspects of the inside contract system, including its innovation, its reduction of costs, its good management systems and its capacity to deliver mass production. What became known as the 'American system' was located in the skilled craftsman's knowledge and innovation. The development of inter-changeable parts by these craftsmen made mass production possible. If one part of a rifle broke, it could be replaced with a similar part from the same factory or from another rifle of the same make. Without interchangeable parts, mass production is impossible. It was worker knowledge and innovation that made it possible, and workers continued to use this knowledge in the second half of the nineteenth century for 'the continuous development of new and better machinery, techniques, and gauges, for only in this way could standards of accuracy be improved' (Clawson, 1980: 77).

One example of this reflects the problem of the inside contract from the point of view of the capitalist. Innovation was often withheld from the capitalist because the release of knowledge would be detrimental to the craft worker, yet capitalists could not make or improve products on their own. For example, in 1861, the Winchester New Haven Arms Company nearly went bankrupt, largely due to its owner's lack of knowledge of his own products (Williamson, 1952: 24). However, a mechanic named B. Tyler Henry, who worked as a superintendent in the factory, had recently been working on improving the capacity of the company's central product – a repeating rifle. In late 1860, due to his work, a patent for the new 'Henry rifle' was awarded and the company began to produce both the weapon and the ammunition for it (also invented by Henry). The rifle was a huge success – so much so that the company bid for (although it did not win) a government contract for rifles and ammunition worth $1.86 million (Williamson, 1952: 30 and 395 n3). Despite not securing the contract, the company still earned $171,335.31 from the government that year. In 1874, it sought to renew its patent for the Henry rifle. As part of its bid, it outlined that Henry would forfeit his annual salary of $1,500 to act as the company's first inside contractor and earn $15,000 over five years (a 100 per cent increase on his projected earnings).

A number of points are worth noting with respect to this story. First, labour's knowledge and invention appear to save the firm. Second, the inside contract system appears to arise from a patent application within which the firm appears to deal generously with its employee–inventor (shades of Schumpeter – innovation is done by he or she who can deliver it to the market). And, third, in relative terms, the income Henry earns from his innovation is dwarfed by that made by the firm and its owner. In 1874, largely from these innovations, the firm's net profit was $265,000, whereas Henry was set to make just an extra $7,500 over five years. For management, profitability would be increased and long-term accumulation made more certain if it could establish a system wherein innovation and production came at a pace it could control and it did not have to deal so generously with labour. Herein lay the weakness of the inside contract.

At the heart of scientific development were the skilled inside contractors because they 'were excellent and ingenious mechanics who operated their own machine shops and had enough time to experiment' (Williamson, 1952: 89). In markets where technical skills were the paramount resource (Williamson, 1952: 85), such experimentation enabled both innovation and the enhancement of that same paramount resource – its owner. The contractors and the skilled craftsmen were today's scientists, creatives, intellectuals, artists or knowledge workers. In contrast, the capitalist/manager 'had neither the training nor the ability to organize the production of such articles as precision tools or guns, nor did he have the inventiveness which was an integral part of manufacturing at this time' (Williamson, 1952: 86). Nevertheless, despite capital's weakness, the system also had other advantages. It delivered cost savings and good management. Contract prices were usually negotiated annually and generally downwards as capitalists asked for the same (or more) for less each year (Buttrick, 1952; Williamson, 1952; Clawson, 1980; Englander, 1987). Indeed, this was a cause of considerable tension, and contractors would hold back innovation in the production process to allow the undercutting of costs to be offset, thereby enabling them to maintain or increase their margins. Nevertheless, reducing costs was a central feature of the system. So too were good 'management relations' among workers. Labour generally saw the contractor as a worker, albeit one with more money, status and power than most (as did management). This view reflected his or her superior technical knowledge, internal power and authority relations, close family, friend and community ties, and the management of production flows, costs, innovations, selection and hiring (Clawson, 1980; Englander, 1987; Perrow, 2002).

When combined, these advantages created a remarkably efficient system capable of mass production. For example, in 1880, Winchester produced 26,000 guns; in 1904, it made 225,000 – an increase of 800 per cent. Singer sold 181,260 sewing machines in 1871; eight years later, it produced 431,167. Output at Colt grew from 73,000 in 1861 to 188,000 just two years later (see Clawson, 1980: 83). It appears that the formal subsumption of labour to capital could – and did – develop a form of proto-mass production. So why was there such a decisive shift away from it? Was it about power and control in the factory or was it a functional necessity? The answer, obviously, is the former. Put plainly, the inside contract and the worker had to be more controlled if profit were to be maximized. But before management could use the division of labour to control this emerging organizational form, it needed to expropriate the workers' knowledge. Management, not worker independence, was deemed necessary for labour, and this required legal theft.

Management's problem remained its lack of knowledge about the production process and also about management itself, hence the appeal of the contract system in the first place (Pollard, 1965: 38–47). *Contra* Weber, Michels or Pareto, before the elite could use the bureaucracy or the organization or the division of labour to lead, they had to learn from those who would be 'led'. As Taylor (1895: 868) puts it: 'The most formidable obstacle is the lack of knowledge on the part of both the men and the management (but chiefly the latter) of the quickest time in which each piece of work can be done or, briefly, the lack of accurate time-tables for the work of the place.' The nineteenth-century management prerogative was to steal this knowledge by expropriating it from the workers who actually understood the production process. Here, we are back in the world of the Amherst Carriage Company. This was the only way in which capital could accumulate, and it meant new undemocratic and irresponsible forms of hierarchy and authority had to be created (Mills, 1951: 109–11). Approving of Thomas Hodgskin's labour theory of value, Marx (2000: III, 266–7; emphasis in original) puts it thus:

> the accumulation of the skill and knowledge (scientific power) of the workers themselves is the chief form of accumulation, and infinitely more important than the accumulation – which goes hand in hand with it and merely represents it – of the *existing objective* conditions of this accumulated activity. These objective conditions are only nominally accumulated and must be constantly produced and consumed anew.

Or as Thomas Edison, the founder of General Electric, would put it over fifty years later: 'an important part of my duties, as a business executive', is to 'make capital' from workers' knowledge (see Jacques, 1996: 143). So how did management glean such knowledge? How did managers steal the right to manage?

Expropriating knowledge

As Marx argues, the inherent driver of capitalism is the need for ever-greater capital accumulation. Accumulation leads to bigger and bigger firms, and with that comes a need for greater management information in order to exploit labour more fully – what Jacques (1996: 47) calls 'scale' and Panzieri (1961) refers to as 'planning'. Accumulation also heralds the 'multiplication of the proletariat' (Marx, 1976: 764). This is not a linear process. For example, the mines of the North East of England were first withdrawn from the subcontracting system to be directly managed in the mid-eighteenth century, only to be subcontracted out again fifty years later (Pollard, 1965: 42). As we saw, this was because the contract system had real advantages that were directly related to capital's weakness and its lack of leadership, organization and knowledge. It allowed capitalists to shift risk to the contractors: they could simply reduce the piece rate and let the contractor sweat labour or innovate (or not) to offset the loss; they could also avoid hiring, firing and disciplining the workforce while simultaneously availing themselves of the labour market knowledge of the contractor; and they could encourage contractors to specialize with knock-on efficiency gains. However, these advantages also highlighted capital's inability to plan or act as the uncontested authority because capitalists were ignorant of the production process (Buttrick, 1952). Management could manage only after expropriation.

However, with bigger firms came the need for greater management information systems concerning issues of costs, sales, inventory control and the profit rates of subcontractors. For example, in the late nineteenth century, firms in the arms industry possessed none of this information (Buttrick, 1952). Indeed, the growth of the accountancy profession stems from this time and is intimately linked to management control strategies within the firm (Armstrong, 1985). As capitalists confronted the issue of controlling the labour process they started to learn more about it, about improving the quality of their products, and about management technique, all of which encouraged them to intervene further (Williamson, 1952; Pollard, 1965: 38; Nelson, 1995: 35–54). By increasing competition, the recession of the 1870s also acted as a catalyst for expropriating knowledge and improving management skill (although, as we saw in Chapter 2, the process had started long before then).

Capital began to expropriate know-how and to control the production process more tightly by enacting new procedures. In the armaments industry, firms started to hire contractors who had knowledge of the production process to act as managers. Williamson (1952: 87) highlights how Winchester became more cost conscious and as a result hired an ex-contractor from Remington to gain more control over the system. In 1892, the firm hired one of its largest contractors as a general super-intendent in order to gain even further control, so that 'it was no small advantage to the company to have the determination of contracts in his hands' (Williamson, 1952: 136). This shift was exacerbated by an increase in hiring managers from engineering schools and colleges – indeed, when T. G. Bennett was appointed the company's new president in 1890, he was the first to have a technical background. This 'qualified' management sought to make innovation and production more 'scientific'; they also resented the power and earnings of the contractors. There were derisory comments about 'contractors who came to work in fancy horse-drawn carriages, wearing frock coats, and sporting diamond stickpins, spats and gloves. These individuals not uncommonly had subforemen under them and supervised their departments at arm's length' (Williamson, 1952: 136). This social antagonism towards men whom owners and managers seem to have viewed as jumped-up workers led to a desire to reorder the social hierarchy and its distribution of wealth along 'proper' lines: that is, more to those who owned or managed. This reflected the fact that management saw contractors as workers first and foremost, as indeed did the workers who sided with the contractors against management (Williamson, 1952; Clawson, 1980: 112). That these workers often earned more than those in the most senior management roles (or even owners) was resented and seen as a management problem. For example, at Winchester in the 1880s, the president earned $14,200 per annum, a top official $7,600, the largest contractor $10,800 and the average large contractor $4,860 (Clawson, 1980: 112). Here and at other firms, such as the Whitin Machine Works, there was a push to lower these salaries to what owners and managers thought was a fair wage for a 'worker' – an income that 'would match the individual's place in the social hierarchy' (Buttrick, 1952: 210). Capitalism may need knowledge workers, but they still need to be suitably reduced and broken because they occupy 'the anomalous position of a belligerent inferior' (Roland, 1897: 995–6).

Thus, the end of the inside contract system was about two related issues: first, diverting surplus away from labour to capital, even if this resulted in a rise in costs, as happened at Winchester (Williamson, 1952: 138); and, second, reducing labour in its capacity to organize production, innovate, plan and earn in order to make it dependent. These processes would enable the creation and legitimation of Adam Smith's unnatural hierarchies and make management the planner described by

Marx – trends that would be reinforced by the work of F. W. Taylor as capital shifted from the formal to the real subsumption of labour.

Taylor and scientific management: reorganizing work

Taylor perhaps represents the culmination of the processes that had been undermining craft workers since the early nineteenth century. Nevertheless, it is important to examine his work because he epitomizes management's attitude to labour and production, and he was active in a key moment in capitalism, wherein capitalist development was becoming ever more explicitly tied to an increasingly 'scientific' application of planning to the social relations of production.[7] (This will be developed further in Chapters 4 and 5 when we move from technology as machine to technologies of the mind.)

Taylor's ideas were rarely fully implemented, but capital and management certainly saw the spirit of the age in them. Although Taylor talks about an almost equal division of work and responsibility and argues that 'his' system benefits the worker and is in the worker's interest, in reality he seeks to obliterate craft, workers' knowledge of production and worker autonomy in the workplace. There is very little original thought in the engineering management theorist's work: the division of labour, the piece rate, the replacing of skilled with unskilled labour, the close supervision of the workplace and the desire to alter worker subjectivity had all existed long before Taylor (Pollard, 1965: 181–92; Thompson, 1967; Braverman, 1974; Marx, 1976: 455–91; Wilentz, 2004). What may have been original (Bendix, 1956: 274–81) was his desire to replace management discretion and judgement – especially the foreman's empire – with what he called 'science' (see Hoxie, 1918: 40 for a clear critique of its 'scientific' basis, but also Stewart, 2009, Braverman, 1974: 104–23 and Nelson, 1995). This may explain why management rarely fully implemented his ideas, but rather cherry-picked even while endorsing his general ideology.

Taylor was perhaps the first systematic management theorist and proselytizer to express a view of what was happening on the ground. In a series of papers presented to the American Society of Mechanical Engineers and in his book *The Principles of Scientific Management*, he outlined how the elite could undermine the craft work ethic and impose discipline on an inferior set of humans who were fit largely only to follow orders. As we saw above, this view was shared by management at the time. Central to Taylor's vision are the following points:

- expropriation of knowledge;
- an increased division of labour;
- the breaking of worker collectivity;
- management's moral agenda;
- redefining management's role so that unnatural hierarchies appear natural, because management itself is the most productive element; and
- a colonizing management logic.

Four elements are essential in establishing the role of 'white shirts and superior intelligence' (Montgomery, 1987: 217):

- centralized planning and routing of work;
- systematic analysis of each distinct operation;
- detailed instruction and supervision of the performance of each discreet task; and
- wage payments designed to ensure workers followed instructions.

Much of this, as we saw earlier, is found in Weber's bureaucracy, and it is equally important in what we might today call 'logistics' (Mezzadra and Neilson, 2013).

Taylor argues that the expropriation of worker knowledge is essential if management is ever to gain control of the production process. Indeed, he sees management's lack of knowledge of production as its major weakness because this means it is unable to get the 'maximum efficiency' from each worker. He suggests that the way to glean worker knowledge is to study the labour process systematically, as it is carried out. Consequently, he engaged in time and motion studies in a variety of plants to determine how to strip workers of their monopoly of knowledge and then improve worker efficiency (largely through the deployment of different workers). This often involved recommending alternative payment systems and individualizing them through the introduction of the piece rate, a further subdivision of tasks, the writing down of instructions for workers explaining how they might improve their performance at work, increasing the pace of work, systematizing work flow, eliminating discretion, establishing a planning department to control and design work, and hiring 'first class' men (Taylor, 1903: 1362).

The whole point of this increased management was to eliminate workers' independence in the production process to render them vulnerable and thereby weaken them in their engagement with the 'cooperation' processes of capitalism. Although it would be 'absurd to talk of time study as an accurate scientific method' (Hoxie, 1918: 51; see also Stewart, 2009 on Taylor's fabrication of evidence), scientific management used time studies to break down tasks and to argue further that this was 'objective'. For example, it divided a planing task in a mill into six timed actions for the worker: from lifting the piece of wood to be planed to cleaning the machine afterwards, with four timed actions for when the planing machine was actually used – from rough cut to finished cut (Taylor, 1895: 871). On this basis, work was monitored, piece rates set and pay decided by management. As Taylor (1903: 1390) comments:

> All possible brain work should be removed from the shop and centered in the planning or lay-out department, leaving for the foreman and the gang bosses work strictly executive in its nature, their duties being to see that the operations planned and directed from the planning room are promptly carried out in the shop.

In consequence, labour was reduced. Weber's 'office files' were constructed and new lines of authority produced. Indeed, now the worker could be trained like an 'intelligent gorilla' to carry out simplified tasks defined by 'a man better educated than he is' (Taylor, 1919: 40). Management meets elitism through the use of the planned bureaucracy (Mills, 1951: 109–11; Clawson, 1980). Here, there is no need for craft, no joy in the production process for its own sake, because – prefiguring Weber's instrumental rationality – Taylor argues that a colonizing management will change the world because 'In the past man had been first; in the future the system must be first' (Taylor, 1919: 7). Skilled work could be – and should be – made unskilled or semi-skilled and workers altered accordingly. On this basis, a better form of cooperation could be engineered. In so doing, Taylor and management redesigned the general intellect because, as Adam Smith had highlighted, they attempted to alter labour's cognitive and affective thinking.

Taylor was building new forms of normation (see the Introduction). He used calculation, science, objectivity, costings, surveillance, coercion and norms to discipline and develop new forms of population and bio-power. He deployed these tactics to develop new types of subjectivity via individualized pay systems, new routines of behaviour, new motivations, new allegiances and new lines of authority. In this sense, Taylor was the founder of the worker as an object of study rather than a subject of knowledge (Jacques, 1996: 117) and of management as a form of subjectivity studies and change. He is an essential part of management theory and must be linked to personnel management, the Employment Management movement, human resources and human capital theory (Montgomery, 1987: 238–43; Jacques, 1996: 118–19). Furthermore, Esch and Roediger (2009: 23; see also Roediger and Esch, 2012) demonstrate his use of personnel-based race management techniques to pit different 'races' against each other. For example, in order to break worker soldiering at the Midvale steel plant, he introduced African-American workers into the gangs across the factory to undermine their unity. He directly follows a line from Descartes and Hobbes wherein the body becomes an object of study that is to be downgraded, regulated and controlled (Federici, 2004: 133–62). In this manner, he reaches into the general intellect and attempts to facilitate the total subsumption of life to work.

The Taylorist organization of work could not be further from that described by Montgomery (1987) at the beginning of this chapter. Taylor understands his Marx (1976: 677) because he recognizes the very real problem of turning labour-power into actual labour. He feels workers cannot be trusted and 'it is one thing to know how much work can be done in a day, and an entirely different matter to get even the best men to work at their fastest speed or anywhere near it' (Taylor, 1895: 871). He believes it is management's leadership and moral role to obliterate that gap. To do so, management must expropriate worker knowledge and reduce labour to performing merely 'a partial function' (Kracauer, 1995). Modern management was forged in these fires of class violence. (On the absolute violence of management towards a recalcitrant labour force, see Pollard, 1965: 255–9.) Taylor epitomizes the elitism of management – he seeks, like the managers in the previous section, to restore what he sees as legitimate social hierarchies based on delivering the surplus created by one class to another.

Having used expropriation and the division of labour to gain control of the production process and the work organization, Taylor (1895, 1903, 1919) further recommends the transformation of value through the piece rate. As we saw earlier, the elite did not control the organization at this point – that had to be stolen. Of course, Taylor introduces the piece rate for good reason because it provides 'an exact measure of the intensity of labour. Only labour-time which is embodied in the quantity of commodities laid down in advance and fixed by experience counts as socially necessary labour-time and is paid as such' (Marx, 1976: 694). Indeed, the piece rate altered the whole work relationship to such an extent that in 1885 the Connecticut Bureau of Labor Statistics called it 'a moral force which corresponds to machinery as a physical force' (quoted in Gutman, 1973: 565). (Yet again, the state was acting as a capitalist state.) Perhaps reflecting on this moral force, Marx (1976: 692–700) demonstrates how the piece rate individualizes and intensifies work by pitting one worker against another and leaving knowledge in the control of capital. As such, speeding up work, lengthening the working day or reducing the rate are presented as being in the interests of the workers. Montgomery (1987: 148–54) argues that piece rates were an older form of pay and, once again, were not uniform in their impact: trades such as bricklaying, carpentry and smithing fiercely resisted their imposition, while others – such as the tonnage men in iron and steel – accepted them. Nevertheless, piece rates are a clear way of comparing and contrasting, of rewarding and disciplining, of simultaneously individualizing and standardizing the worker. They are normation enacted.

Taylor (1903: 1352–4) argues that the piece rate as it was implemented by capitalists encouraged workers to be deceitful because if they increased their productivity the piece rate would be lowered, thereby giving the full benefit to the capitalist. He recommends an approach based on more accurate management knowledge that could be gleaned from time and motion studies, wherein the 'correct' objective work intensity could be mapped, a piece rate set and, as a result, workers could work harder and earn more without fear of the rate being reduced (Taylor, 1903: 1355–8). The piece rate should remain as it was first set unless technological or some organizational change altered the productivity of the process. To alter it arbitrarily because workers achieved the rate would dishearten them and lead them to resist. If Taylor's method is followed, he argues, workers and owners experience a rapturous unity and both benefit from productivity increases. Workers also improve morally because they are persuaded to give up 'soldiering' – that is, collectively and systematically underperforming at work.[8] As a result, they start to accept authority, they are more motivated, productive and honest, they are fairly rewarded and they become dependent. However, although workers were to be 'fairly' rewarded, in no sense were they to be *equally* rewarded. Taylor provides an example of workers producing a 100 per cent increase in productivity for a 30 per cent increase in pay. (See also Montgomery, 1987: 227 for examples of how piece rate systems gave workers progressively less the more they produced, and Brody, 1965: 15 on how the steel industry had one iron rule – 'the denial of productivity as a guide' for wages.) Taylor (1903: 1412) argues:

At first workmen cannot see why, if they do twice as much work as they had done, they should not receive twice the wages. When the matter is properly explained to them and they have time to think it over, they will see that in most cases the increase in output is quite as much due to the improved appliances and methods, to the maintenance of standards and to the great help which they receive from the men over them as to their own harder work and they will realize that the company must pay for the introduction of the improved system, which costs sometimes thousands of dollars and also the salaries of the additional foremen and of the clerks etc. in the planning room as well as tool room and other expenses, and that, in addition, the company is entitled to increased profit as much as they are.

As was suggested in Chapter 2, in this managerial view, labour does not create the value of a commodity; it merely commands a wage. Workers should receive what their position in the social hierarchy merits. Having broken worker knowledge, a free contract of cooperation that detaches value and wages can be imposed so that workers inch towards work and wages simply as a means to consume – Mills's (1951) 'coin of fun'. Here, although management introduces new layers of control, destroys the self-organization of workers' production and introduces new costs, it is somehow made productive (see Montgomery, 1987: 227). Management is no longer a drain or 'mere superintendence' (Pollard, 1965: 250; Wilentz, 2004: ch. 1). Like Adam Smith's 'middlemen', Taylor's managers now 'create' wealth by controlling knowledge. Workers and capital pursue a unitary purpose despite the employment contradiction emphasized by many at the beginning of the nineteenth century (Hodgskin 1825; Ricardo, 1996). In order to enter such a world, craft worker culture had to be broken. There was thus an emphasis on specialization from the early 1860s onwards as the piece rate system was rolled out. Taylor merely intensi-fied this because 'This inherent tendency to specialization is buttressed, broadened in its scope and perpetuated by the progressive gathering up and systematizing in the hands of the employers all the traditional craft knowledge in the possession of the workers' (Hoxie, 1918: 126).

However, there was also another benefit. This process mystified the relationship between value and wages – it was ever more difficult for workers to understand their contribution to the finished product, hence it was ever easier to link wages to local labour market rates rather than the value of the commodity and to make capital the source of managerial planning and authority, thereby further undermining the labour theory of value endorsed by craft workers (Hoxie, 1918: 126; Marx, 1976: 475–6; Montgomery, 1987: 149–50). Organizing production became an attribute of capital and managerialist planning rather than labour. Indeed, Montgomery (1987: 193) suggests that machinists were more radical than most workers in the late nineteenth century because they produced handmade capital goods and hence more accurately understood and witnessed the difference between the value created by their labour, the wage they received and their role in organizing production. The same was true of the contractors at Winchester, who refused the debased role of foreman with its lower wages and status. Of course, if wages were high, workers often refused work, so delinking wages from profit became important to enable capital – which is only interested in profit – to link workers' reproduction to local wage rates (Thompson, 1967). To 'get on', to embrace progress, to seek improvement meant embracing dependent wage work. The piece rate thus encapsulated specialization, intensifying work rates, the lengthening of the working day and the power of managerial authority, and it decoupled value and profits from wages. It was at the very centre of the emerging regime of accumulation and its disciplining tendencies (Montgomery, 1987: 150), hence Taylor's (1895: 879; 1903: 1367) repeated stress on it. This also explains his belief in the need to create new organizational cultures and a 'mental revolution' on the parts of both workers and managers (Taylor, 1947: 26–33). Management would create new cultures and subjectivities (Taylor, 1919: 48) along the lines of organizations, natural hierachies and elitism.

Central to this organizational change was the brutal imposition of management authority, the breaking of collectivity and, as we have seen, the undermining of worker skill and knowledge. Although Taylor himself (1903: 1421) argues that his system is actually one of upskilling and related to justice, not severity (1947: 9), he knew that he was engaged in a form of class violence. For example, in his description of his time as a gang boss at the Midvale Steel Company in the 1870s, he highlights how 'the shop was really run by the workmen not by the bosses' (Taylor, 1919: 48–53) and how he set about undermining this over three years of struggle (Taylor, 1947: 79–88). Having been promoted from machinist to gang boss, the workers confronted him to ask whether he would maintain the existing system of management. Taylor's answer was that he was 'on the side of management'.[9]

He claims two advantages in this struggle. First, the bosses trusted him rather than the workforce because 'he happened not to be of working parents' and shared the owners' class background and prejudices about the status of workers as inferiors. Second, he did not live among the community but 'in a fine home far from industrial neighborhoods' (Montgomery, 1987: 190); hence, he and his family did not experience the pressure of living in a collective culture (see Gutman, 1973 for examples of this culture and work). His bourgeois origins gave him the advantages of his class and these were important in his struggle to shift the balance of power from workers to management. What we experience in Taylor's parable (irrespective of whether it is true) is an individualizing bourgeois culture located in the prioritization of capitalist work meeting the resistance of a collective working-class culture that he and management deemed inferior. A central element of Taylor's task was to individualize and standardize the culture of the workshop. His whole approach was to harmonize the interests of the individual worker with management and the capitalist and from there to the society in a free contract. However, in this desire he could only ever see a capitalist, elitist, managerial, productivist, work-centred, efficiency-led and profit-driven logic (see Weeks, 2011: 37–92 on this logic), which was continually undermined by the 'work-shy' collective culture. It was this collectivist refusal that led to Taylor's continued obsessions with 'soldiering', individualizing workers and his absolute fear of worker knowledge.

For Taylor, soldiering epitomized all that was wrong with worker knowledge, craft collectivism and the workplace. By this, he meant the workforce's ability and desire to work at their own pace and to hide their capacity to produce more from management. Taylor is very explicit about it in his writings. Furthermore, he was not expressing a unique view at the time. Bendix (1956: 254–74) outlines just how rabid American capital was in its attitude to workers and their desire to refuse work. Successful capitalists viewed themselves as the 'fittest' and workers were held responsible for their own failings because they were weak and lazy. Echoing Weber, Michels and Pareto, leaders led because of their abilities while 'salaried men' were merely there to follow and accept orders within the emerging bureaucratic form. For management and capitalists, the idea of independence or autonomy had to be destroyed so that the 'new' worker merely accepted. Indeed, a cult of individual effort, work ethic and charisma was espoused through programmes such as that of the New Thought movement, wherein anyone could achieve anything if only they had the right attributes. In line with the thinking of elite theorists, for managers and capitalists, workers lacked these qualities while leaders exhibited them. Just as today, self-help books sold in their millions and suggested individuals could and should achieve more if only they tried harder. Large swathes of US public opinion endorsed a mixture of Samuel Smiles, Thomas Malthus, Herbert Spencer, Charles Darwin, Vilfredo Pareto and Robert Michels and believed in the virtues of working hard, the vices of the working class, the incessant struggle to exist, the inevitable success of the fittest and the deserving misery of the worker (see Mills, 1951: 77–111). (However, it must also be said that large swathes of US society rejected this (Gutman, 1973).[10]) The elite embodied all that was good and the workers all that was bad. Central here, for Taylor, was soldiering and the inability or unwillingness of workers to work at the 'correct' pace that sprang from a misguided collectivism and an implicit or explicit refusal of work. Yet again, management was about reconstituting the subject. As Taylor (1895: 866) comments:

> Cooperative experiments have failed, and I think are generally destined to fail, for several reasons, the first and most important of which is, that no form of cooperation has yet been devised in which each individual is allowed free scope for his personal ambition. This always has been and will remain a more powerful incentive to exertion than a desire for the general welfare. The few misplaced drones who do the loafing share equally in the profits, under cooperation.

Taylor presents an essentialist account of human motivation and one that is in contrast to the craft ethic discussed earlier. He has individualized labour and is establishing the worker as an individualized, economically incentivized subject by assuming those who cannot – or do not wish to – keep up are drones and loafers and therefore pathological. (We will return to worker pathology in Chapter 4.) He ignores the fact that the piece rate discriminates against the old, the ill and the less able and that, in light of this, collectively, worker survival is necessarily linked to resisting it. He also ignores the fact that his aim is to reduce labour to a mere 'appendage of the machine' (Montgomery, 1987: 153; Marx, 1976). The body is downgraded. Taylor (1903: 1361–5) is aware of fatigue issues, and in a Darwinian fashion suggests that in one of his successes only 20 per cent of men could keep up the pace of work set for them. These were his 'first rate' men of 'initiative'. All of them were 'sober', saving, well paid – but not paid *too* well, of course, as this would lead to indolence, a poor attitude and refusal (Taylor, 1903: 1346) – and, finally, they had embraced a changed mental attitude to their work.

Taylor (1919: 15–16) was in the business of creating a new industrial subjectivity that would not succumb to the pernicious influences of the collectivist soldiering 'condition'. This condition emerged from: the fallacy propounded by workers that increased productivity would lead to job losses; flawed management systems; and existing 'rule-of-thumb' methods used by workers that needed to be replaced with management 'science'. Soldiering itself took two forms – 'natural' soldiering (the tendency of workers to refuse the pace of work set by management and to take things easy) and 'systematic' soldiering, which had its roots in the workers' 'relations with other men' (Taylor, 1919: 19). Soldiering is a refusal of work – a working-class act of insubordination against capital and capitalism which, for Taylor (1947: 19), equates to stealing from the poor because it lessens efficiency and hence increases costs. These relations to other men hamper production because even the fastest workers slow down when working alongside slower men (Taylor, 1903: 1340; 1947: 7–33). In such a world, a culture of mediocrity arises which then has to be broken by management expropriating knowledge, developing better personnel techniques of hiring and firing (the latter was an essential element of Taylor's system; see Taylor, 1903: 1375), exerting authority over the workforce, pitting worker against worker and creating appropriate incentive systems. The creation of this new organizational environment would refashion the individual and make him or her a bourgeois subject. It would also enable positive elite control through the organizational division of labour. It was about destroying the collective traditions, experiences, affects, cognitive understandings and knowledge of workers, and indeed of the general intellect, and replacing them with new forms and owners of knowledge. It ignored the innovation, good management, mass production and high wages of the inside contract in favour of a spurious argument of functional necessity.

Management's endeavour was based on its political project of expropriating knowledge and subdividing the labour process so that it, rather than the 'mutilated' labour force (Marx, 1976: 480–91), was responsible for organizing production. As such, it bore the burden of responsibility, authority, leadership and the creation of work as a goal in itself – a burden that was a real sacrifice on the part of management (Taylor, 1919: 37; 1947: 40). (See Chapter 6 on the mirage of the burden of management and its links to neo-liberal management.) Managers would use this position to implement systems that would mould workers. As with all violence, the perpetrator claims the subject of the violence is actually the cause of it through their rejection of responsible behaviour: so workers 'force' managers to be violent.[11] Of course, there is some truth in this: workers sought control and did resist management's demand for a higher pace of work or the extraction of the value they created. But Taylor argues that workers eventually came to see what was good for them through management (a theme picked up in Chapter 6). For example, speaking of his own achievements (a perpetual habit), he comments:

> It was most interesting to see these men, principally either former gang-bosses or the best workmen, gradually change from their attitude of determined and positive opposition to that, in most cases, of enthusiasm for, and earnest support of, the new methods.
>
> *(Taylor, 1903: 1417)*

In a similar vein, he suggests that workers now

> work more cheerfully and are more obliging to one another and to their employers. The moral effect of the writer's system on the men is marked. The feeling that substantial justice is being done them renders them on the whole much more manly, straightforward and truthful.
>
> *(Taylor, 1895: 881)*

This is management's goal – reshaping worker subjectivities so that they are more pliant, will deliver ever-greater efficiencies and will embrace work. (In this sense, Taylor was proposing nothing new, because this was the essential violence of the Industrial Revolution described by Pollard (1965).) However, this reshaping via the 'one best way' (Taylor, 1919: 25–6) is pursued for profit. The ideal subject is the bourgeois subject: one who values work, is thrifty, individualistic, sober, ambitious, has initiative, is efficient, saves and who is obedient and realizes that his or her bosses act 'not as nigger drivers[12] forcing them to work extra hard for ordinary wages, but as friends who [are] teaching them and helping them to earn much higher wages than they [have] ever earned before' (Taylor, 1919: 72). Here, Taylor perhaps deliberately taps into the white worker fear of being an unfree 'wage slave' and hence potentially equates paid employment with being in the lowly position of the African-American (Roediger and Esch, 2012).[13]

As suggested earlier, accompanying this elite leadership role was the belief – prevalent in middle-class America at the time – that there was a natural order (Michels, 1915; Pareto, 1991; Sellers, 1991). Worker knowledge had to be expropriated and subdivision had to take place for profits to be delivered. Although Taylor (1947: 36) acknowledges that craft skill is a worker's 'most valuable possession. It is his great life's capital', he is prepared to obliterate it – today's human capital – in the interests of everyone! Workers had childishly opposed progress and put their sectional interests (assuming they could recognize them) above the universal interest delivered by capitalist management, the market and the factory. Linking into the popular ideology of the time, Taylor argues at various points that workers are childlike: for example, he compares the role of the manager to that of the school-teacher trying to explain a lesson; he argues that workers need immediate praise or criticism because they operate on a short time span and lack the ability to think in the abstract (Taylor, 1903: 1372); he suggests that they have a limited capacity to comprehend and hence reach the 'level' to which they are best suited (Taylor, 1919: 40–1); and he accuses them of concealing things (Taylor, 1919: 104). The role of management is to match the workers' (limited) abilities to specific tasks so that the latter can achieve the highest potential available to them (Taylor, 1903: 1347). Again, a common theme in management is to allow the worker to achieve the best he or she can be (see Chapters 4 and 5). As Taylor puts it:

> It becomes the duty of those on the management side to deliberately study the character, the nature and the performance of each workman with a view to finding out his limitations on the one hand, but even more important, his possibilities for development on the other hand; and then, as deliberately and as systematically to train and help and teach this workman, giving him wherever it is possible, those opportunities for advancement which will finally enable him to do the highest and most interesting and most profitable class of work for which his natural abilities fit him, and which are open to him in the particular company in which he is employed.
>
> *(Taylor, 1947: 42)*

Taylor may have read Marx, but he obviously ignored Smith. Having argued for the mutilation of the worker, he adds insult to injury by blaming the worker for his or her low position and low abilities in a manner that Smith (1981: 28) never did (see Chapter 1). He attempts to make unnatural hierarchies natural while arguing that management violence is prompted by the workers themselves and simultaneously suggesting that this violence is perpetrated to help them by unleashing their energies so they may achieve their full potential.[14]

Taylor tries to universalize scientific management and argues that most, if not all, work should be subject to it and to the intensification it encapsulates. As the organization grew and as ever-greater control of the production process was demanded, management itself would have to be subdivided (in this sense, Taylor echoes Michels on organization). Indeed, his planning department had sixteen different functions and he divided the traditional foreman's job into eight separate positions (Taylor, 1903: 1394–400).[15] The skilled workers who would henceforth be unnecessary once the new system was broken down into simpler tasks were either promoted into some of these positions or replaced by men of 'smaller calibre and attainments and who are therefore cheaper' (Taylor, 1903: 1395). Taylor's beneficence would deliver a small elite and a large, unskilled mass. He recognizes that these new systems will need to be 'enforced' via supervision and sackings (Taylor, 1919: 83), and, as stated above, he asserts that all work is potentially subject to this process, even management itself (Taylor, 1903: 1394). (See Hoxie, 1918: 59 for an early rejection of this assertion.)

In his testimony to the United States Commission on Industrial Relations in 1914, Taylor argued strongly that scientific management would lead to social harmony because – through rational laws, the roles and positions his system mapped out for how a job should be performed, the pace and productivity that should be used, and the equitable sharing of rewards between capital and labour – everyone would gain (see Hoxie, 1918: 7–11). In this, hierarchy would be natural and meritocratic, the manager/expert would be productive of value, and management would perform the crucial leadership role – Michels's (1915) elite would be legitimated. By so doing, he argued, Taylorist management enhanced democracy within industry and ruled out arbitrary decision-making because the worker, rather than the position, was rewarded, and selection, training, work organization and supervision ensured that each worker achieved his or her appropriate role (although one worker in any one role would be a facsimile of the other). In this sense, Taylor outlined what Weber would discuss as 'bureaucracy' and 'rationality', and what Weber, Michels and Pareto labelled 'elitism'. Taylor, then, was the first of many management theorists ideologically to outline the rise of the manager as a (violent) social saviour.

Taylor and the modern organization

Katherine Stone (1973) describes how the organization changed as a result of management developments after 1890.[16] Her argument is that the modern organizational form developed out of the struggles at the end of the nineteenth century. Her work describes a form that lasted for almost a century (and still exists in large parts of the contemporary world, both near and far, despite discussions about networked or post-bureaucratic forms). At its heart is the transferring of knowledge of the production process from workers to management, the emergence of the semi-skilled worker, the development of internal labour markets, the new importance of promotion and spurious career paths, the increased use of technology, the rise of the problem of motivation, the attempt to individualize the workplace and the increased use of formal education to hire management cadres. The steel industry between 1890 and 1920 was one of the sites where this modern organization was born.

In 1860, the US steel industry employed just 748 men in 13 establishments; by 1901 US Steel was the first billion-dollar corporation; and in 1919 the steel industry employed half a million workers, 50 per cent of whom were on strike that year. It was a truly remarkable period of change (Brody, 1965: 113; Stone, 1973: 21). In achieving this change, the industry had to destroy the traditional craft pattern of working. As described by Montgomery (1987) and above in our discussion of inside contracting, the craft way of working essentially brought together capital and labour as more 'equal' partners. For example, in the steel industry, skilled craft workers were paid on a 'sliding scale' by the tonnage produced. Workers' wages were tied not to local wage rates but to the market price of steel, so they rose or fell as the market price rose or fell. As mentioned above, capitalists contracted with the craftsmen, who then organized the production process and hired the necessary labour; capital did not confront labour as the organizer of production. In addition, craft workers controlled the pace of work, training and apprenticeships, the pay rates for different grades of worker and trades within the production process, the allocation of tasks, the amount of product produced per worker, the quality of the product and the proportion of scrap that might be used in running a furnace. The workers controlled production and, because their remuneration was tied to the market price, the employer could not use wages as an incentive or a disciplining mechanism to intensify their work (Stone, 1973: 21–5; Montgomery, 1987: 9–57). Worker refusal was hardwired into the system of production because of their knowledge. In one sense, this was a form of competitive capitalism where workers were collective, simultaneously attuned to the market and to commercial life, to risk and to calculation, and able and willing to refuse work. In some respects, Smith's market had been brought into the factory – the very last place the capitalists wanted it to be (Clawson, 1980: 124). It was anathema to large capitalists who were structurally tied into profit, but for craft workers it was about life not solely as the valorization of capital.

As we know, this system of working and 'partnership' between workers and capitalists was set to change. In the 1880s, competition increased within the steel industry as demand grew rapidly because of ever more railway building and the United States' determination to compete with Britain and Germany on the world market. However, because of labour's control of the production process, capitalists could not easily increase production to meet this demand; nor could they easily drive down costs in order to steal a march on their competitors. Indeed, because of labour's power within cooperation, it could resist attempts to lower wages or increase workload despite the declining price of steel. Labour could largely control its own social reproduction and push risk and cost back to capital. Because of this, labour costs as a percentage of revenue continued to rise (Stone, 1973: 24–6). As with Keynesianism fifty years later, labour's wages were the independent – not the dependent – variable, albeit in craft this power was located in knowledge of the production process, rather than 'class' strength.

In light of these developments, Andrew Carnegie used his capital to set about destroying the craft workers and their union (which represented 25 per cent of the skilled workforce) at their strongest point – the Homestead steel plant (Stone, 1973; Montgomery, 1987: 36–43). The firm appointed Henry Clay Frick, a noted union foe, director at Homestead. He immediately built a three-mile fence topped with barbed wire. The recent steel boom was over and mills were laying people off. In this environment, the three-year deal based on the sliding scale that labour and capital had negotiated in 1889 was coming to an end, and the company now rejected union proposals for a new sliding scale and demanded wage cuts. The union refused, so management began shutting down parts of the mill before closing it completely on 2 July 1892 and declaring it a non-union mill. It then hired 300 guards from the Pinkerton National Detective Agency and locked out the workers. The Homestead strike (or lockout) had begun in earnest. It lasted until the end of November. With help from the Pennsylvania State Militia and a ninety-five-day military occupation of the mill, the company began to hire scabs. By November, after scores of deaths and through the use of the state police, Pinkerton's private guards and the courts, the workers were finally defeated. All involved knew what had been at stake. The state police chief was horrified to think that the workers 'believe the works are theirs quite as much as Carnegie's', while Pennsylvania's Chief Justice Paxson sided with the mill owner and against 'men receiving exceptionally high wages … resisting the law and resorting to violence and bloodshed in the assertion of their imaginary rights' (Montgomery, 1987: 38–9). In short, and echoing the feeling of management and owners at Winchester and other organizations that these men were being paid and making demands above their station, Paxson was aghast that they refused to allow capital to confront them as the organizing force or authority in production matters. Property rights, work intensification, labour as a commodity, management's right to manage and the capitalist class as a class in the face of worker resistance were all to be defended. The knowledge workers of their day would now know their (inferior) place. They no longer owned the work, and capitalists now owned that and the product of that work – new lines of authority, hierarchy and cooperation were put in place through state and private collusion as well as state violence.

The Homestead strike led to a restructuring of the steel industry and ended the previous relationship between capital and labour. Between 1892 and 1898, the membership of the Amalgamated Association of Iron, Steel and Tin Workers declined from 25,000 to 10,000 (Stone, 1973: 28). Over the next thirty years, the industry was radically transformed through a minute division of labour. It sought to enforce three resolutions: the use of new technology to change production processes and the job structure; as a result of this, the implementation of new systems of motivating and disciplining the labour force; and, finally, the establishment of lasting control over the entire labour process. Just as Winchester Repeating Arms had done, the steel industry accepted extra costs, new problems and new management layers, and it set about restructuring work by destroying worker self-organization and worker control of knowledge. The knowledge worker was to be stamped out, made dependent; and, following Michels (1915), the division of labour would allow for a new university-trained, elite-led authority (see Taylor, 1947: 60–4; Mills, 1951: 77–111; Williamson, 1952: 136–7). As noted above, Montgomery (1987: 9–58) queries Stone's account of the extent and pace of this process. Nevertheless, Stone's work is important because, while the scale and timing are questionable, the outcome on the nature of management into the twentieth century is not. What emerges is something akin to what we know today as the bureaucratic organizational form (Mills, 1951; Edwards, 1979; Clawson, 1980).

Stone (1973) argues that the Homestead strike was only the prelude to a more sustained, systematic attack on craft work. Employers used the period after the strike to engage in a class struggle for knowledge of the production process. This culminated in the transfer of knowledge from workers to management in ways outlined by Taylor.[17] (Although the steel industry did not accept his recommendations completely: for example, mills frequently reduced the piece rate arbitrarily to extract more value from labour.) Because it was operated by semi-skilled workers, technology could be used to weaken the organizational power of skilled workers and reduce the amount of unskilled work. It was also central to narrowing wage differentials within the mills by lowering the wages of skilled workers and increasing those of the semi-skilled. Thus, despite increasing productivity per worker, the pay of skilled workers declined. For example, a roller at Homestead in 1899 could expect to earn $14 per tonnage; yet by 1908 he could expect only $4.75. Hence, the steel industry broke the connection between productivity and wages (Brody, 1965: 15). Within the same period, unskilled and semi-skilled men saw their pay rise, and indeed they experienced some social mobility (Stone, 1973: 33). The composition of the labour force changed significantly to reflect this (as did the composition of the US working class during the same period). From 1890 to 1910 the total labour force grew by 129 per cent. However, native-born skilled white workers grew by only 55 per cent, and immigrants from Germany and the British Isles (from where overseas skilled workers generally originated) declined by 18 per cent. In contrast, the number of African-American workers grew by 165 per cent. Most remarkably, the number of Southern and Eastern European workers grew by 227 per cent: in 1890, they made up less than 10 per cent of the workforce; by 1910, they comprised nearly half of it (Montgomery, 1987: 42). Race management and scientific management combined (Roediger and Esch, 2012), but in so doing, and however disjointedly, they laid the seeds of the mass industrial worker.

These shifts marked a transition from skilled and unskilled to semi-skilled labour; they also led to increasing tension between skilled and semi-skilled workers in the plants (see Montgomery, 1987: 42). Indeed, the arrival of so many Eastern and Southern Europeans had a damaging impact on Pennsylvania's black working population and on black migrants to the region. Bodnar (1976: 228) argues that any upward social mobility black workers may have experienced was halted to such an extent that the black community experienced a decline in population. Again, these changes can be viewed as part of the systematic use of race management and the pitting of one group of workers against another (Esch and Roediger, 2009).

However, controlling the labour force became a bigger management issue. Under the contract system, skilled workers had controlled the production process, training and the labour force. Fundamentally, these were self-organized workers. Now, workers had to be motivated to work: they needed to be instilled with desires and potentialities, opinions, ambitions, routines and motivations so that they might be manipulated as a population.

Another problem was created because deskilling meant workers were increasingly homogenized and hence more likely to experience collective grievances and see themselves as a mass. Hence, they might be collective in new, inappropriate ways. Taylor – who advocates simultaneously standardizing and individualizing workers – explains:

> When employers herd their men together in classes, pay all of each class the same wages, and offer none of them any inducements to work harder or do better than the average, the only remedy for the men lies in combination; and frequently the only possible answer to encroachments on the part of their employers is a strike.
>
> *(Taylor, 1903: 1440)*

Management's solution to this problem involved using the calculative, norm-inducing piece rate to individualize pay, thereby pitting worker against worker, as Marx, Weber and Taylor had all highlighted. This led to the development of an internal labour market with an elongated promotion ladder designed to stoke desire, develop certain potentialities and inhibit others, and entrench a world of competitive individualism. (See Taylor, 1903: 1415, who discusses something like an emergent internal labour market.) Both tactics were designed to suggest that the workers were competing with one another and that their individual interest and that of the company were one and the same, even – or especially – as workers became interchangeable and dependent. These systems were simultaneously about discipline, standardization and individualization; they were about trying to create Weber's disciplined organization now that the worker had finally been stripped of control, independence and access to his or her means of production outside his or her wage dependency. Edwards (1979) calls this a more totalitarian organization. Of course, given the nature of the emerging job structure, this competition among workers had little, if anything, to do with skill as it had previously been understood.

Following the Homestead strike, steel firms began to realize that apprenticeships and training (which Taylor, 1903: 1419 argues are no longer required) were not occurring because until then they had been the responsibility of craft workers. Importantly, the socialization of the next generation into work – a free gift of the general intellect – was not forthcoming in the ways that management required, so it was obliged to devise new disciplining techniques (see Chapter 4). Firms also began to create new forms of skilled work. However, these were invariably firm specific and developed through short courses or company training. Workers were not allowed to develop a *general* knowledge of the production process because to do so would lead to worker empowerment. If capital was to confront labour as the organizing force of production, enforce the new division of labour and create the new hierarchy, general knowledge of the production process had to be denied to workers. It must remain firmly located within management. By 1920, new managers were being hired from outside the steel firms. They increasingly arrived from formal education institutions (Jacques, 1996: 124–34).

These new college-educated management employees were trained in a general knowledge via an apprenticeship system whereby they spent time in each department working under a foreman. (Evidence of similar training and the very limited levels of mobility in the emerging internal markets of large-firm Germany can be found in Kracauer, 1998: 47–52; and see Mills, 1951: 161–78 on the US retail industry.) Thus, the education system was explicitly linked to selection and to moulding cognitive maps about work and authority. It comprised a class-based transfer of knowledge from workers to management and so was deeply implicated in the emerging expropriating corporate form of monopoly capitalism. As Stone (1973: 52) comments, 'The knowledge expropriated from the skilled workers was passed on to a new class of college trained managers. This laid the basis for the perpetuating class divisions in the society through the education system.' All of this was 'a strategy to rob workers of their power' (Stone, 1973: 58). Indeed, speaking of Germany's business schools, Weber (1994: 116) argues that they were merely a mechanism for social climbing without any real educational or technical value (perhaps we should take note). But certification is also a way into managing the general intellect – a road, however unfinished and bumpy, to reshaping cognitive and affective potentialities. Michels's (1915) elite organization is created by the new division of labour, bureaucracy and moulding the general intellect, much of which is located in the expropriation of worker knowledge (see Mills, 1951: 106–11).

It was through this expropriation that management developed its planning authority. The new division of labour left both the skilled craft worker and the unskilled and semi-skilled workers unable to organize production. The craft worker could not now 'understand the science of that trade without the kindly help and co-operation of men of a totally different type of education, men whose education is not necessarily higher but of a different type from his own' (Taylor, 1947: 49). And the semi-skilled or unskilled worker was simply too 'stupid' (Taylor, 1947: 49–50) to understand. The worker required college-educated management 'to teach him the best way and show him the easiest way to do his work' (Taylor, 1947: 62). Such managers at Winchester and US Steel would act as 'brothers' to labour.

Stone (1973) describes the emergence of the bureaucratic or monopoly capitalist corporation. Increasingly, corporations were made up of semi-skilled workers; management controlled the knowledge of production; it used this power to reduce worker autonomy in the factory; worker motivation and discipline became key issues; management was tied ever closer to the formal education system, and from there to class; worker training was increasingly specific rather than general; and wages were linked to local labour market rates rather than the labour theory of value. The mass industrial worker was born.[18]

The new labour relationship

These shifts led to new forms of relationship within production. But they also led to the rise of a new industrial subject – the mass industrial worker. In short, although it had many good qualities, craft was a miserable base from which to build an equal society. Craft workers were hierarchical, self-contained, arrogant, sexist and racist while also collective. As Virno (2004) highlights, craft or skill is used by those workers who monopolize it to create hierarchy, and this then protects them from capitalist valorization. Certainly, these workers shared elements of the general intellect, especially those tendencies that led to refusal of life as simply the pursuit of profit for capital. However, by its nature, hierarchical skill in the division of labour is not universal. In this sense, craft is always going to be incapable of building a mass society of equals – of the social individual with his or her shared inheritance and their individuated development. The craft workers' defeat was, for them, an inconsolable loss; but it also reflected the ushering in of massive change.

At the heart of this change was the rise of the operative and the labourer; the migrant and the immigrant; men and women; African-Americans, Eastern and

Southern Europeans, Chinese, Japanese and Hispanics. This transition had severe implications for skill, class, gender, migrant and race relations. It helped to forge what Montgomery (1974) calls the 'new unionism'. Essentially, this was an industrial union wherein the grass roots were often more militant than their leaders. Thus, the defeat of craft gave rise to a different working-class movement, one that would alter the twentieth century. It was a form of movement that in many respects defied belief and it formed in the factories, infrastructure, the mines, mass production and working-class communities. Roediger and Esch (2012: 87–97) suggest it was forged in places like the Colorado Fuel and Iron Company of the Rockefellers and of the Ludlow massacre infamy, where, despite race management, company welfare systems, violence, intimidation, harsh living conditions, astronomical levels of industrial accident, state hostility and the fact that upwards of twenty-five languages were spoken and people came from up to thirty-eight different countries, the workers still combined, refused management and demanded *more* – primarily more money for less work. This endeavour to demand more for less created the mass industrial worker who confronted capital as a more powerful and innovative force than the craft worker ever had.

But this worker also increasingly relied not on skill in the craft sense but on the cognitive, affective and communication abilities of the general intellect; that is, his or her skills were ever more universal. As management replaced living labour with machines, labour rejuvenated its subjectivity in disposable time outside the factory. This was what happened in Colorado. The universal experience of the social individual enabled the formation of a wider, more egalitarian collectivity than craft skill could. As the division of labour eradicated difference, the mass industrial subject formed.

Nevertheless, workers still experienced an increase in technical and social discipline and control, rising rates of unemployment and a decline in real wages between 1890 and 1920. These working conditions led immigrant and semi-skilled workers to seek more control in the factories, down the mines and on the railroads, and to seek higher wages. In many respects, this became the embryo of Keynesianism or Fordism, and it led labour into conflict with capital in the early 1920s and again in the 1930s. What emerged in the first thirty years of the twentieth century was a new working class, often divided by race and ethnic conflict (Brody, 1965: 163–4, 181; Bodnar, 1976; Montgomery, 1987: 42; Esch and Roediger, 2009), but nevertheless formed through its struggle with capitalist planning and its desire to eschew individualism for class or family, ethnicity and community (Montgomery, 1974; Bodnar, 1980). These struggles often led to various forms of welfarism on behalf of companies (Brody, 1965; Nelson and Campbell, 1972; Gitelman, 1988; Barley and Kunda, 1992) but also, and more importantly, to much industrial warfare. However, this is not to say that the United States went radical or, indeed, that it was even consistent (Montgomery, 1987: 411–24). For example, the 1920s can be seen as a decade of retreat from progressive politics on the part of organized labour as it fell under capital's hegemony (Gramsci, 1971: 277–320; Montgomery, 1987: 423–4). In a different vein, Tronti (1965: 22–3) argues that the collapse of industrial unrest from the immediate post-First World War era until 1929 came about because labour gained a great deal from capital without having to struggle. Either way, militancy certainly declined. Similarly, the period from 1929 to 1933 was not conducive to making gains, hence a lack of unrest. Simply to categorize the lack of struggle as defeat is therefore problematic.

As we saw in the Introduction, worker resistance did alter industrial relations and, eventually, capitalism's future as it led to Keynesianism. Certainly, it was obvious that labour had to be negotiated with and managed – this lay at the heart of welfare management (Brody, 1965: 147–78; Nelson and Campbell, 1972; Montgomery, 1987: 438–57; Gitelman, 1988), scientific management (Taylor, 1895, 1903, 1919), employment relations management (Jacques, 1996) and, indeed, all of the management theories that emerged from 1910 onwards (see Bendix, 1956 and Chapter 4). The new bureaucratic organization claimed to be fair, meritocratic, to motivate workers, to deliver on their desires and potentialities, and to produce. Of course, the reality was somewhat different: primarily, the bureaucratic organization sought to deliver the valorization of capital. For example, General Electric, influenced by the Taylorite French theorist Charles Badeux, epitomized this bureaucratic corporation with its modern management techniques, huge productive potential, elongated divisions of labour, new hierarchies, and desire to accumulate worker knowledge and instil a work ethic in its workers (Montgomery, 1987: 438–57; Jacques, 1996). If modern labour relations were forged in steel, they were finessed in electrics. Here, the piece rate and fatigue (to which we shall return with Elton Mayo in Chapter 4) were monitored and studied; steadiness, not maximum effort, was prized (see Jacques, 1996: 112–24 on this personnel-led transition); rogue workers were to be isolated not by management but by worker self-management via committees and norms relating to safety, productivity and earnings; workers were to be increasingly tied to the firm so that in times of hardship the unmarried, the transient and the non-local would be fired first; labour forces were to be homogenized; the worker's welfare and identity were to be linked to the firm's success (and hence to work); work was to be controlled and made firm specific and semi-skilled; and social and technical control were to be separated in ways described by Mayo, yet both were to become 'scientific' as capitalism moved ever closer to planning (see Panzieri, 1961; Montgomery, 1974; Chapter 4). In short, everything should be used to achieve discipline and adherence to the 'common cause'. These were key management objectives and management was often successful in delivering them. Nevertheless, even at General Electric, a paragon of the new bureaucratic management, workers struck and white-collar workers joined unions. (The firm was not necessarily hostile to unions and even invited the American Federation of Labor to organize its workers; see Marens, 2013.) Indeed, welfare policies in the Taylorized workplace did not solve the labour problem, and workers were not easily convinced to identify with their employer, with work in general or with their job – another key management theme (see Jacques, 1996: 121–3). In fact, General Electric was a centre for industrial conflict and perhaps the first location for a sit-down strike in the United States (Montgomery, 1987: 445). Management was necessary simply because workers resisted and refused the new regime of accumulation, even though capital faced them as the elite organizing authority. The workers who proposed the sit-down protest were sacked after the company's 1918 strike, but what they had proposed was used to devastating effect in the car factories of Michigan in the 1930s (see Chapter 5).

One can also see the changing composition of the working class in the nationwide steel strike of 1919. This strike was divided by issues of craft, skill, control, race and ethnicity, all of which served to undermine it. And yet, by the 1930s, labour's subjectivity in steel had altered so that it was more homogenized and less divided by such issues. Hence, it could (and did) win major concessions from capital and force it to change (Brody, 1965: 181). Craft gave way to a new, more inclusive political subject – the mass industrial worker who fought back to influence the social individual of the general intellect, too. New demands for autonomy would come with this more expanded (if still flawed) idea of inclusiveness, desire and potentiality, as would many of the things that shaped the late twentieth century, including health, education, pensions and seniority. Although individual and sectional gains, these demands were also implicitly located in a refusal of life as work or as the valorization of capital. However flawed, they marked a refusal to be subjected to the criticism of the labour market and capital's free contract in perpetuity. As such, with the transition to post-Fordism, management has systematically sought to repeal these concessions and return labour to the capricious criticism of the labour market and the work organization.

And loss or gain? The real subsumption of labour to capital

Antonio Gramsci (1971: 277–320) describes the emerging system as 'Americanism and Fordism'. He sums it up as a shift from competitive capitalism to monopoly capitalism, and from individualism to planning within which management is central to the new regime of violence. It occurred in the United States precisely because that country did not have the elite structure of Europe, which was backward-looking and parasitic. As both Michels (1915) and Weber (1994) predicted, in the United States the bureaucratic corporate form delivered a new way of entrenching the elite – a new aristocracy. In its factories, worker homogeneity – so feared by management – was potentially the norm, hence the need for techniques of obfuscation such as the recreation of the meaning of 'race' in race management (Roediger and Esch, 2012: 170–203) and of spurious hierarchies and skill differences (Stone, 1973). This homogenization gave birth to a new type of person – a new subjectivity suited to the new work and the emerging regime of accumulation. The attack on the craft unions was thus progressive, in its own way, because craft workers were hierarchical and could not give birth to a new society or new and better forms of collectivity (see Montgomery, 1987: 9–57).

Again, we return here to subjectivity and new ways of being. Within this transition, the state and capital combined to break craft workers because they opposed work intensification. This transition also gave rise to many other changes, such as a change in gender relations and what Gramsci (1971: 294) calls the 'sexual question'. Thus, in its need of, and desire for, a new form of worker, American management focused much more of its energy on policing of the worker *outside* of work – in terms of his or her sexual behaviour, alcohol consumption, leisure time, drug use and need to be 'productive' both in and out of work. This was not, as Weber suggested, simply Puritanism or a Protestant work ethic; rather, it was necessary because of the new regime of accumulation. For example, central to it was the pattern of consumption for the factory worker (see Mills, 1951; Montgomery, 1987; Weeks 2011; Lears, 2000). Thus, the disdain of the work ethic as ever more intensification that Gutman (1973) noted, had to be replaced with an embrace of the work ethic as steadiness (see Montgomery, 1987: 438–57; Jacques, 1996: 113–17). This was (and remains) the function of management, the policing and disciplining of life. As Gramcsi (1971: 297), commenting on sexuality, puts it:

> One should not be misled, any more than in the case of prohibition, by the 'puritanical' appearance assumed in this concern. The truth is the new type of man demanded by the rationalisation of production and work cannot be developed until the sexual instinct has been suitably regulated and until it too has been rationalised.

After all, it may be difficult, but it is not impossible, to have spontaneous fun with an individual in a factory where you need permission to go to the toilet. The killing of 'spontaneous enjoyment' was central to the work ethic (Weeks, 2011: 48). Thus, the early twentieth century saw the creation of a new subject who emerged out of coercion, resistance and acquiescence. Taylor's desire for a 'first rate' man was specifically linked to this end of the non-drinking, non-hedonistic, bourgeois subject (as is much leftist thinking; see Weeks, 2011: 79–92). This is what Jacques (1996: 142–7) refers to as the 'Second Industrial Revolution'. The disciplining, socializing and mining of subjectivity are essential to management because they are essential to capitalist accumulation. As such, they have a long history based on subsuming life to work (Federici, 2004). But to achieve this, capital has to shape the skills of the general intellect because delivering a consistent capitalist subjectivity is a managerial priority. We will return to these issues in later chapters.

Conclusion

The labour–capital struggle of the late nineteenth and early twentieth centuries recomposed the working class by stripping labour from its means of production and hence from control of its own reproduction and by eradicating the craft worker as a political subject. In so doing, it gave rise to a new form of worker – the mass industrial worker who was increasingly subject to the prioritizing of life as work and from there to wages and consumption (Weeks, 2011). This was the essence of Fordism (Gramsci, 1971: 302–5). As such, the labour struggle in the workplace shifted to wages and productivity and away from control of production and value

(Tronti 1965, 1971; Baldi, 1972). Unlike the steel employers who wished to keep wages and productivity separate (Brody, 1965: 15), workers increasingly forced this relationship on to the agenda and were often much more radical than their leaders (Montgomery, 1974). In one sense, they regulated themselves via the creation of consumer needs, debt or mortgages, but in another sense their role as renewing subjects and as consumers led capital and the state to Keynesianism. The working class became more, not less, central to capital just as it was increasingly replaced by technology in the factory as capital pursued its futile attempt to end its dependence on labour. Nevertheless, discipline remained:

> Coercion has therefore to be ingeniously combined with persuasion and consent. This effect can be achieved, in forms of the society in question, by higher remuneration such as to permit a particular living standard which can maintain and restore the strength that has been worn down by the new form of toil. But no sooner have the new methods of work and production been generalised and diffused, the new type of worker been created universally, and the apparatus of material production been further perfected, no sooner has this happened than the excessive 'turnover' has automatically to be restricted by widespread unemployment, and high wages disappear. In reality American high wage industry is exploiting a monopoly granted to it by the fact that it has the initiative with the new methods. Monopoly wages correspond to monopoly profits.
>
> *(Gramsci, 1971: 310)*

As Silver (2003) and Arrighi and Silver (1984) have demonstrated, this was indeed the case. As US workers demanded and refused more from the monopoly profit derived from their subjugation in the factory (Braverman, 1974), as they rejected the new discipline because it was more 'wearying' (Gramsci, 1971: 311; Hamper, 1986), as they developed new subjectivities, as management theories failed to deliver, and as they abandoned discipline for consumption, flight or avoidance, corporations moved to new locations and new workforces to escape their dependence on this labour. As we will see more clearly in Chapter 4, this new industrial worker required 'new' management by both the state and the bureaucratic corporation because subjectivity and motivation were becoming an intensified frontier of management while they also embodied the real and growing subsumption of labour to capital (Tronti 1965, 1971; Marx, 1976: 1035–8). Central to this new management was the rise of manipulation to capture the soul (Mills, 1951: 109–11). This was labour not formally under capital and left to organize production itself. Now organizational forms, authority, management, technology, capital, routines, procedures, consumption and cooperation were organizing the worker. Organization was subject to what appeared to be more 'scientific' forms of technical and human control as capitalist development became increasingly concerned with planning. Although capital expenditure rapidly increased, it is the element of management planning that focuses on people – and the class struggle embedded within it – that we explore in

Chapter 4. This also takes capital and management ever further into their reliance on the free gifts of sociality and the general intellect.

Notes

1 This quote is taken from F. W. Taylor's (1919: 37) *Principles of Scientific Management*.
2 Gutman (1973) warns us against using the US Civil War as a transition point and suggests there were continuities before and after, including immigration and the attack on craft.
3 Jacques cites Elbert Gary and Alfred Sloan as exemplars of this new management style, but both were ruthlessly hostile to labour. Gary's anti-labour views are evidenced by his hard lines on unions and on providing pay and conditions improvements for workers (see Brody, 1965; Gitelman, 1988).
4 For example, following the Ludlow massacre, the Rockefellers, who owned the Colorado Fuel and Iron Company, financed industrial relations departments at Princeton, Michigan, Stanford, CalTec and Queen's in Ontario as part of a bid to increase understanding of the labour question and the capacity to shape it. The massacre occurred in 1914, when financed police shot at strikers and their families, killing twenty-four men, women and children. It would be interesting to know the origins of all business school specialisms, as presumably they will leave a mark.
5 It should be borne in mind, however, that the workers on the ground were more radical than the union leadership. See, for example, the relationship between John D. Rockefeller, Jr., Mackenzie King and Samuel Gompers at a time of industrial strife for the Rockefellers (Gitelman, 1988: 264–304).
6 It is important to note here that in practice the contract system could be exploitative of workers (see Chapter 1; Buttrick, 1952; Pollard, 1965: 38; Clawson, 1980; Wilentz, 2004), management also systematically used the contract to divide workers on race lines (Esch and Roediger, 2009) and, where there was a strong craft culture and tradition, or local and family ties, it could and did empower workers and generate community norms and values (Wilentz, 2004; Montgomery, 1987; Clawson, 1980).
7 Importantly, as we shall see, this science is spurious. For example, the lack of science in management was evident in management's inconsistent and unresearched use of race management theories that were often located in the rule of thumb of the foreman's empire. Unscientific scientific management was used alongside unscientific race management (see Roediger and Esch, 2012: 139–69).
8 This term was also used on the slave plantations to describe the 'sluggishness' of slaves in their work, which further links the slave economy to modern capitalism and modern management (see Cooke, 2003: 1905–10). Indeed, the word 'factory' itself was used for the West African staging posts where the recalcitrant bodies of slaves were housed before being shipped to their fates (Roediger and Esch, 2012: 23).
9 Taylor was born into a very wealthy and prominent Quaker family in Philadelphia (Stewart, 2009; Roediger and Esch, 2012: 146).
10 Elite schools and universities perpetuated this social Darwinism by the manner in which they trained engineers. These engineers then went overseas in large numbers to use their race management techniques globally, with one example being US President Herbert Hoover (Esch and Roediger, 2009: 17–21).
11 This has certain parallels with the way in which apologists for slavery often blamed the slaves themselves for their inability or unwillingness to work harder and hence for forcing the overseers to manage them via the lash (Esch and Roediger, 2009: 12–13). The overseer with the whip was also extorted by plantation management writers to control his emotions while whipping a slave because one should 'never display yourself before [slaves] in a passion; and even if inflicting the severest punishment, do so in a mild cool manner', using the whip 'slowly and deliberately' (quoted in Roediger and Esch, 2012: 46). Despite Illouz's (2008) enthusiasm for the controlling of passion and its liberating

potential, it has a dubious history in management, as those deemed irrational and out of control – women, slaves, the colonized, the proletariat – will attest (see Chapters 4 and 5).

12 This was apparently how Midvale steelworkers referred to Taylor himself as he continuously sought to quicken the pace of work (Esch and Roediger, 2009: 23).

13 Interestingly, in Taylor's morality tale, managers can legitimately hide the stopwatch so the worker is unaware of his own monitoring. However, if workers conceal anything, they are deceitful. Management, in its pursuit of ever-greater expropriation and extraction, therefore seems immune from immorality.

14 This degrading of the worker as childlike or feminized is, of course, a common theme in all subjugation attempts, whether they are based in gender, race, sexuality, colonization or class (Federici, 2004).

15 These were the route man, instruction card man, time and costs clerk, disciplinarian, gang boss, speed boss, repair boss and inspector.

16 Montgomery (1987: 41, n99) acknowledges the influence of Stone's essay but suggests that she 'seriously overestimates both the pace and the extent of the steel industry's adoption of a job hierarchy based on "scientific management" principles'. Nevertheless, Stone highlights the emergence of many of the management tactics and organizational strategies that went on to dominate much of the twentieth century.

17 It should also be noted that Taylor worked in the steel industry and it was where he developed many of his ideas. While working at Bethlehem Steel, he and a colleague, Maunsel White, invented a technique for making harder steel that could then be used in cutting tools. This technique rendered the machinist's knowledge of cutting speeds obsolete, thereby empowering management in its ongoing conflict with the machinists in the early 1900s (see Montgomery, 1987: 230–2).

18 It is in light of this productivity and deskilling that we should view Lenin's reaction to Taylor. Initially, Lenin (1913) argues that Taylorism was 'scientific' sweating. However, a year later, his verdict is more nuanced (Lenin, 1914; Devinatz, 2003) when he suggests that productivity rises will reduce the need for workers to labour and will enable worker committees to assume control of social production. Later still, Lenin (1918a, 1918ba) goes further to argue that, alongside the Soviet reintroduction of the piece rate, Taylorism will enable the country to increase its productivity, while re-hiring expert managers familiar with managing Taylorist production processes in large plants will allow labour to gain knowledge about the control of vast, complex factories. In essence, Lenin appears to view Taylorism – and piece rates (for workers with bourgeois subjectivities derived from their work experiences) and the re-hiring of bourgeois experts – as a means of reappropriating the knowledge of mass production for the workers. As such, his view is more a pragmatic transitional endorsement (Devinatz, 2003) than a permanent one (Scoville, 2001). On Lenin and a Marxist productivist tradition, see Weeks (2011: 83–5).

4

'SPONTANEOUS COOPERATION'[1]

Excavating the soul

The shaping of conscience, the internationalization of new belief systems and the altering of subjectivity are all aspects of the Cartesian Enlightenment project to shape the 'complex "social inheritance" – language and culture but also the "technical" environment and practical technical know-how – that functions as a medium of humanisation' (Haug, 2010: 201) or the general intellect. As we saw in Chapter 3, elements of this were central to management, and indeed to Taylor's project, alongside the race management of the time and other techniques for sifting the population. However, the management school that is perhaps seminal in attempting to shape the conscience – or to manipulate it, to use C. Wright Mills's (1951: 109–11) term – is Elton Mayo's human relations school. Mayo makes communication – or what, following Foucault, we might call 'the confessional' – a centrepiece of management in his attempt to change the cognitive and affective potentialities desired by labour.

Communication, opening up, revealing and disclosure became ever more significant elements of modern life and management (Townley, 1993; Illouz, 2008; Weeks, 2011) in the twentieth century. Importantly, for our discussion, communication is also highlighted by Michels in his book *Political Parties* and by Weber in his analysis of leadership. Michels (1915: 1–12) argues communication is less important in aristocratic societies than it is in democratic societies. He suggests that in the latter, if the aristocrats or the natural elite are to continue to rule, they have to learn how to communicate with the masses in order to appear sympathetic while actually continuing to act in their own interests. Equally, Mayo highlights the need for managers to communicate with workers as a means to build a cohesive, pliant and productive workforce (without actually acting on that communication). Communication becomes a key feature of control, legitimation and manipulation – and this is also a central theme of neo-liberalism (see Chapter 6).

To return to Foucault, he (1981: 61) describes the confessional in the following manner:

The confessional is a ritual of discourse in which the speaking subject is also the subject of the statement; it is also a ritual which unfolds within a power relationship, for one does not confess without the presence (or the virtual presence) of a partner who is not simply the interlocutor but the authority who requires the confession, prescribes and appreciates it, and intervenes in order to judge, punish, forgive, console, and reconcile; a ritual in which the truth is corroborated by the obstacles and resistances it has had to surmount in order to be formulated; and finally, a ritual in which the expression alone, independently of its external consequences, produces intrinsic modifications in the person who articulates it; it exonerates, redeems, and purifies him; it unburdens him of his wrongs, liberates him, and promises him salvation.

The confessional, with its impact on the worker's conscience, as we saw in the Introduction, makes him or her both master and slave (Federici, 2004). This gets to the heart of Mayo's human relations school, which acted as a precursor for contemporary management practices, such as human resource management (Weeks, 2011). Anyone who has ever been appraised has entered this bureaucratic confessional world, wherein the appraisee is asked to recognize the authority of management and capital not only in the organization of production but now in his or her conscience, too. This is the Catholic confessional Foucault describes, in the sense that pressure on the subject means the confessional–appraisal is avoidable only through unemployment, which has been turned into a form of social death (Gorz, 1999; Weeks, 2011). Unburdening oneself, bearing one's soul, altering one's soul and the human need to communicate enable management to expropriate one's inner desires and frailties and thereby manipulate one's conscience. Management tries to capture and mould potential and, accompanying this, attempts to demarcate what has been left behind or is not of any use to capital as non-valuable. Here, management is the authority that judges, approves, punishes, forgives, consoles and reconciles one's desires and potentialities to the needs of valorization while discarding the residue.

Planning, discipline and labour

As we saw in Chapter 3, the craft worker as a central political subject was dead by the early twentieth century. However, this death did not herald industrial peace; far from it. Between the 'American Terror' of 1890–1910 and the 'Second Industrial Revolution' of the 1920s (see Jacques, 1996: 61 and 142–7) we witness the formulation of a planned capitalism aimed at the real subsumption of labour to capital and from there on to total subsumption. Although management's specific tactics may have changed, it essentially persisted with what Taylor had attempted to do – to mould the worker's individual and collective subjectivity to the interests of capital (Weber, 1948: 253–63).

This period was defined by many of the words and concepts proposed by Taylor – partnership, cooperation, responsibility, commitment and motivation. However, management increasingly turned its attention to emotion and psychology in the belief that these would unlock human nature's secrets and allow management to manage (Mills, 1951: 110). Its interest in the world outside of work started to grow. As Mayo (1923a: 420) puts it: 'Human emotions determine human destiny; life must be sufficiently interesting to the average man or woman if civilisation is to endure.' Capitalism heretofore had largely concentrated on developing society technically, but its capacity for understanding human behaviour and human emotions was paramount if 'civilisation [were] to endure' (Mayo, 1923a: 420). Science was put at the disposal of management (Panzieri, 1961; Federici, 2004: 145–55). Mayo and others attempted to shape the human personality and make the mass industrial subject pliant. Such a task was absolutely essential because, as we saw at the end of Chapter 3 – with the destruction of craft, the emergence of mass production, mass consumption, rapid urbanization and new forms of social relationship – a new subject was needed, one who would exhibit:

> a new kind of human discipline. This discipline, to be industrially effective, must not be imposed but immanent; it should not be collective but individual; and it ought not to be external but internal. Such a regimentation of the human spirit must be austere, in order to command respect; this-worldly, so that the daily task will not go untended; empirical, so that new learnings will issue; and exacting, so that obedient self-sacrifice will be generously forthcoming … The industrial man is justifiably acquisitive and industrious because he is, after all, a steward of the great Manager–Mathematician. He must be rational and efficient, like the machine itself: his techniques must match industrial technics! He must be leisure-less, for his time is hired: unhired time is indulged only in so far as it increases the productivity of the working hours; he is unfortunately unlike the machine, he must be re-created. He must be restless, looking toward the future, for which his acquisitions are made: otherwise how can the machine come into existence or multiply? He must be money-minded, for how else can he be related to the machine, his products disposed of, machined commodities secured, the imponderables of his existence 'controlled'?
>
> (Meadows, 1947: 363–4)

Society needed a new individual and it was the task of management to generate this subject. Such important matters could not be left to chance. It was also its task to discipline those who were recalcitrant, those who desired radical social change and those who refused to acquiesce – such groups were deemed to suffer from pathology. Management entered further into the normation of the soul. Through this process it hoped to ensure the acquiescence and the degradation of the worker and to repackage it as the potentiality the worker desired. Over two or perhaps three generations, the worker would be turned from a public-sphere-oriented knowledgeable subject with a political role in the community to a private-sphere object of study by others, deemed to be pathological if politically active and therefore to be policed, managed, educated and, if deemed a subject of no value, increasingly rejected as worthless (a theme picked up in Chapter 6). Capitalism sought the unthinking, pliant subject. But to achieve this, it had to redraw the subject's cognitive and affective maps. As we shall see in the second half of this chapter, Elton Mayo and the human relations school were central to this project.

The mass industrial worker and resistance to management

The real subsumption of labour to capital that had occurred meant that capital and management now controlled the production process and had imprinted it with techniques and processes located in the pursuit of profit. This knowledge was located in machinery, the division of labour, science and bureaucracy. Efficiency gains through the direct control of the production process became central to modern capitalism (Thompson, 1967). As we saw in Chapter 3, this shift meant that capital developed a more intense, directive and constantly changing relationship to labour and the production process, and in its wake came the real subsumption of labour to capital (Marx, 1976: 1019–38). Capital and management presented themselves to labour as the organizing force of production. The story of management theory is largely one of this subsumption – of how, within the workshop, management and capital can control and revolutionize the production process in the search for ever more efficiency and profit. Management theorists are basically seeking ways to maximize management's control of the labour process in an attempt to extract efficiency gains through technology, psychology, discrimination, conscience, subjectivity or identity. And much critical scholarship has aimed to highlight the ways in which these struggles over the production process unfolded (Thompson, 1967; Braverman, 1974; Marglin, 1974; Edwards, 1979; Gordon et al., 1982).

That this real subsumption occurred in the late nineteenth and early twentieth centuries seems unarguable. For example, 30 per cent of manufacturing capital consolidated from 1889 to 1904; capital per worker increased by 36 per cent between 1920 and 1929; real value added per worker increased by 75 per cent; plant size grew rapidly, from a maximum of 1,500 workers per establishment in the 1880s to as many as 60,000 in the 1920s. (And this trend has continued: today, Foxconn has a million factory workers producing, among other things, perhaps the most iconic product of our generation – the iPhone.) All of this gave rise to the 'drive system' of production to extract ever-greater productivity (Gordon et al., 1982: 107–40). However, despite this massive expansion of constant capital and the growing concentration of capital, labour remained the dominant actor because, with real subsumption, the crisis of motivation became ever more acute – the crisis of turning labour power into actual labour and of creating a new subject simultaneously became both more difficult and more necessary. Indeed, as the economy moved increasingly to services, the modulation and planning of personality became one of its central features (see Chapter 5).

The extent of the resistance to management's attempt to 'habituate the worker' (Braverman, 1974) to these new disciplines and motivations was impressive. This refusal and resistance led directly to management's obsession with partnership, cooperation, responsibility, commitment and motivation. As Marx highlights, such refusal and conflict are inherent and never-ending within the capitalist system. For this reason, management theory has a tendency to repeat itself (see Jacques, 1996: 146–91).

Resistance to the new organizational and productive form was demonstrated in a variety of ways – strikes, sabotage, absenteeism, turnover, lock-outs, unionization, unemployment and the pursuit of pleasure. Then, internationally, came the Bolshevik Revolution of 1917; various revolts by communists in Central Europe; and massive waves of industrial unrest throughout the rest of Europe, including occupations of factories in Italy, the UK's general strike of 1926 and ongoing industrial turmoil in France. In the United States, the unrest included a general strike in Seattle in 1919; a steel strike in the same year; a coal strike in 1917 and almost continuous agitation in the mines from 1920 to 1923;[2] the record militancy of 1912–13, 1915–16 and 1917, when over six million work days were lost to strikes (which encouraged the further formation and collusion of the capitalist class, as we saw in Chapter 3); calls for miners' ownership of the mines and the nationalization of the railways, rather than their re-privatization after the state had commandeered them during the war (Montgomery, 1987: 370–411); bombs sent to leading industrialists and politicians; and, in Boston, three days of looting following a police strike (O'Connor, 1999a). Concerned by the extent of the agitation, President Wilson established industrial conferences between the state, labour and capitalists to try to establish better relations and open up some prospects for more industrial democracy in response to labour's demands for a greater say in production (Tronti, 1965; Montgomery, 1987; Gitelman, 1988; Bruce and Nyland, 2011). This period also witnessed the state's desire to embrace unions during the war effort in much the same way as had happened in Britain and France (a form of proto-Keynesianism); the rise of a progressive bloc and a socialist party; and their subsequent decline as the century wore on (Montgomery, 1987: 352). This militancy, the war effort and the growing complexity of production convinced the state and large corporations that a two-pronged approach to labour was required – appeasement and an attack on 'militants'. Management theorists were at the forefront of both.

Resistance to the new regime often manifested itself as labour turnover – people simply refused and walked off the job in droves. The Employment Managers Association, which grew substantially after 1910, was rightly obsessed with this issue (Bloomfield, 1915; Willits, 1915; Alexander, 1916; Nichols, 1916; Williams, 1917; Douglas, 1918). Turnover for industrial firms in the early twentieth century could reach 400 per cent per annum (Douglas, 1918). This was due to

> The monotony of modern factory labor. This is rarely mentioned as a cause of labor turnover, but on *a priori* grounds we must infer that it exercises tremendous influence. Specialization and routine labor have rendered industry so dull that it is no wonder the modern artisan frequently throws up his job and seeks another plant from sheer weariness.
>
> *(Douglas, 1918: 313)*

Having created modern work, capitalism had created its own crisis of motivation – and management was made increasingly aware of this. Another two areas of resistance were the ever-present threat of unionization and a successful attack on the open shop (see Bendix, 1956: 267–74) and workers' sabotage of production. Given all of these various forms of resistance, capitalism was clearly in trouble, and the mass industrial worker was simultaneously refusing work and demanding a say in production. Civilization needed to be saved.

The emergence of large-scale capital, the increased division of labour and its accompanying bureaucracy led to an important shift in the ideology of US management and the way it viewed both the worker and itself. As we saw in Chapter 3, the worker was no longer a subject with knowledge. He or she had become an object to be studied, a bundle of work routines, skills, knowledge, emotions, ideologies, motivations, interests, affects, relationships, desires and potentialities, living in a culture that itself needed to be examined, approved and harnessed by management. As Fordism and real subsumption instituted shifts in the work ethic (Weeks, 2011: 37–98), in ideas about relationships and intimacy (Illouz, 2008: 58–104), in concepts about the relationship between labour and value (see Chapter 3), in consumption (Gramsci, 1971; Meadows, 1947) and finally in thinking about the body as a commodity (Kracauer, 1998: 33–40), they also changed management thought (Bendix, 1956: 287–308). Increasingly, capitalism had to be planned, regimented, managed, normalized and standardized both within and outside the factory; and science was invoked to achieve this. Management itself would be a science, both the workers and management would be subjected to the scientific gaze and, on the basis of this 'scientific' legitimacy, new lines of hierarchy would be created which suggested to labour that, as its knowledge had been expropriated, it was now deemed to be a largely unknowing cog in the machine. Central here was the general intellect as management and bureaucracy let slip class war (Mills 1951: 109–11).

Managing and planning cooperation in capitalism

The Employment Managers Association perhaps encapsulates the embrace of so-called 'science'. As we saw in Chapter 3, Taylor also sought to hitch science to his management wagon, albeit with limited results. Thus, cinematography was used to record movement, workers were subjected to time and motion studies (often without their consent or knowledge), notes were compiled, quotas assigned and piece rates set, all in the name of objectivity and efficiency. As we know, Taylor's scientific credentials (and those of race management theorists) were quickly called into question (Hoxie, 1918; Stewart, 2009), but his claim to science also heralded a change in how management came to view itself. Management ideology shifted from a belief in the manager/owner as a Darwinian winner who vanquished the weak to a view that management was about planning and especially about empowering and/or allowing the worker to achieve his or her correct level now that those achievements and levels were believed to be conducive to the valorization of capital. Management would also stifle industrial unrest because, as one manager expressed it, 'management should explain company policy and fundamental economics to its workers, simply and clearly, just as a parent explained the family program to the children: and that would win their cooperation' (see Bendix, 1956: 293). Childlike, irrational workers – like colonized peoples, slaves, women, children and indeed any dependent group – merely needed their role in the hierarchy explained to them.

As management in the twentieth century responded to the crisis of production and motivation it was facing, it turned ever more to science in the form of analysis. The army's use of psychology and intelligence testing played a central role here. Its research into morale was increasingly used by psychologists in relation to business (Illouz, 2008: 67), with Mayo, for example, carrying out a great deal of psychological research on soldiers in Australia (Smith, 1998). Management was increasingly subjected to analysis. Central to this was the belief that workers were not solely driven by money but had relationships, emotions, motivations, respects, personalities, attachments and desires and potentialities, and that these were increasingly important at work and in the consumer sphere. One might think here of Maslow, McGregor and Herzberg (McKenzie, 2001). Hence, in the white-collar occupations of both the United States and Weimar Germany, hiring on the basis of anticipated consumer reaction and attachment to the worker, and therefore the company, was beginning to take place. This was, of course, gendered, racialized and sexualized (Mills, 1951: 161–88; Kracauer, 1998: 33–9). Furthermore, managers could not behave like the self-made industrialists of the past, who had supposedly thrived in a survival-of-the-fittest world. Rather, leadership and management were now concerned with 'workers who failed to produce efficiently and cooperate fully' (Bendix, 1956: 298). It entailed a manager being 'worthy of his authority, eager to acquire new information, willing to learn from subordinates, anxious to see them develop, able to take criticism and acknowledge mistakes' (Bendix, 1956: 303). Management was about enabling others – what Jacques (1996: 109) might call 'stewardship' or Illouz (2008) 'therapy'. However, although this signalled a change from Taylorism, it was still about 'human engineering' (Bendix, 1956: 289).

Central to this was that the 'new' management should be located in relationships: that is, managers increasingly had to demonstrate an ability to communicate to various groups and interests – both above and below themselves – if they wished to progress up the corporate ladder. The way to success in the bureaucracy was granted to those who could communicate leadership, hence the importance of communication to the elite (Michels, 1915). (As evidence of this new importance, one might highlight the runaway success of Dale Carnegie's book *How to Win Friends and Influence People*, which told readers how to communicate with others.[3]) Accompanying this stress on communication was the management belief that workers were not part of this system: they merely wanted to labour; and although they could perhaps develop within that sphere, they could not communicate because that entailed possessing the ability to control their emotions, something which they – along with colonized peoples, non-whites, women and children – lacked. Naturally, this lack of worker 'ambition' reflected not a rejection of management but an inability to appreciate it because of the workers' lower acumen (Bendix, 1956: 302–8). The bureaucratic management career as class war was now being waged in earnest.

This career was intimately linked to the organizational form that had emerged out of the division of labour, as we saw in Chapters 2 and 3. At its heart were pseudo-science, planning and analysis, which were used to smooth out the modulations of capitalism – this was the second reason for the new form for the emerging elite and ideology of management. For example, an employment manager (Alexander, 1916) at General Electric published a paper emphasizing the lack of science when it came to understanding the labour turnover problem. He thus asked for firm- and plant-level figures on employee hirings and replacements as a result of (1) death, (2) long-term illness, (3) unsuitability for the work, (4) a lack of fitness on account of personal characteristics, (5) the departure of workers of their own accord for reasons of congeniality, climate or other factors, (6) the departure of workers who had been taken on to cope with a temporary spike in demand, or (7) the simple fact that no firm can achieve a perfect match between hiring and need, hence there was a 'normal' turnover. He goes on to segment the workforce according to skill and price, outlines the various damages that hiring, training and turnover of staff from each category can cause, and seeks to put prices on them: for example, the costs of (1) clerical work, (2) instruction of new employees by foremen and assistants, (3) increased wear and tear of machinery and tools due to inexperienced new hands, (4) reduced rate of production compared to experienced employees, and (5) increased spoiled work by new employees. He then divides these costs by grade of worker and, because firms often rehired former employees, divides these costs again by new as opposed to repeat hires. (Incidentally, without these figures, he puts the turnover rate at 633 per cent; see Alexander, 1916: 130.) Science, ratios, norms, costs, averages, comparisons, contrasts and evaluation – these are the order of the day. Foucault's normation and Panzieri's planning were in the ascendant as work and workers were ever more categorized, segmented, modulated and moulded.

To achieve this required an organizational change – another push against the rule of thumb so hated by Taylor and indeed by Mayo (1924b: 591). This science suggests management needs to take over the function of hiring and firing from the foreman, embrace the scientific selection and placement of personnel, and create training and development so managers will act as leaders who motivate the workforce to achieve targets for both the company and themselves. And workers will simultaneously uncover life or their full potentiality in the service of capitalist valorization (see Bloomfield, 1915; Alexander, 1916; Nichols, 1916; Redfield, 1916). Yet again, science and management will replace the arbitrary foreman's empire (see Nelson, 1995) and ensure capital and labour's unitary interest in a wondrous moment of the scientific matching of the worker and the work. This is capitalist cooperation wherein workers' recalcitrance disappears and capital becomes the super-ordinate active agent.

Management used science to claim objectivity and present a unitary view of the organization. However, as with Taylorism and the race management theories mentioned earlier, questions were soon raised about whether any of this deserved to be called 'science' (see Bell, 1947; Moore, 1947).

Managing and planning at Ford

In reality this 'new' management was not so new. Rather, it was a complement to systematic (Litterer, 1963) and later scientific management; and, as is well known, many of its principal components were developed further by Henry Ford. It is Ford who is most associated with the mechanization of labour, although it must be noted that the whole of US business was becoming more aware of technology's possibilities: for example, trade magazines such as *Factory* and *Iron Age* had been running eulogies to the machine and control since the very early years of the century (Montgomery, 1987: 233). So when Ford opened his Highland Park plant in 1910, it was viewed as a technological wonder confronting the worker as science, planning and capital in action. As Marx had foreseen, it designed the control of production directly into the technology. Thus, the routing and directing of operative tasks were assigned to engineers and supervisors, 'but also to an astonishing degree had been incorporated into the machinery itself' (Montgomery, 1987: 233). The factory operated via chain-driven sub-assembly and final assembly lines, using machinery that was designed to make a single cut on a single part and was often unable to perform any other task.

Such a productive plant required a huge capital investment, which proved to be its weakness (Silver, 2003). In 1927 Ford retooled in order to construct a new product and the firm closed down the entire plant for the reconstruction, leaving 100,000 workers idle. (By then, of course, management had discovered ways to measure and calculate the costs of idle plant; see Gantt, 1915.) The level of monotony was simply staggering: for example, one worker reamed bushed the T-225 for stub-axle arm left T-270 850 times in an eight-hour day (Montgomery, 1987: 234). Accompanying this level of monotony, routine and technological control was a new version of the foreman's empire: overseers had absolute authority to fire at will, a system that developed alongside an increased emphasis on the human side of management that was discussed earlier.[4] As John R. Lee, a Ford manager, put it:

> we began to realize something of the relative value of men, mechanism and manufacturing, so to speak, and we confess that up to this time we believed … that somehow or other the human element of our men was taken care of automatically and needed little or no consideration.
>
> *(Quoted in Meyer, 1980: 69)*

Man literally was an appendage to the machine.

In actuality, Ford was made to realize the human element of workers' refusal – he was made to recognize labour's active status. In 1913, on any given day, 10 per cent of the workforce was absent, and the firm had a labour turnover rate of 370 per cent. It needed to hire 52,000 workers to keep 13,600 employed throughout the year. The new factory system needed ever greater work and time discipline, which proved difficult to achieve: even among wage-dependent immigrant workers, refusal was exhibited as the crisis of motivation. Using what Foucault would later describe as normation, Ford managers realized that the highly sophisticated factory system was working below capacity because of the 'human element'; hence, the working population had to be further recast. This need gave rise to Ford's sociology department and to the profit-sharing plan that heralded the five-dollar day in 1914.[5]

While Ford's welfare capitalism was a particular entity, it was not completely unique, and it provides an insight into how capitalism was managed and developed at the time. What Ford did was blend management techniques from the very Taylorist emphasis on work standards and efficiency with an emphasis on subjectivity and, in particular, Americanization (Meyer, 1980). Approximately 75 per cent of the workforce were immigrants (more independent US-born workers refused Ford's factory discipline) and, as part of the firm's race management, Ford disproportionately hired African-American workers (Montgomery, 1987: 381; Esch and Roediger, 2009). In its profit-sharing programme, workers were evaluated on the standard of their work but also on the manner in which they lived their lives, their families and their willingness to learn English. In different ways this is aligned to what Mayo (1924a: 249) called the 'psychology of the total situation', what German management labelled the 'total personality' (Kracauer, 1998: 36) or what Mills (1951: 182–8) termed 'the personality market'. To benefit fully, one had to be a good worker, a good family man and a good citizen. Central to this was the necessity of being a worker who submitted himself to the norms and routines of the new factory discipline, of the future, of consumption, of being money-minded and of being obedient – the new capitalist subject. Here it was management's role to uplift the worker and turn the subject into a better worker and hence a better subject. If the worker did not rise to this challenge, he was pathological or a failure and dismissed after six months. In short, Ford's system was an intensification and extension of Taylor's political agenda.

As is well known, Ford's political agenda included living in a suitable house (ideally away from the city centre), being clean, having a family home, not sharing a room if single, being thrifty, saving and working hard. The aim of Ford's management was to create the ideal individual in terms of routines, family life, desire, potentiality, consumption and production. Thus, the lessons given were divided into a Domestic Series (getting up in the morning, table utensils, washing, welcoming a visitor); a Commercial Series (buying and using stamps, pay day, going to the bank, buying a lot, building a house); and an Industrial Series (beginning the day's work, shining shoes, looking for work, finishing the day's work). All of these courses (which were compulsory for immigrant workers) were aimed at creating the subject of the Fordist citizen–worker–consumer and thereby breaking the immigrant's connection to other forms of community: 'The Ford managers and engineers devised a system wherein men were the raw materials which were moulded, hammered and shaped into products which had the proper attitudes and habits for work in the factory' (Meyer, 1980: 74). Also inherent in the system was race management. Workers were managed by white, middle-class Americans who viewed them as childlike and in need of civilizing. Indeed, Boris Emmett of the US Bureau of Labor Statistics highlighted the class and ethnic bias of the profit-sharing programme (Montgomery, 1987: 242–4; Esch and Roediger, 2009; Roediger and Esch, 2012).

Ford is interesting because it highlights the terrain upon which management was taking place. This was not new terrain – as we have seen, Taylor had advocated moulding the subject several decades earlier – but it was both growing and intensifying. Human engineering became more important in light of industrial struggle, turnover rates, worker sabotage and the need to control the worker's community life. In this context, personnel management shortly after 1910 reached into the worker–subject to shape attitudes and ethics as manipulation became the new form of management (Mills, 1951: 110; Meyer, 1980; Weeks, 2011). Management was extending Taylorist interests in new ways and digging deeper into the general intellect.

Ford was seeking to develop a particular set of cognitive and affective skills or potentialities within work. Capital tried to recast the social individual of the general intellect. It attempted to shrink the critical distance to social relations that the general intellect requires to act as a universal liberating force so that the social individual became the capitalist social individual, thereby transforming the general intellect to 'particular intellects' pursuing profitability and the valorization of capital (Haug, 2010: 215). When this happened, its free gifts were radically enhanced as the worker was socialized into the factory, the office or the department store before they had even reached them by family, friends, community, education, union, the church, media and the state, so that a life of work and valorization would be desired because all of those potentialities that actually mattered were guided towards it. The universal of the social individual would be privatized and made safe for capital, and resistance would become both futile and pathologized.

This extension to the general intellect took many forms, from the welfare capitalism and technological control of Ford (Meyer, 1980) to Rockefeller's experiments with company unions (Rockefeller, 1916; Gitelman, 1988), the call for greater dialogue between workers and management (e.g. from future Canadian Prime Minister Mackenzie King, a key adviser to J. D. Rockefeller following the Ludlow massacre; see Gitelman, 1988), the emerging links between elements of the trades union movement and the Taylor society (Jacoby, 1983) and the development of internal labour markets based on selection, seniority or credentials (Edwards, 1979). Running through many of these developments was an increased awareness that subjectivity had to be moulded to make it easier to co-opt. As Bendix (1956: 297) writes:

> Taylor's work in scientific management, the work of industrial psychologists in selection and job placement, and the entire open-shop campaign had for their common denominator the endeavor to enlist the cooperation of workers in a manner that would combat unions and increase efficiency.

In so doing, the myth of scientific neutrality was invoked and there were calls for greater levels of expertise. Indeed, one version of this was that capital and labour should both be run by experts because matters of production were becoming technical rather than political issues (Jacoby, 1983) – an early form of Bell's (1973) post-industrial society. Science and cooperation would solve the problems of the new industrial order. Of course, these practices often failed; as the levels of industrial unrest and capital's assault on labour after the recession of the early 1920s indicate capital was only ever interested in cooperation on its own terms (see Montgomery, 1987; Gitelman, 1988; O'Connor, 1999a; 1999b).

As we saw earlier, like technology, capitalist cooperation is never neutral. Both are utilized to render production more efficient, to extract surplus value and to curtail the independence of workers. Thus, the question is not simply one of deskilling but of gaining command over and modulating the entire capitalist process (Hanlon and Mandarini, 2015). The early twentieth century was precisely about this modulation. For example, management began using routines, norms, procedures, rules and regulations to gain control over labour turnover (Bloomfield, 1915), idleness of plant (Gantt, 1915), selection and training of employees (Alexander, 1916), home life and its impact on workers (Bloomfield and Willits, 1916), underemployment, unemployment and remuneration (Nichols, 1916), and labour–capital dialogue (Rockefeller, 1916). The key issue for industry was deemed to be the 'problem of handling men' (Bloomfield, 1915: 122). This was important for the whole economy, and increasingly so as the economy became more services based because 'Business may be essentially impersonal but it is highly personal in services (Bloomfield, 1915: 124). Hence, human resource management, its development, selection and, most importantly, control were essential and too important to be left to foremen or the old organizational forms. Human resources needed to be handed over to university-trained professionals who, using scientific methods, would select, develop, promote and remunerate the workforce. In such a way, 'whim and prejudice are eliminated' (Bloomfield, 1915: 125; see also Mills, 1951: 77–112). These calls reinforce Bendix's (1956: 288–308) claim that management ideology shifted in its evaluation of management itself and began to prize scientific approaches, analysis, communicative skill, adaptability and team-building. By so doing, capital would receive 'spontaneous cooperation' – it would be offered free gifts willingly. What was being proposed was ever more reaching into the worker's subjectivity. As US Secretary of Commerce William C. Redfield (1916: 11) expressed it:

> We say we employ so many 'hands'. The very use of the word shows that we do not appreciate the situation. We are not employing 'hands'; we are employing brains and hearts and dispositions, and all sorts of elements that make for personality – we are employing them all.

Industry, like war, was about winning and remoulding hearts and minds. This was the agenda of management. Perhaps no one expressed this concept more clearly than Elton Mayo – the founder of human relations and perhaps the most significant management theorist of the twentieth century (Illouz, 2008: 65–77).

Elton Mayo, the spontaneous and the general intellect

In his writings, Mayo touches on a range of issues that are still with us. Although, like Taylor's, his ideas were never completely implemented, his work remains central to management ideology in the United States and Europe (Bendix, 1956: 319–40; Illouz, 2008: 68; Bruce and Nyland, 2011). His work has been popular and important because it explains the shift in management that became necessary with the advent of large-scale, bureaucratic organizations, mass production, the increasing polarization of the labour market and the importance of a greater concern with 'consensus' between firms rather than 'wasteful competition' (see Jacques, 1996: 109). As suggested, this form of management put more emphasis on certain forms of communicative skills. Mayo explained to the ever-increasing number of managers how they might better manage their own careers through an understanding of human relations and the need to cooperate. He also endorsed management as an elite activity and provided managers with a rationale for rejecting labour's claims to be involved in managerial decisions: workers should be listened to, but they were incapable of managerial insight.[6] Finally, he identified the eliciting of cooperation in complex organizations as the central and growing feature of management, so that 'it is reasonable to expect a constant and perhaps an increasing concern with inducing a cooperative attitude' (Bendix, 1956: 338). Inclusion, listening, talking, analysing and explaining would become ever more important features of management.

At the core of Mayo's notion of human relations are cooperation and group activity. We are not individuals but rather socialized into groups. Capitalism profoundly disrupted our social groups and our traditions and therefore put civilization in peril. It was management's duty to save this civilization (Bendix and Fisher, 1949: 316). Mayo propounded the same thesis from his first book *Democracy and Freedom: An Essay in Social Logic*[7] in 1919 until his death in 1949. Essentially, he argued that workers or ordinary people were not rational, self-interested individuals but rather often non-rational, irrational and group-oriented. As such, they cooperated spontaneously. In this context, 'spontaneous' did not mean voluntarily; in fact, almost the opposite. It meant that people unwittingly followed routines and traditions and that they did so non-rationally, in contrast to what Mayo viewed as the actively thought-through, rational, self-interested form of thinking and being promulgated by liberal thought historically. Indeed, rational, self-interested thinking was what occurred when routine and tradition lost their way or when an individual hit a crisis. Thus, rational, self-interested action reflects a breakdown in order. It is in light of this that we must view the eighteenth and nineteenth centuries and the growth of capitalism, which destroyed routine and tradition and replaced spontaneous group behaviour with a dangerous, individualist logic (Mayo, 1919: 1–14).

Mayo was particularly exercised by a fear of social conflict – as were many in the Harvard–Pareto circle in which he moved (Keller, 1984; Scott, 1992). He argued that the nineteenth century opened up society to conflict and that this brought social dislocation and disunity alongside great productive and technological improvements. As he puts it:

As a result of this individualism, even so able a philosopher as J. S. Mill was reduced to an economic gospel of anarchical competition and a political belief in salvation at the ballot box. Theories such as these cannot explain social growth. Man, considered merely as an individual, alters little from age to age; it is in respect of knowledge and power to use, of social custom and tradition for depth of vision – it is in respect of these qualities that man changes; and it is these changes which make history. Individualism failed to see that man, socially speaking, holds his past and future in his present. And individualism consequently, though it gave us an economics and a politics, failed to give us a science of society and government.

(Mayo, 1919: 5)

Although Mayo is talking about individualism here, capitalism is also a source of concern because it is a system of constant change – 'creative destruction', 'constant revolutionizing' – thus the past is quickly dismissed (if never entirely forgotten), thereby further undermining social cohesion. In what appears initially like a Durkheimian twist (see Appendix), this flux leaves the individual exposed to the will of the state. Mayo (1919: 5) goes on to comment:

By opposing society, described as a mere formless anarchy of persons, to the unity of the State, democracy has made it seem that social unity can only come by way of state activity. Socialism, without attempting a more adequate analysis of social institutions, has come to this conclusion; so also have the majority of present-day politicians. Much as some of the latter dislike the tenets of *lassier-faire* [*sic*], they show by their actions that they look to State intervention for the cure of social ills. So the political science which sought to place social authority beyond the State, ended by relegating all authority to the State. The social philosophy which began by repudiating the right of one man to control others, concluded with the inference that 'social construction' will make state control and the power of the politician absolute.

Like Durkheim, Mayo proposes the need for groups and functions to intervene with the state. However, his understanding is different to Durkheim's. Durkheim (1957, 1984) sought to use professional associations, workers' organizations and occupational associations to mediate between the state and the individual and, in some respects, between capitalist organization and the individual. Mayo sought to use small social groups and work groups created *within* the capitalist organization as intermediaries between the small state and the individual – for him, private capitalist bureaucratic organization was obviously not a Hobbesian Leviathan, even though it was responsible for disciplining and socializing labour. As we will see in Chapter 6, Mayo has more affinity with Hayek than Durkheim.

Hayek (1948) rejected the French Enlightenment view of rationality, arguing that, because it was constructivist, it returned us to a form of collectivism and planning. He instead praised the Scottish Enlightenment, because it was based on scepticism about how much we know and what we could know. Thus, Hayek's question was not individualist or not but rather whether the citizen is guided by what he or she can know, which itself is derived from tradition, routine, family, friends, the market price and interests. A lack of complete knowledge means the state can never know or plan completely (Hayek, 1945), thus we need to limit its coercive power. This is not anarchy but reliance on tradition, routines, habits, practices and markets – so that we find real consensual democracy in cultural inheritance. Central here is also Hayek's espousal of the marketplace. He accepted that this was not fair, but argued that it was unbiased in how it treated people in its unfairness: it did not discriminate against anyone because they were a worker or a woman or non-white; it just did or did not want the skills a person had to offer. If properly organized, society and markets need and engender a common culture, shared routines, social cohesion and traditions that stop people from indulging in destructive behaviour. They need what Hayek calls 'spontaneous order' (Hayek, 1944, 1948; Gamble, 1996; Foucault, 2008). What they generate are benign particular intellects that have power and elitism built into them.

For Mayo, the modern democratic state is a constructivist state in the way that Hayek describes and rejects. That is, it does not reflect the will of the people but seeks to impose its will on them – more accurately, the will of certain irrational groups and collectivities. True freedom comes from allowing routine and tradition to evolve unhindered, rather than trying to create it. As Mayo (1919: 6) puts it:

> Since the special business of the State is to record and enforce moral relationships, it cannot take the lead in the manner of changing them ... Social growth is the accretion of slow centuries, each one of which endows humanity with some new legacy. We live and move and have our being in the achievement of our predecessors to such an extent that none can tell precisely where tradition ends and originality begins.

Tradition, routine and the institutions 'provide mankind with motives, and we cannot begin to understand the nature of the social will until we know something of the manner in which one generation communicates its social discoveries to the next'; thus, the individual learns and develops through fellowship and as part of a group, which 'combine to aid and stimulate his powers of self-development' (Mayo, 1919: 7). The state's role is very limited, based simply on conserving the freedom for this communal growth and its central institutions – the market and the work organization (see Chapters 5 and 6). But this also entails moulding the individual and the group.

Mayo (1919: 10) feels that the state often steps beyond its proper function. It regulates in ways that are 'incompatible with the extra-political expansion of social activities which is apparently to be the outstanding feature of a reconstructed civilisation'. The cause of this problem in the early twentieth century was party politics, against which democratic government, as it stood at that time, had no safeguards.

> The inadequacy of mere party-politics to the wider social problems of the present is already painfully apparent. *Primâ facie*, it would seem that democracy, in the existing condition of the world affairs, is as liable to become tyrannical as any historic monarchy. We may yet see democratic governments, in the name of social enfranchisement, obstructing the efforts of society to over-come the difficulties which racial and geographical remoteness place in the way of social unity.
>
> *(Mayo, 1919: 10)*

Mayo's fear of democracy is actually a fear of the mass industrial worker. He argues that 'class conscious' theories of the working class are a 'direct outcome of modern extension of the wage system' (Mayo, 1919: 12). As such, because they have lost all economic self-determination, the working class are seeking to recreate their autonomy and function through politics and the capture of the state. Here again, there is neo-liberalism with its need to capture the state to secure the 'spontaneous order' and oppose the planning Mayo so fears (see Foucault, 2008 on neo-liberals and the state). Mayo argues that there was real exploitation, but that the doctrine of indi-vidualism and laissez-faire left it untouched, except through the political system and hence the rise of working-class parties that sought to control the market via the state. Again, this is a neo-liberal strategy to argue that the mass industrial worker was left wage dependent and hence sought to limit this dependency by capturing the state in order to avoid the market (see Chapter 6). Mayo (1919: 12) writes:

> This is, of course, a logical enough remedy if it be assumed that the State is the only real source of social unanimity and co-operation. But the falsity of this assumption is bringing a nemesis to our civilisation. The workers have drawn the obvious conclusion that political or quasi-political organisation is the only means of securing the adjustment of their grievances; they believe their future to depend upon their capacity to control the State.

Such a strategy jeopardizes the institutions of the market and private property upon which Mayo builds routine and tradition. For him, this would be a disaster because only market-based private property gives rise to 'personal responsibility for social use to the privileges of ownership' (Mayo, 1919: 12). Furthermore, a democracy increasingly built on discussion, on 'trusting the people', and an extension of the franchise leads to the emergence of 'collective mediocrity' and a form of government that is increasingly shaped by distrust between the people and their representatives, which in turn engenders less discussion and more appeals to fear and hate (Mayo, 1919: 18–20) – or, as neo-liberal theorists such as Lippmann call it, 'a war economy' (see Chapter 6).

Within this, the public good of the general intellect, its free gifts, or its basis for a genuine spontaneous cooperation is also an opportunity for capital, if it can be shaped. Mayo is caught between acknowledging this need for sociality, fearing it and wanting to shape its multiplicity of potentialities so that they are individualized, privatized and guided towards the valorization of capital. In this sense, he reflects a long tradition of right-wing thinkers – Becker (1962), Lucas (1988) and Hayek (1948). For Mayo, a wider franchise, democracy, is shaped by forms of rabble rousing. (The title of the second chapter of his 1947 book *The Social Problems of an Industrial Society* is 'The Rabble Hypothesis'.) 'So far we have elicited the fact that the "completely popular government" which is the very essence of democracy has, in practice, led to control by "collective mediocrity" and the more so, the more widely the franchise is extended' (Mayo, 1919: 24). Hence Mayo's desire for a private bureaucracy led by the elite – the only form of bureaucracy that could outmanoeuvre the state (Weber, 1948). Echoing the neo-liberals (see Hayek, 1945; Röepke, 1948, 1992), Mayo feels that the state cannot be trusted because of the people – we need constituted not constituent power (see Chapter 6). Also like the neo-liberals, he never directly addresses the manner in which routine, tradition or the spontaneous may be actively shaped by management elites (see also Bernays, 1928; Marx, 1976; Lears, 2000).

This lack of trust in the mass industrial worker is based on the view that they were in some sense broken by the emergence of capitalism, and this pushed them into an irrational collectivism because it deprived them of their autonomy and traditional socialization processes (see Chapters 2 and 3). For neo-liberals, the state needs to be captured and then used to reinvigorate property rights, entrepreneurship and competition in all areas of life (Foucault, 2008). For Mayo, workers must be given a function – they must be made to feel socially useful as they ream bush the T-225 for stub-axle arm left T-270 850 times a day (Montgomery, 1987: 234). Thus, the issue is one of reconciling (Foucault, 1981: 61) the mass industrial worker to the new society with its new forms of hierarchy (Mayo, 1949: 26–9). The bureaucratic organizational form becomes the mechanism for enforcing and legitimating class structuring (Mills, 1951: 108–11).

Mayo argued that society had shifted gear and moved from a world wherein established traditions dominated – what he referred to as 'established society' – to a more flexible one that required individual workers to compete and adapt – his 'adaptive society' (Mayo, 1949: 11). Influenced by anthropology – and in particular Malinowski, with whom he had a close relationship (see Smith, 1998) – Mayo suggested that in the past traditions had shaped our behaviours, routines and practices, and often did so in an unthinking manner. However, capitalism had restructured society so that it undermined these traditions, if it did not eradicate them altogether. This meant that citizens were lacking in social skills. Previously, individuals had been socialized into the routines of work and life without necessarily being aware that this was happening. Thus, as we saw in Chapters 2 and 3, craft workers had long apprenticeships that included educational and moral aspects, then they became journeymen and were further socialized into ways of being before becoming masters themselves and assuming, in many respects, the role of passing on the traditions and routines of their craft.

Building on Henry James, Mayo distinguishes between this established form of learning – 'knowledge-of-acquaintance', located in experience – and the 'knowledge-about' forms of adaptive society that came primarily from abstract learning and the use of symbols that could be accumulated so that it could be passed on easily (Mayo, 1949: 14–18) – what today might be called 'knowledge management'. The former knowledge was more beneficial for society because it also passed on tradition, routines and a way of living as was evident in craft. Critically, it also put skill first, so that a skilled worker, in a reflective moment, would make the implicit knowledge in his or her repertoire explicit. But this also meant it was a free gift that could be captured and written down for capital. For Mayo, skill is the precursor to abstraction. As he puts it: 'The point to be remarked is that scientific abstractions are not drawn from thin air or uncontrolled reflection: they are from the beginning rooted deeply in a pre-existent skill' (Mayo, 1949: 16). One of management's tasks was to make this rule-of-thumb knowledge explicit. In this sense, Mayo's thinking was much the same as Taylor's or management's generally.

However, as we saw in Chapter 3, capitalism had systematically made explicit and undermined this structure of learning and with this, Mayo argued, the working class in particular had lost its socialization mechanisms – or its social skills. Thus, while the technical knowledge and skills of society had advanced to an unparalleled degree, its social skills had remained static at best, or even declined. Furthermore, the emphasis on technical skill had become ever more pronounced, to the detriment of social skills, and this was dangerous – specific skills were subsuming the generic skills needed for leadership. (See also Weber, 1994: 115–18 on this point.) Mayo describes the situation as follows:

> [I]n the area of social skill there seems to be a wide gulf between those who exercise it – the actual administrators – and those who talk about it. The fact that the United States has developed a successful series of tests for technical skills does not provide any extenuation of psychology. Within its narrow limits this is useful and, indeed, excellent. But the general effect is to concentrate attention on technical problems and to blind us to the importance of the problems of human co-operation – social skill. The blindness has unquestionably contributed to the advent of calamity.
>
> *(Mayo, 1949: 18–19)*

This weakness of socialization and the resultant increasing inability of the individual to communicate were 'beyond all reasonable doubt the outstanding defect that civilisation is facing today' (Mayo, 1949: 20–1).

So far, so cuddly, and one can certainly see why Illouz (2008: 65–80) praises Mayo for opening up management to relationships and emotions. Mayo also argues that the collapse of methods of working-class socialization have left workers irrational. Furthermore, although capitalism destroyed the craft skills and work routines of (some) workers and replaced them with the monotony described earlier, this was not the cause of worker dissatisfaction. In fact, Mayo explicitly rejects this as a possibility, commenting:

There is no great evidence of that 'deadening' effect of machine minding or routine work which literary critics commonly suppose to be the chief problem of the mechanical age. There was no reason to suppose that the personal or human quality of the supervision was essentially defective. But many 'conflicting forces and attitudes' were 'working at cross-purposes with each other'. This conflict centred upon 'the focal point' of an industrial situation; namely, the work and the manner of its performance. Somehow or other, no effective relationship between 'the worker and his work' had been established; and since a community of interest at this point was lacking the group failed to established an integrated activity and fell into a degree of discord which no one could understand or control.

(Mayo, 1933: 118–19)

The problem was thus not structural but managerial. Contrary to Marx, good management would lead to positive and spontaneous cooperation – to an effective relationship between the worker and his work. Thus, Mayo describes how managing requires an ability to understand the total subject both inside and outside of work. It needs to understand and mould his or her cognitive and affective contours. He describes a plant suffering from erratic productivity where the manager or the expert interviewer employed by the firm ascertains through interviews and communication the workers' different individual total situations: for example, one has children, reflects on life, has few friends and is middle aged; another is eighteen, lives at home and wants to break away but is dominated by her parents. If management gains awareness of and acts on these different situations, it can make the workers feel part of a supportive community, alternate rest routines, improve the social atmosphere and encourage communication, whereupon productivity will rise and then remain stable (Mayo, 1933: 99–122).

Foucault's confessional is central to the process of unburdening. Moreover, not only will productivity be restored and a work culture fostered, but the individual's total life will improve. Work will ameliorate life:

Indirectly, of course, her improvement is due to the change, but so very indirectly that it cannot be entirely credited to rest-pauses or even to improvement in the human atmosphere. The change is an outcome of social comradeship and discussion in some degree; more than this, it is due to a consequential and major change in method of living. The changed method of living not only frees the worker from a perpetual interference with her personal development unjustified by anything in the Chicago adolescent milieu; it also puts her in a position that she can talk to her immediate relatives and seniors on a footing of greater comparative equality.

(Mayo, 1933: 107)

The capitalist firm, not the state or workers' self-organization, has the power to free the soul, but only if management organizes it correctly.

The corollary of this positive story is, of course, that any problems are maladies of the individual worker. Mayo (1933: 107–22) uses Pierre Janet's work on the obsessive personality and Freud's on neurosis to argue that workers often have lives outside the organization that debilitate them and make them incapable of action. Furthermore, management should not accept workers' views of their work situation because they are irrational and in need of 'reeducation or psychological "analysis"' (Mayo, 1933: 107). Central here is Mayo's view that reverie can cause an inability to act or allow workers to succumb to a deluded politics. Thus, he links the problems of work not to the nature of the work itself, nor to capitalist cooperation, but to the individual. The individual, not society, is pathological. Indeed, his discussions of political activists are interesting in this regard (Mayo, 1949: 23–9), and his analysis of the Industrial Workers of the World labour movement quite breathtaking (albeit typical of the views of US management at the time). He pathologizes the members of this movement and explicitly links them to Hitler, claiming that 'one cannot fail to be interested in the close similarity of attitude and history' (Mayo, 1949: 25). When describing how activists participated in the movement's meetings, he states:

> the men had no friends except at the propagandist level … They had no capacity for conversation … Everything no matter how insignificant, was treated as a crisis,[8] and was undertaken with immense and unreasoned 'drive' … They regarded the world as a hostile place.
>
> *(Mayo, 1949: 24)*

In light of these 'scientific' observations, Mayo dismisses the social relations of production with which these activists were concerned as irrational and pathological. Contrary to Durkheim (see Appendix), the 'crisis' invoked by the change from an established to an adaptive society was largely one in the mental health of the working class as maladjusted individuals. As we shall see, it was the role of management to palliate these dislocations between the worker and his or her adaptation to the new society.

All of this obviously makes work central, because Mayo argues that we are in large part shaped by our work and occupational experience. This makes work both the problem and the solution, provided workers will accept being habituated to their new social position through their cooperation in the productive process on capital's terms. This is the leadership job of management. Work is one of the key factors in our attempt to give a total meaning to the individual because it helps to give

> some kind of total meaning to the world, a total meaning which reflects his past experiences, his life and character; and this total meaning goes far to determine the meaning of every lesser object to him – his attitude to any problem which may present itself for consideration.
>
> *(Mayo, 1919: 36)*

Thus, if the total meaning can be shaped and moulded, the 'lesser objects' can be eradicated or mitigated. This moulding lies at the heart of Mayo's desire to study the whole subject both inside and outside of work, and it places the work organization at the heart of the neo-liberal project (see Chapters 5 and 6). The worker is turned into an object of study as part of management's search for the disciplined conscience.

How do we restore meaning to industrial life? This was Mayo's main question and the task he set himself. His answer was a return to a form of cooperation that had strong overtones of Röepke (1948, 1992), as the following extract indicates:

> Viewed from the standpoint of social science, society is composed of individuals organized in occupational groups, each group fulfilling some function for society. Taking this fact into account, psychology – the science of human nature and human consciousness – is able to make at least one general assertion as to the form a given society must take if it is to persist as a society. It must be possible for the individual to feel, as he works, that his work is socially necessary; he must be able to see beyond his group to society. Failure in this respect will make disintegration inevitable. Social unity must be a conscious unity, known and recognised by every group and individual; the alternative is disruption. The last century has seen immense social expansion, accompanied by an increasing allegiance to democratic forms of government. The question we have to ask is whether democracy has enabled a society of enlarged extent and expanded powers to preserve its integral unity. With the development of society, has its power of internal cohesion correspondingly increased? In effect this question asks if it is possible for the individual to feel, under conditions imposed by the present social order, that his daily task aids the fulfilment of a social function – it asks if it is possible for him to see beyond his group to society.
>
> *(Mayo, 1919: 37)*

Mayo answers that it is not, and then suggests some of the reasons why this is the case. For example, class is opposed to community because it does not enable one to see beyond one's own group, except to see enemies. Laissez-faire has created disunity. Industrialization has led to workers – men, women and children – being treated merely as machines. Indeed, he mentions that the desire to lower adult wages encouraged employers to recruit workers' children and use them against their parents. These children then grew up and were 'the persons responsible for the formation of the social tradition of the present working class ... the average worker of the present sees industries not as social functions but as the scene of "class-war" between the employing and the working class' (Mayo, 1919: 40). Similarly, the rise of the joint-stock company and the shareholder were causes of disunity because both served to make management and ownership irresponsible. (As noted in Chapter 1, much of this echoes the neo-liberal attack on a decadent bourgeoisie that pauperized the working class, thereby creating the travails of capitalism.) In these circumstances democracy itself generated disunity. Mayo (1919: 41) suggests that, without

> a radical alteration in respect of these ruling ideas, 'social unrest' may be expected to continue. The workman is put on a level with the machine he operates. No increase in wages or improvement in working conditions can atone for the loss of real autonomy and of all sense of social function.

Taylorism, welfare capitalism or the employment manager's selection and training would not solve these problems. Capitalism needed human relations, management and leadership.

At the core, then, of Mayo's understanding of work and the worker is this reassertion of traditions, routines, hierarchy, community and function in a natural unity of leaders and led. This suggests some affinities with Durkheim, but in actuality, where Durkheim saw alienation and anomie as social problems suffered by the worker, Mayo saw them as symptoms of individual worker irrationality and maladjustment. Despite Mayo's analysis that industrialism, as he called it, had stripped the worker 'of all sense of social function', the individual worker, not society, was the problem because the individual was essentially irrational because he or she failed to adapt. If management could restore cooperation and community, it would save civilization. As Mayo puts it:

> The urgent problem of the present is that our administrative *élite* has become addicted to a few specialist studies and has unduly discounted the human and social aspects of industrial organization. The immediate need is to restore effective human collaboration; as a prerequisite of this, extension of the type of research I have reported is the major requirement. An administrator in these days should be qualified as a 'listener'; many of our *élite* are so qualified, but are not able to treat the various 'echoes' they catch in conversation to anything beyond their own experience ... the most melancholy fact of our time is that the appropriate inquiries – biological, anthropological – are so little developed that their findings are relatively unavailable for the training of an administrative *élite*. England has for some time required her younger colonial officials to study anthropology – and that is all that can be reported for the world of the twentieth century.
>
> *(Mayo, 1933: 183)*

Mayo makes three notable points in this quote: an organizational and managerial elite will guide society, ameliorate its tensions and manage the worker's subjectivity; yet again, 'objective' science should be used to expand this elite, and management itself will become subject to study and hence meritocratic (see Mayo, 1933: 174, where he invokes Pareto explicitly); and the British colonial service is the model of leadership. The new bureaucratic organizational form, with its extended division of labour, its new forms of knowledge and mystification based on the expropriation of worker knowledge for the pursuit of profit, would now be led by an elite that could both act in its own interest and improve the lot of the irrational working class. Once again, we are not far removed from the periphery, colonized peoples, the treatment of women, non-whites or children. Always there are some who are of value, seem to know and should lead, and others who should merely follow and remain obedient.

Mayo's position on worker irrationality is most cogently expressed in a series of papers produced between 1922 and 1924. (For insightful readings of these papers, see Bendix and Fisher, 1949; Bendix, 1956; Bourke, 1982; O'Connor, 1999a, 1999b; Bruce and Nyland, 2011. It is important to note here that Mayo produced no evidence for his scientific claims in this series.) In these writings he outlines the idea that people are not naturally sane. As he expresses it: 'Sanity is an achieved, rather than a merely natural condition of the mind' (Mayo, 1923b: 424). Thus, to be sane, an individual has to adjust their individual predicament to the environment within which they find themselves. Sanity is a balancing act:

> Happiness, sanity, success, mental harmony – these things are indicative of a successful compromise between the demand of life made by the racial self and the conditions of living imposed by the environment. Our mental capacities are originally racial; the life we lead must recognize the existence of such capacities and provide them with means of direct or indirect expression. At birth we are neither sane nor insane; sanity is a mental condition we achieve or miss.
>
> *(Mayo, 1923a: 122)*

He continues to state that no individual person achieves full sanity but that we are all, more or less, further away from this perfect balance between the individual and the environment. In the wrenching of society unleashed during the nineteenth century, our ability to cope with this individual–environment relationship was impaired. This now manifests itself as irrationality.

By 'irrationality', Mayo (1923a: 121; 1923b: 425) means our inability to access the cause of our mental symptoms. As he (1923a: 121; emphasis in original) comments:

> It is not so much the thing we see that determines our thought, it is rather the background against which we see it. *And for every individual this background is different.* Although in actual fact the same for everyone, the world about us is nevertheless interpreted by each of us in the light of his past life and previous experience.

Such thinking leads him to a series of assertions about the worker:

> For the psychologist the outstanding feature of the present situation is the fact that civilisation is facing a very heavy task with a badly damaged morale. The worker is not sure that he wants to increase production; he is uncertain

that it will be in his interest to do so ... This attitude has been carefully fostered for some years by his labour press and his political leaders, not with any fell intent, but simply because the party system seemed to demand it. And now his suspicion is extended to embrace his own leaders.

(Mayo, 1922a: 16)

He then comments:

Ideas such as these are obviously subversive of morale; it is impossible to find interest or to take pride in his work if he believes himself to be deluded and enslaved. If these doctrines gain ground our civilisation cannot live. We must solve the problem of industrial peace or be crushed by circumstance. It is obvious that the worker, generally speaking, is not facing the tasks which present and future hold with courage and determination; on the contrary he views the part allotted to him with suspicion and dislike. This attitude of dislike, suspicion and fear must be eliminated.

(Mayo, 1922a: 16)

This is the stupendous task facing management: to save civilization, the worker must be persuaded to his or her fate; his or her circle of irrationality must be squared.[9] The worker must be helped to adjust to society and to consent to its form. In this sense, Mayo stresses cooperation and equilibrium – central ideas for the Harvard–Pareto circle of which he was a member (Scott, 1992). As we saw earlier, he stresses the breakdown of socialization, the decline of apprenticeships, the emergence of crisis, which can be seen in the mounting need to control human nature (1923b), labour strikes, turnover and industrial unrest (1923a), increasing levels of nervous breakdown (1922b) and monotony (1924b). Control of the worker, not the eradication of capitalism's structural problems, was the order of the day.

Mayo argues that humans instinctively seek to control their environment and their own nature – this is fundamental to our behaviour. However, capitalism unbalanced this when it removed people's autonomy. As such,

We are forced to the conclusion that the minds of the majority of individuals are relatively disintegrated, not because some shock has served to break up or scatter, as it were, the various capacities, but because the individual has never discovered how to achieve self-control and sanity. It is as if one who possessed a ten-acre field were to cultivate only two or three perches of it.

(Mayo, 1922b: 63)

He continues:

There is nothing so dangerous individually and socially as a mind which has escaped individual conscious control; it is such minds which are the cause of crime, war, and social revolution. Yet as a society we tolerate the existence of industrial and political practices which serve to extend and intensify mental instability and disintegration. We also do little or nothing to discover and make plain the causes of all the various forms of mental disorder. The causes are only rarely organic; they are nearly always to be found in mistaken or neglected education. The psychologists of the United States Army ... discovered 45,653 men in the ranks whose intelligence was below that of the average child of ten years. This dangerously low level of adult intelligence was caused in the great majority of cases by early neglect and repression, factors of upbringing which must be eliminated if civilisation is to continue.

(Mayo, 1922b: 63)

Leaving aside the issue of tolerance for political practices that intensify mental instability – presumably left-leaning ones – yet again having hinted that the cause of this instability or 'low intelligence' is capitalism, Mayo (1922b: 63) quickly moves on to blame workers: '"Industrial unrest" is not caused by mere dissatisfaction with wages and working conditions but by the fact that a conscious dissatisfaction serves to "light up", as it were, the hidden fears of mental uncontrol.' This 'uncontrol' manifests itself most when

the worker is energetically pursuing will-o'-the-wisp phantasies with all the energy of his starving intellect and will. Dispossessed from his place in the social will and structure, totally unaware of the real social and psychological causes of his dissatisfaction, he has lost touch with reality. Like the neurotic individual, he is compensating his loss of contact with reality by constructing phantasies which give him the illusion of power and control where none exists. What else is socialism but an endeavour to regain a lost sense of significance in the scheme of things.

(Mayo, 1922c: 160)

The worker is thus irrational and pathological, and somehow needs to be reconciled with his or her environment. This is the job of management – a very directly political task. Mayo (1924b) advocates studying the whole worker and their life inside and outside the factory and the need to mould the conscience so that the will is developed, because the 'mind's supremacy over the body implies that the will can (in principle) control the needs, reactions, reflexes of the body; it can impose regular order on its vital functions, and force the body to work according to external specifications independently of its desires' (Federici, 2004: 149). Ideally, this would lead to 'The development of self-management i.e. self-government, self-development because an essential requirement in a capitalist socio-economic system in which self-ownership is assumed to be the functional social relation, and discipline no longer relies purely on external coercion' (Federici, 2004: 149). The general intellect, with its collective intellectual and social power, needs to be bent to the will of capital so that, instead of developing collective multiple potentialities, it develops particular capitalist ones (Haug, 2010).

However, Mayo also feared the worker's lack of discipline at work. The factory was a place of monotony and fatigue because work had been deskilled and stripped of meaning. Nevertheless, for Mayo (1922c: 159), the economic and technological breakthroughs of capitalism were beneficial, even though they had destroyed a world wherein 'The individual worker was able to feel that he was fulfilling a social function in the exercise of his calling.' This might appear to be an endorsement of something like the Artisan Republic (see Chapter 2), but Mayo quickly suggests that we must acknowledge where we are now and accept that society has progressed. Science and expertise have left the worker behind intellectually because

> His inability to keep abreast of scientific advance in knowledge and skill has put him outside, as it were, the real freedom of the age. His refusal to be scientifically interested has led to his enslavement by the social will. This method of expression must not be supposed to convey any imputation of blame to the worker, or to the scientist. That the situation is so, that it has unexpectedly but inevitably happened, is all that is intended. This is the really dangerous feature of the so-called 'capitalistic' organization of industry – that science has, at least temporarily, dispossessed the worker from his place in the social will and structure.
>
> *(Mayo, 1922c: 159)*

Here, the innovation, good management and mass production of the worker-organized production process under the inside contract is utterly obliterated, despite the fact that it was eradicated a mere ten to twenty years earlier. Furthermore, there is no reflection on how deskilling occurred, nor any embrace of Smith's notion that this process would destroy workers' capacity to be 'scientifically interested'. Instead, Mayo presents the elite, progressive and scientific emergence of the division of labour and its bureaucratic organizational form. The expropriation, social conflict and thoroughly unscientific nature of management are all forgotten as hierarchy is made meritocratic and natural through the division of labour and bureaucratic organizational forms (Michels, 1915).

The factory was the embodiment of these changes precisely because, as Panzieri (1961) notes, it was where capitalist science, technology and planning confronted the worker. This was what Mayo noted and feared. In the papers of 1922–4 and his book *The Human Problems of an Industrial Civilization* (Mayo, 1933: especially 1–55), Mayo discusses fatigue, monotony and reverie at length. For him, fatigue was a physical problem (as it was for Taylor). Studying it required science, but it could be solved from a management point of view with adequate selection of workers for physical activity, rest periods, improved conditions and greater communication. However, monotony was a more dangerous problem. It was also a problem of the twentieth century's relentless drive to subdivide work, embrace time and motion studies, mechanize the productive system and all of the other issues laid out in Chapters 2 and 3. If the work situation becomes monotonous, the worker can and will drift away into reverie, and this is potentially harmful. One of Mayo's clearest statements on this issue was presented to the Taylor Society in 1924, when he expressed the view that

> Taylor confined his attention, upon the whole, to the problem of irrelevant synthesis or mistaken coordination in our muscular apparatus; there is an urgent need to extend this inquiry to discover what irrelevant syntheses of emotions and ideas are imposed upon workers by indifferent education and unsuitable conditions of work.
>
> *(Mayo, 1924a: 258)*

Here, Mayo extends Taylor to the mind or the soul.

In the same paper, he distinguishes between dispersed and concentrated thinking. The latter – what he had previously called the 'day mind' (Mayo, 1923a) – was the rational thinking that took place when a person was actively thinking. Dispersed thinking (the 'night mind') was reverie during which workers (or others) day-dreamed and allowed their unconscious emotions – their backgrounds – to shape their thoughts without being aware of it. The night mind was characterized by an inability to understand one's situation fully, and one 'problem for civilisation is to extend the area of understanding and to diminish the area of night-mind control' (Mayo, 1923a: 123). Both shape meaning, but the night mind, because it is unconscious, is often stronger. Industrial life (post-Taylor and others) encourages dangerous reverie because of the monotony of the tasks, and

> too much reverie thinking of an irrelevant type tends to diminish the indivi-dual's hold on reality. Concentration is possible only when supported by the well ordered total situation. It is the business of total situation psychology in industry to investigate and eliminate conditions which lead to disharmony in the individual's mental background, and to promote that orientation which alone makes reasoned adjustment to the job possible.
>
> *(Mayo, 1924a: 255)*

Edwards's (1979) totalitarian bureaucratic form inches ever closer. It is important to note here that Mayo is not alone in his thinking in this regard. Kracauer (1998: 45) quotes a Professor Heyde to highlight that similar ideas were propounded in 1920s Germany:

> One must not fail to appreciate, you see, that through the monotony of an unchanging activity thoughts are set free from other objects. Then the worker thinks of his class ideals, perhaps secretly calls all his enemies to account or worries about his wife and children. In the meantime however his work goes ahead. The female worker, especially so long as she still believes like a young girl that employment for her is only a transitory phenomenon, dreams during monotonous work of teenage novels, film dramas or betrothals; she is almost less susceptible to monotony even than the male.

Kracauer (1998: 45) caustically points out 'that behind these pastoral meditations there undoubtedly lies the pipedream that workers might really think about their class ideals only in secret'. For Mayo and his German counterpart, to mould reverie, one had to study the worker as a totality – both inside and outside of work. Hence, one had to understand the worker's

1 physical condition and medical history;
2 personal history, including dominant reveries;
3 domestic situation; and
4 adaptation to work.

Management, through the industrial confessional, had to excavate the subject's soul to make him or her safe for capitalism. One could explain absenteeism, strikes, turnover and industrial unrest (refusal) through reverie. Mayo goes on to suggest that 'monotony becomes a problem for the management of a concern only when it is obviously giving rise to pessimistic reverie, not merely in individuals but over wide areas of the personnel' (Mayo, 1924a: 256). Management should understand and shape our unconscious just as marketers, advertisers, leaders and demagogues shape it – the general intellect – through our unconscious. If it is not moulded by management, workers could behave irrationally because they have a pathology located in their loss of function. Reverie, or modern monotonous work, extends the dangerous night mind like 'Witchcraft, sorcery, reassurance without under-standing' (Mayo, 1923a: 123). In true Enlightenment fashion, Mayo fears witchcraft, sorcery and reassurance without understanding (luck, fate and magic, perhaps) because all three are 'an illicit form of power and an instrument *to obtain what one wanted without work*, that is, a refusal to work in action' (Federici, 2004: 142; emphasis in original).

As we saw earlier, Mayo's means to circumvent this is to understand the whole person (Mayo, 1923b), because 'Productive efficiency, like the capacity for con-centration, is a product or expression of a total mental situation' (Mayo, 1924a: 250). To limit (or even better to mould) the night mind and extend the day mind, we need to understand the total person – in and out of work, at home, at leisure, their anxieties, their fears, their hopes, their dreams, their loves and their dis-appointments. This is management's task, its leadership role. It is about creating 'a factory of smiles and visions' (Mills, 1951: 167). Mayo was in the business of desensitizing the workers to the damage done to them by capitalism through confession, the bearing of one's conscience, and management shaping of the con-scious and the unconscious. He was following on from Taylor and ensuring that the individual worker would succumb to capitalist organization, its monotony, its refusal of social meaning and its discipline. Central to this was managing life outside of work or total subsumption.

It was the role of management to ensure that this happened. This could be done through rotating rest periods, creating small cooperative groups, listening, using scientific research on workers to inform their decisions, analysis, and by providing space and skilled personnel for workers to express themselves and both divulge and potentially divest themselves of their irrationalities. By using these skills, the manager could mould the worker and hence enter his or her conscience:

> [W]e moved onwards. The efficiency experts had not consulted the workers; they regarded workers' statements as exaggerated or due to misconception of the facts and therefore to be ignored. Yet to ignore an important symptom – whatever its character – on supposedly moral grounds is preposterous. The 'expert' assumptions of the rabble hypothesis and individual self-interest as a basis for diagnosis led nowhere. On the other hand, careful and pedestrian consideration of the workers' situation taken as part of a clinical diagnosis led us to results so surprising that we could at the time only partly explain them.
>
> *(Mayo, 1949: 58)*

Although he claims to be in opposition to the 'efficiency experts' (Taylorists), Mayo invokes science just as they did (for which, like Taylor, he was castigated; see Chapter 5). Again, workers are treated as objects of study, not as knowledgeable subjects, and although Mayo acknowledges that they can learn – acquire technical skills – he feels that they can rarely lead because of their lack of social skills and self-control. It is the manager who will be trained to adapt in this regard, so that

> The administrator of the future must be able to understand the human–social facts for what they actually are, unfettered by his own emotion or prejudice. He cannot achieve this ability except by careful training – a training that must include knowledge of the relevant technical skills, of the systematic ordering of operations and of the organization of cooperation.
>
> *(Mayo, 1949: 109)*

Managers could be given the general skills denied to workers in the new organizational form (see Chapter 3) because they have self-control and have adapted to the dislocation caused by the capitalist pursuit of profit. Managers are disciplined.[10] Because of the overwhelming importance of social skills, they should be obeyed, thereby opening up an authoritarian element in Mayo's thinking. Managers, unlike workers, can control their emotions and this enables them to lead. Here, as with management theory more generally (Bendix, 1956: 301), skilfully manipulating the emotions of others is central to managing, and this became even more important as the bureaucratic organization (Bendix, 1956: 303), bureaucratic control (Edwards, 1979), the increasing rise of affective labour (Mills, 1951: 182–8) and the segmentation of the labour market (Gordon et al., 1982: 165–227) meant that there was a growing primary labour market with core workers in the firm – both white and blue collar – who increasingly expected some form of 'career' but also suffered monotony and frustration (see Mills, 1951: 77–111; Kracauer, 1998).[11] In order to limit this frustration, managers needed to control group dynamics. Thus, Mayo (1949: 67) comments:

[F]or the individual worker the [problem] is really much more serious. He has suffered a profound loss of security and certainty in his actual living and in the background of his thinking. For all of us the feeling of security and certainty derives always from assured membership of a group. If this is lost, no monetary gain, no job guarantee, can be sufficient compensation. Where groups change ceaselessly as jobs and mechanical processes change, the individual inevitably experiences a sense of void, of emptiness, where his fathers knew the joy of comradeship and security. And in such a situation, his anxieties – many no doubt irrational or ill-founded – increase and he becomes more difficult both to fellow workers and to supervisor. The extreme of this is perhaps rarely encountered as yet, but increasingly we move in this direction as the tempo of industrial change is speeded by scientific and technical discovery.

Although he did not use these terms, the real subsumption of labour to capital and capitalism's constant revolutionizing of the production process meant anxiety, insecurity and isolation were inevitably set to increase – one might think of the increasingly rapid change inherent within the contemporary labour market. Yet, despite this, as with human resource management, Mayo still seeks to identify the workers' well-being with this management and organizational form and feels workers are irrational when they see the relationship more clearly than he does.

These developments meant the world needed

an administrative *élite* who can assess and handle the concrete difficulties of human collaboration. As we lose the non-logic of a social code, we must substitute a logic of understanding. If at all the critical posts in a communal activity we had intelligent persons capable of analyzing an individual or group attitude in terms of, first, the degree of logical understanding manifest; second, the non-logic of social codes in action; and third, the irrational exasperation symptomatic of conflict and baffled effort; if we had an *élite* capable of such analysis, very many of our difficulties would dwindle to vanishing point.

(Mayo, 1933: 185)

Thus, the manager can understand the non-logic and irrational exasperation of the workers. In this sense, as with Michels, Pareto and neo-liberalism, there is an authoritarianism to Mayo's management that finds its way into much management theory about organizational culture – workers will cooperate 'only when they accept the objectives of management' (Bendix and Fisher, 1949). In this sense, Mayo provided management with much more authority than Taylor. He provided it with a rationale for refusing to allow labour a say in production that remains with us today (Bruce and Nyland, 2011: 387). But he also pushed towards a total subsumption of society to capital with his desire to expand capital's remit into the conscious and the unconscious, the cognitive and affective realms, and the general intellect. He took management down the path towards human resources, human capital, emotional labour and the entrepreneurial self.

Cooperation and irrationality

Mayo epitomizes a desired transition from the real to the total subsumption of labour to capital. Having subjected the worker to Taylor's division of labour, time and motion study, the piece rate and then to Ford's technological control within the formal structure of the organization, Mayo seeks to enable management to gain greater control of the informal work culture of the organization through the creation of small-group camaraderie in the workplace and by encouraging workers to communicate their discontent. But he also attempts to understand and shape the realm outside of the workplace in order to recast or remould Descartes's conscience so that the universal traits of the general intellect are not just offered as a public good but privatized and particularized within capitalist social relations and hence made available for capitalist valorization. Taylor sought to pull the worker's subjectivity in one direction; Mayo did not necessarily challenge that, but sought to add control in a bid to 'extend this inquiry to discover what irrelevant syntheses of emotions and ideas are imposed upon workers by indifferent education and unsuitable conditions of work. I use the term workers to include proprietors and managers as well as machine operatives' (Mayo, 1924a: 258). Mayo – like the neo-liberals who followed him – felt that capitalist social relations should not be left to chance (see Chapter 6).

Of course, around the time Mayo was writing, the 'irrational' and 'pathological' workers were cooperating with each other to reject their subsumption, and they understood better than Mayo that their cooperation was even more important within monopoly capitalism. For example, they were developing new techniques to challenge management. Perhaps the most spectacular of these was the sit-down strike, which, as mentioned in Chapter 3, was first adopted at General Electric. However, it reached its zenith in the United States in the highly Taylorist, technologically controlled automobile industry. This industry exemplified the problems Merton (1947) outlines as creating industrial strife – jobs without a recognized social function, a growing gap between management and workers, a lack of promotion opportunities and ever-greater demands of industrial discipline. However, technical control via the assembly line, rules, procedures and office files also made the typical automobile factory very susceptible to labour. Capital needed living labour to cooperate and this it often refused to do. As Silver (2003: 47–69) suggests, a small number of activists could and did halt production simply by barricading themselves into the factories. Thus, although capital confronted labour as the organizing authority and the organizational form supposedly presented to the worker was unknowable, this was not in fact the case. Labour quickly learned how to resist the factory and use the major control processes of the industry – the technology – to halt production, tie up vast resources and leave capital idle. For example, during the Flint sit-down strike at the General Motors Fisher Body Plant No. 1 in 1937, only 1,000 of the 7,000 workers took part. However, because of the integrated nature of production and the fact that this was a 'mother plant' supplying three-quarters of the company's sixty-nine other US factories, some 135,000 workers out of the total production force of 150,000 were left without work. The newly created and irrational mass industrial worker clearly had power.

Thereafter, the automobile industry remained vulnerable to this tactic across the globe. Each time it relocated to avoid the militancy of local labour, it enjoyed only a short period of respite before the same unrest began again in the new location – from Flint, Michigan, to Europe, Brazil, South Africa and now South Korea. Its central weakness was that technical 'control linked the entire plant's workforce and when the line stopped every worker necessarily joined the strike' (Edwards, 1979: 128). Given its impact, it was unsurprising that the sit-down strike spread to other leading industries, too, including aviation and metalworking (Torigian, 1999).

These strikes were often spontaneous, the workers' demands were frequently more militant than those of their union leaders and they were increasingly 'political', rather than 'industrial'. Thus, the Flint protest won support from politicians who were championing Roosevelt's 'New Deal', and it led to the unionization of US heavy industry and the completion of the transition to Fordism (itself in many ways a political defeat for the working class; see Hardt and Negri, 1994 and Gramsci, 1971). Something similar happened in France during a sit-down strike in 1936 in which 150,000 metalworkers (half the workforce) occupied their factories to push for concessions beyond those negotiated by their union with employers and the government. The subsequent 'Matignon Agreement' granted union recognition and sanctioned large wage increases, a shop steward system, a forty-hour week and two weeks' holiday pay. The strikers had won 'workers' rights and benefits enjoyed by no other working class' (Torigian, 1999: 327). Two days after this agreement was signed, 25 per cent of French workers were on strike, and they returned to work only when the Communist Party, a partner in the government, lost its nerve and ordered its activists to do so. An opportunity for the radical restructuring of French politics was thereby lost.[12]

Sit-down strikes developed as a tactic, in the United States at least, in response to management violence against picket lines (Torigian, 1999: 333), and they were a fundamental element of the Fordist compromise that endured until the 1970s. Once again, capitalist planning had to be enlarged. As Torigian (1999: 334) puts it:

> Without the advantages afforded by the sit-down strike – and this gets to the core of my argument – it is doubtful if the labor movement, even after it shifted to an industrial model of unionism, would ever have established itself in the Fordist–Taylorist factory system.

Equally, in the United States, middle-class reformers in urban and rural areas were not nearly as important as labour unions, working-class people and immigrants, who used their political and industrial clout to demand better wages, more leisure time, greater job security, widows' pensions, shorter-hours legislation, tenement laws, labour reform, child protection regulations and workers' injury compensation. These groups (along with middle-class progressives) also supported 'progressive' politicians, such as Senator Robert Wagner (Huthmacher, 1962; Nelson, 1995: 136–52). In short, Huthmacher argues,

> it may not be too much to say that in all three fields of reform – the political, the economic as well as the social – indications are that the urban lower-class approach was more uniformedly 'advanced' than that of the middle class, in the sense of being more in line with what has become the predominant liberal faith in modern America.
>
> *(Huthmacher, 1962: 239)*

These few examples demonstrate that, yet again, the mass industrial worker was capable of resisting and, in so doing, was able to change society. It was on the basis of these and other working-class actions that the mass industrial worker was to meet capital in the compromise of Keynesianism, which then secured capitalism's continuance but also its significant change and the initiation of mass healthcare, education, pensions and many struggles relating to gender, race, sexuality and class. However, all of this came about not because of Mayo's small-scale group dynamics under the assured guidance and leadership of management but because of large-scale collectivity in opposition to capital. Without denying the many reactionary moments or the very real prejudices of the times, far from being irrational and unable to adapt to their new environment, working people rationally set about constructing an environment that would enable them to prosper, desire, develop potentialities, enjoy and, in turn, improve the lives of others, even though this potentially weakened the possibility for more radical change. And through their labour struggles, they forced capital to migrate, thereby contributing to the development of working classes elsewhere (Silver, 2003).

Mayo, quite simply, was wrong. But that does not mean he is irrelevant to management thought or that he did not understand the push towards total subsumption; far from it. As we shall see in the next chapter, if Taylor was the management theorist of the factory, Mayo was the first management theorist of society. This was because the growth of constant capital and the development of disposable time made him realize that value would increasingly be harnessed from the worker's subjectivity. As such, it and the realm outside of work had to be shaped – total subsumption was essential.

Notes

1 This term comes from Elton Mayo's (1949: 120) unfinished book, which appears as an appendix to *The Social Problems of an Industrial Civilization*.
2 This agitation culminated in between 10,000 and 14,000 armed miners fighting with armed company militia for a week until the US government sent in the 88th Bomber Squadron to suppress the miners. The state is a capitalist state.
3 In the twenty years after its reissue, it sold four million copies (Bendix, 1956: 302, n110). Mills (1951) also comments on its influence.

4 The foreman's empire, scientific management and race management were regularly deployed systematically (Roediger and Esch, 2012: 139–69).
5 Refusal has been an important element of the automobile industry throughout its history via counter-planning, sabotage, strikes, absenteeism and so on (Watson, 1971; Silver, 2003).
6 As we saw in Chapter 1 and will return to in Chapters 5 and 6, the suggestion is that irrational workers and democratic processes are suspect and should be rejected in favour of the emotional control of managers not subject to the opinions of the rabble.
7 This book was written as a tract for the Workers' Educational Association in Australia, which published widely on social and political problems in that country. Mayo was interested in worker education but his 'broader theoretical assumptions reveal a radically different set of propositions from those advanced by W.E.A. contemporaries' (Bourke, 1982: 218). In 1922, he went to Wharton on a Rockefeller Foundation scholarship, and from there to Harvard Business School, again with Rockefeller money, to embark on a range of projects. His private sector funding 'was renewed again and again, and his work remains, to this day, one of the most generously funded research programs in the social sciences' (see O'Connor, 1999b: 122). He received money from Rockefeller (both as personal donations and from the foundation) for almost all of his academic career in the United States, with the total amounting to over $1,500,000 (Smith, 1998: 239).
8 Given Mayo's own propensity to invoke the crisis of civilization and calamity, this is rather unreflexive.
9 Astonishingly, Mayo (1949: 28–9) discusses some of the steelworkers of Pennsylvania, where Taylor himself did so much damage, and comments:

> Quiet suddenly, after the depression of ten years ago, the method of manufacturing tin plate was radically changed, and these men, many of them in later middle age, found themselves without an avocation and without the means of continuing to support themselves and their families in a way of life to which they had become accustomed. This was for them a personal calamity of the first magnitude; as former pillars of society they did not lapse easily into revolutionary attitudes. And they drifted downwards towards unemployment as their savings became exhausted and towards profound personal depression. Their attitude to themselves and to society might be described as a complete loss of confidence. In some respects this echoes that aspect of the European situation which led the German people to hail Hitler as deliverer.

He then immediately goes on to say:

> In stating these facts, I must not be supposed to be arguing for the placing of any limitation upon scientific advance, technical improvement, or, in general, change in industrial methods. On the contrary, I am entirely for technical advancement and the rapid general betterment of standards of living.

Better social skills and the adjustment of the individual to his or her environment are needed, not revolutionary attitudes. Echoing Hayek's thinking, Mayo seems to suggest that these 'changes' might be unfair but they are never discriminatory.
10 Perhaps Huxley's Gammas, Deltas and Epsilons are to be found in management? It is they who have given up refusal and individuality.
11 Indeed, Alexander (1916) had indicated the push towards core–periphery workers, internal labour markets and the segmentation of labour. A version of the flexible firm was mooted in 1916. We should not, however, see a unicausality. After all, the slave overseer was also encouraged to control his emotions while administering the lash (Roediger and Esch, 2012: 46).
12 These occupations only partly reflected the Italian factory occupations of 1920, wherein the social and political order was fundamentally challenged. The French and US occupations, although political as well as industrial, did not seek to alter the social order fundamentally (Torigian, 1999).

PART III

Management, neo-liberalism and a history of violence

5

'CONFISCATE THE SOUL'[1]

Taylor, Mayo and the fundamentals of management

The conventional explanation of the relationship between Taylor and Mayo is that there is very little to relate. Scientific management and human relations are often juxtaposed as opposites. This is sometimes done in Mayo's favour, so that the human relations school (HRS) tries to humanize the damage inflicted on work by Taylor and the scientific management movement. Boddewyn (1961) questioned this distinction as simplistic over fifty years ago, and more recently Bruce and Nyland (2011) have again questioned the validity of the position while noting its prevalence. This chapter continues in this vein and argues that the two are not opposites but complementary and linked. It is not a choice between Scylla and Charybdis – to humanize or to dehumanize. Rather, it is more like a chemical compound wherein, depending on what you want to produce, you alter the mix of the constituent elements. Thus, in that most Taylorist of industries – automobiles – one can see elements of Mayo's human relations. For example, in 2012, an internet search for 'Volvo and Total Quality Management' led to this on the car company's website: 'Daily quality management is decentralized, and handled in our product development processes in manufacturing and in the market and sales organizations. Key terms are total quality and participation by everybody, through dialogues and clear objectives' (Volvo, 2015). The work processes were all ISO 9001 certified, where ISO stands for International Organization for Standardization. The aim of the certification process is to standardize and audit quality throughout an organization in line with other organizations – a classic Taylorist process. However, it also involves taking an interest in the employees within the organization, communicating standards to them, encouraging inclusion and continuous improvement. Volvo was also famous for introducing greater dialogue as well as job rotation, job enrichment and job enlargement practices in the 1970s and 1980s in order to 'humanize' the Taylorist work practices of its factories. Mayo and Taylor were thus combined.

In fact, the two had been combined even in their heydays. Kracauer (1998: 40–7), in a vignette entitled 'A Short Break for Ventilation', which describes a modern German factory in the late 1920s. In it were rational systems, such as scripting human activity, route work, written instructions, a control room, paper records and technology, all as Taylor would have wished (see Chapter 2):

> From the flashing and dimming of the tiny bulbs, the manager can at all times deduce the state of work in the individual departments. In the course of the tour through the offices that the commercial director makes with me, we gradually pace out the network of lines on the walls of his room. The marvellous thing is that the operation of the plan is set in motion by real people.
>
> *(Kracauer, 1998: 41).*

Kracauer (1998: 42) then describes how, 'Thanks to the intellectual labour invested in the equipment, its handmaidens are spared the possession of knowledge; if attendance at a commercial college were not compulsory, they would need to know nothing at all.' As in the United States at the same time, German labour was confronted by the authority and knowledge of capital, spurious certification was required to legitimate elongated careers, promotion ladders were rooted in the similarities between grades, rather than skill differences, and constant capital continued to expand as a factor of production.

However, lest we think it was all Taylor, the story quickly proceeds to the needs of the people:

> The girls … punch for only six hours and during the remaining two hours are employed as office clerks. In this way we avoid overtaxing them. All this takes place in a predetermined cycle, so that each employee encounters all tasks. For hygienic reasons moreover from time to time we slip in short breaks for ventilation.
>
> *(Kracauer, 1998: 41)*

Monotony, fatigue, rationalization, deskilling, job enrichment and rotation were all there, just as they are in both Taylor and Mayo. Although Mayo – unlike Taylor – does not discuss the division of labour, he too is interested in rotation, ventilation, fatigue and monotony. The two men complement each other because both are first and foremost interested in the extraction of surplus value and worker compliance.

Thus, to see them as opposites is incorrect. Worse still, to see one as 'good' and the other as 'bad' is unfair to Taylor, who in many respects was more honest and open about what he was trying to achieve. He also understood why workers would reject what he and others were attempting to do: unlike Mayo, he never accused them of being irrational, pathological or part of a rabble, despite all of the harm he sought to inflict on them.

Lines of similarity

Ultimately, Taylor and Mayo both hoped to assert management's right to manage, to break the will of working people in the factory or office, and to remould these workers along management lines so that they would embrace the valorization of capital. In this sense, they are members of a long and violent tradition which, despite its claims to the contrary, is all about disciplining and remoulding workers to the interests of capital (see Chapter 6). In different ways, these theorists have been explicitly linked to modern management theory through human resource management (Townley, 1993; Bruce and Nyland, 2011), expectancy theory through Drucker (see Locke, 1982), return on investment studies (Locke, 1982), organizational behaviour (Boddewyn, 1961) and organization behaviour modification (Locke, 1982), or management by objectives (Locke, 1982; Townley, 1993). Is there thus something in their work that gets to the very essence of management? Both of them, and management more generally, seek to close the gap between turning labour-power into actual labour and solving the employment contract's indeterminacy in the interests of capital. That is, they try to enforce the supposedly free and voluntary cooperation of capitalism and they use the division of labour and the bureaucratic form to entrench elite power (see Chapter 6).

Both writers set off to remould the worker in the following ways:

- by stressing the moral (in reality, political) role of management;
- by falsely invoking science and objectivity as inherent to management;
- by creating a new subject within and without the workplace;
- by reshaping the organizational culture; and
- by using the division of labour to generate new lines of authority.

All of these issues have their worker 'other':

- the immoral nature of workers;
- the rejection of a 'better' subjectivity;
- the resistance to organizational change;
- the eschewing of 'better' lines of authority based on the division of labour and property ownership; and
- the unintelligent subjectivity and selfishness of workers refusing management's right to manage.

None of this would look unfamiliar to the average worker today. In its denial of its own subjectivity and its desire to transfer resources from one class to another (Mills, 1951: 109–11), management knowledge continuously repeats itself (see Jacques, 1996 for examples of this repetition).

The moral and political role of management

For both Taylor and Mayo, and for the schools of management thought they embody, management is first and foremost a moral and very political project.

Taylor felt a moral need to reorganize work because he thought that workers were invariably dishonest when they controlled the production process. Thus, he notes in his testimony before the Special House Committee on Scientific Management:

> Whatever they [the workers] are or are not, they are not fools. That is straight ... It just takes one cut [in the piece rate] like this – just one – to make them soldier for life ... I did not even have to have it before I started soldiering. I never got my cut. I was too keen. The boys informed me beforehand, when I was an apprentice.
>
> *(Quoted in Boddewyn, 1961: 101–2)*[2]

Similarly, in 'Shop Management' (Taylor, 1903: 1351), he comments:

> It evidently becomes for each man's interest, then to see that no job is done faster than it has been done in the past. The younger and less experienced men are taught this by their elders, and all possible persuasion and social pressure is brought to bear upon the greedy and selfish men.

Furthermore, he states: 'My anger and hard feeling were stirred up against the system; not against the men' (Taylor, 1947: 83).

Thus, Taylor saw the group culture of the workshop as located in a refusal to submit to capitalism's discipline and hence as inherently immoral, collectivist, anti-profit and in need of change. This is sometimes traced to his Puritan frame of reference, his Quaker and Unitarian background (Boddewyn, 1961: 104). Certainly, as he saw it, workers were being unfair to both owners and consumers. He also held the view that if owners cut the piece rate, they were behaving badly because this would encourage soldiering. However, within this, as we saw earlier, Taylor always came down on the side of capital. He also wilfully ignored the fact that the piece rate and working flat out are impossible for workers over the full course of a working life – regardless of whether it is pleasant. Work in such physical environments inevitably favours the young and the strong. But older workers also socialized younger workers into not being 'greedy and selfish' because being collective and generous were more admirable qualities of mutual care. This resistance was, as Taylor acknowledged, not an individualistic act. At its heart was the simple matter of workers' ability to reproduce themselves and their lives and a refusal to valorize capital without question. As we saw earlier, even Taylor himself estimated that only 20 per cent of workers could work in the type of system he advocated; yet, despite this knowledge, he pushed for his brutal labour system as being in the universal interest.

Kracauer's (1998: 53–9) analysis of labour exchanges in Weimar Germany provides ample evidence of what happened to older workers in the type of environment Taylor sought to establish (with 'older' being a worker in his or her thirties). Put simply, an employee moved from a good to a worse job, from there to the labour exchange, and then into despair for themselves and their families. However,

Kracauer notes that managers rarely followed a similar downward path because they protected themselves from the very systems they were implementing. As we saw in Chapter 4, Mayo acknowledges as much in his analysis of the fate of Taylorized steelworkers, even though he rejects any structural redress. For Mayo, these individuals were simply maladjusted.

Taylor argues that both managers and workers need a different way of thinking about production. Thus, he claims:

> Scientific management is not an efficiency device ... Not a system of figuring costs, ... not a piecework system, ... Not a bonus system, ... Not a premium system, ... it is not holding a stop watch on a man and writing things down about him ... It is not time-study, it is not motion study, ... it is not any of the devices which the average man calls to mind when scientific management is spoken of ... in its essence scientific management involves a complete mental revolution on the part of workingmen ... And it involves an equally complete mental revolution on the part of those on the management's side ...
>
> The great revolution that takes place in the mental attitude of the two parties under scientific management is that both sides take their eyes off the division of the surplus as the all-important matter, and together turn their attention toward increasing the size of the surplus until the surplus becomes so large ... [t]hat there is ample room for a large increase in wages for the workmen and an equally large increase in profits for the manufacturer.
>
> *(Taylor, 1947: 26–30)*

Taylor here espouses the unitary vision of the firm located in a universal interest because it would lead to cooperation, harmony and mutual prosperity. Of course, as we saw in Chapter 3, the spoils were not to be divided evenly, it entailed the subdivision of labour and it replaced expensive skilled workers with less expensive unskilled workers. However, despite these tendencies, Taylor argues forcefully that this is a more moral system that enhances the worker both financially and morally (see Chapter 3).

Mayo too saw his role as a moral and a political one. If anything, he gave managers an even higher calling than Taylor. The latter argued only that management was productive. Mayo, however, suggested that management would save civilization from the irrationality of workers and that, by so doing, would enable workers to develop towards sanity as they better adjusted themselves under management's leadership. Management would accommodate workers to the new industrial environment that had been created for them by the onslaught of capitalism. Only through more social control could workers' potential be released. Indeed, on this elite role for management, Mayo hints that the left and right could agree, provided they were led by educated people:

> Marx detested 'the bourgeoisie': on grounds that will some day probably have been shown to be personal, he regarded the bourgeois as a greedy

profit-making exploiter of labour; he considered that the classless society could well do without him. And the revolutionary society speedily discovered that this is doctrinaire nonsense. No society can do without the man who is educated and, moreover, possessed of what is termed nowadays the *know-how*. It is this knowledge that keeps the wheels of industry and agriculture turning. A high official in the English Labour Cabinet, himself a man of education, told his trade union supporters not many months ago that none of them was eligible for the appointment to some reorganization board because none of them had the necessary knowledge of the principles of management.

(Mayo, 1949: 120)

Only by allowing managers and leaders who were educated to 'keep the wheels turning' could the individual worker be habituated to his or her position and achieve something like sanity. Having violently expropriated knowledge, subdivided work, reduced labour in ways Adam Smith had feared and created bureaucratic organizational forms to reflect these new lines of authority, Mayo elevates managers to the role of saving the workers from themselves. Only good management can adjust workers to capitalism. A successful society would be based upon effective cooperation, and it was management's role to ensure that this occurred. Self-organizing and workers' contributions were possible and could be encouraged only as long as management set the terms of engagement, because of the latter's superior knowledge, leadership and moral qualities (Bendix and Fisher, 1949: 317; see Chapter 6). Hence, Mayo sought to reach further into the worker's conscience. Furthermore, this cooperation was to be attained in the private sector and through small groups, and it must entail a rejection of socialism or state planning. Mayo explains:

> For the socialist 'the nationalization of industries' solves every economic problem – which, plainly stated, means that the only remedy for industrial chaos is to place the politician in charge. On this view national, or social, control means political control and no more. Socialism, in effect, asks society to return to that evil *regime* from which *lassier faire* [*sic*], with all its faults, delivered civilization.
>
> *(Mayo, 1919: 47)*

There are resonances with Hayek or Röepke here (see Chapter 6). Importantly, Mayo rejects individualism and competition in favour of the emerging monopoly capitalism, with its emphasis on private sector management and the planning of production (Edwards, 1979: 72–89). This private system would be morally better than any system run by the state. State-run organization, he suggests (while discussing arbitration courts), is 'a subtle form of state control; its decisions are inevitably moral rather than technically skilled, from a strictly industrial point of view' (Mayo, 1919: 48). Private sector technical and bureaucratic skill is morally superior to the politically informed decisions of the state – Weber's democratic bureaucracy is put to sleep and reawakened as a system of elite control (see Chapter 6). Seemingly, the corporation has no politics, only spontaneity, whereas the state 'can do nothing to bring about a condition of whole-hearted and spontaneous co-operation' (Mayo, 1919: 48). This private, corporatist, spontaneous cooperation under a management elite is the ultimate form of civilization. And yet, Mayo never highlights the logical flaw in his position: that this spontaneous cooperation needs to be manufactured by management (Bendix and Fisher, 1949: 317).

For both Taylor and Mayo, management has this moral and political role, which it exercises, at least partly, through its use of science and expertise. This moral agenda is about restructuring the polity to strengthen capital further as a social relation. Management is politics and class war from above.

Objectivity, science and expertise – the basis of management's right to manage

That management appeared on the scene in the late nineteenth and early twentieth centuries claiming to be a science should not be a surprise. Economics (Gane, 2013), sociology (Durkheim, 1984), psychology (Illouz, 2008), accountancy (Armstrong, 1987) and a host of others (Abbott, 1988) did likewise. As with these other areas of expertise, management claimed a scientific basis. As we saw in Chapter 3, Taylor was adamant that he was replacing the rule of thumb with the objective knowledge of management science. As he expressed it to the Special House Committee:

> First, the development of the science, i.e. the gathering in on the part of those on the management's side of all knowledge which in the past had been kept in the heads of the workmen; second the scientific selection and the progressive development of the workmen; third the bringing of the science and the scientifically selected and trained men together; and fourth, the constant and intimate cooperation which always occurs between the men on the management's side and the workmen.
>
> *(Taylor, 1947: 48)*

This quote resonates with what we saw in Chapter 3: Taylor's belief that his time and motion studies, his selection policies, his matching of workers to tasks were all located and upholstered by his claim to objectivity and science.[3] This was supposedly the end of poorly informed, prejudicial management, and workers would stroll into the light of science and willing cooperation. Hoxie (1918) dismisses these scientific claims out of hand and argues Taylorist management continued to operate on an unscientific basis (just as race management did; see Roediger and Esch, 2012). It must be said, Taylor (1895, 1903, 1919) never showed how his time and motion studies or his breaking down of tasks would be achieved in anything like a scientific manner. He used the terms 'scientific' and 'objective', but never explained what either might look like in the subdivision of tasks or the setting of piece rates.

However, this did not stop him from claiming that all of production could be put on a neutral 'scientific' basis and hence would be depoliticized. To quote from his Special House Committee testimony again:

> I have tried to point out that the old fashioned dictator does not exist under scientific management. The man at the head of the business under scientific management is governed by rules and laws which have been developed through hundreds of experiments just as much as the workman is, and the standards which have been developed are equitable; it is an equitable code of laws that has been developed under scientific management and those questions which are under other systems subject to arbitrary judgement and are therefore open to disagreement have under scientific management been subject to the most minute and careful study of which both the workman and management have taken part, and they have been settled to the satisfaction of both sides.
>
> *(Taylor, 1947: 189)*

Four points should be noted about this statement: it is a falsehood because management itself had never submitted to Taylorism at the highest level; on the basis of this falsehood, Taylor renders all protest pathological or unscientific; it overlaps with Weber's bureaucratic form, hence Clawson's (1980) linking of the two; and it appears to be an attack on the foreman's empire (Nelson, 1995). Taylor ignores the undemocratic nature of bureaucracy that so worried Weber and so enthralled Michels. As we saw in Chapter 1, rules, procedures, techniques, protocols and an extended division of labour enabled experts (often without much expertise) to hijack organizations, legitimate their control and act in a politicized, sectional interest. Taylor helped to deliver this violence through his unscientific 'scientific' management. Far from encouraging equity or justice, he delivered class sectionalism.

Mayo also invoked science, falsehoods and pathology. His whole theory of irrationality, which was designed in the early 1920s, was 'constructed – without any evidence whatsoever – [to provide] an interpretation of high labour turnover, linking it to psychological reveries due to fatigue owing to absence of rest breaks' (Bruce and Nyland, 2011: 389). Furthermore, at the time, Bell (1947) and Moore (1947, 1948) dismissed Mayo's studies as 'cow-sociology' (Bell, 1947: 88) that uncritically adapted man to the machine in the name of expertise.[4] Writing in the *American Sociological Review*, Moore (1947: 652) doubts the objective legitimacy of Mayo's work, commenting:

> In writings of one of the major exponents of social inquiry in industry, Elton Mayo, there is a recurrent emphasis on intuitive familiarity with the intimate details of organization, a sort of synaptic 'understanding' of the unique case in all its particulars. One finds a consistent confusion of the role of the problem-solver, the diagnostician or clinician, with that of the analytic researcher. This confusion not only reveals insensitivity to problems of interests and

values ... but also indicates a failure to understand the basic logic and methodology of science.

Thus, the 'science' upon which Mayo was advocating the reorganization of working life was called into question and dismissed by his contemporary social scientists. This begs the question why management has since continued to buy into human relations and, indeed, scientific management so vehemently? Perhaps we should look elsewhere, beyond science and objectivity – incongruously assuming that these are ever neutral – to the nature of the management project? Management and management scholarship have never been scientific or objective; they have only ever been – could only ever be – political because they are about organizing human life in particular ways and for particular elite interests. What could be more political than that (see Chapter 6)?

Creating the new subject?

In line with much of the Enlightenment since Descartes and Hobbes, Mayo and Taylor both attempted to create a new subject. They struggled with workers over practices, routines, behaviours, norms, rules, regulations, emotions and affect in order to recreate the subject through coercion and the worker's own conscience – essential tools of the Enlightenment (Federici, 2004). As we saw in Chapters 3 and 4, they felt the need to recreate the subject because 'the ultimate object of capitalist production is not commodities but social relations or forms of life' (Hardt, 2010). They were always operating within the capitalist mode of planning (Panzieri, 1961) and hence happily invoked management in an attempt to develop the capitalist subject, with the ultimate intention of deepening the real subsumption of labour to capital and generating a total subsumption of society to capital. And they did this, at least partly, through processes that Foucault would have described as 'normation' – encasing power into knowledge, encasing power into routines, encasing power into organizational forms and encasing power within the conscience. (This issue of subjectivity is discussed further in Chapter 6.)

For example, both writers rejoiced in the power of selection. Taylor was very explicit about this; hence his emphasis on 'first class men' (Taylor, 1903: 1362). For him, the ideal work situation was one where workers, if they were first class men, were interchangeable facsimiles of one another. When he turned his attention to the world beyond of work – the total subject – it was simply as an addition to work. Thus, sober, industrious, thrifty and responsible men in their lives beyond of work would make better workers who would keep up with the pace of work, seek the highest wages and be responsible in the workplace because of their responsibilities – presumably supporting a wife and children – outside of work. One is reminded of human capital theory and the American neo-liberal Gary Becker's (1962) list of non-work-specific issues that add to an individual's employability: education, health, migration, training, vitamin consumption and the acquisition of information about the marketplace. All of these become forms of human capital because they all add to the industriousness of the subject. This is Taylor's interest in subjectivity – a cog in a machine but one that adds value through how he or she lives by being able, willing or needing (and Taylor did not care which) to keep to the pace of work and serve oneself up to capital as human capital or a subject of value – the ideal of total subsumption (Tronti, 1971). But for this to happen, capital has to shape, particularize and privatize the general intellect (Haug, 2010). As we saw in the Introduction, an attempt was made to do this in the earliest period of Fordism, in what Mills (1951) describes as the 'personality market'. It is not particular to diffuse intellectuality (Virno, 2004), immaterial labour (Lazzarato, 1996) or cognitive capitalism (Vercellone, 2007), although it may be exacerbated today as capital further subsumes society. The person is individualized via the piece rate in work and the improving of human capital in external life; and, in another sense, he or she is simultaneously standardized and rendered replaceable.[5] As we saw in Chapter 1, work discipline requires the obliteration of the individual work subject, and this obliteration at work will be compensated for by consuming one's way to individuality outside of work. Often this was done to refuse work itself as a meaningful practice (Weeks, 2011: 79–112).

Similarly, with a hint of eugenics, Mayo's whole approach is to match the right person to each position, and this becomes even more important in an adaptive society because of the employee–situation disequilibrium or fatigue that occurs. This happens for two reasons:

> The first is the commonplace that increasingly in industry the machine does the work and man merely directs it. The second reason is that where industry still demands muscular effort there is a tendency to develop a species of natural selection of those who, like the athlete in training, can undertake the work without any significant disturbance of organic balance. This is accomplished in normal times by what is known as 'labor turnover'; those who find the work unduly distressing leave it. In other industrial situations where special muscular effort is not required this type of natural selection is wasteful by comparison with systematic vocational selection. But where 'oxygen debt' is involved a natural selection works sufficiently well.
>
> *(Mayo, 1933: 18)*

Management theory sought to provide – alongside unemployment, moral attacks on the working class, deskilling and immigration – another 'coercive force' to compel wage labour not just to work but to do so in particular ways. 'Hunkies' (Roediger and Esch, 2012) (i.e. immigrant labourers or navvies; essentially a term of abuse) could be race managed in their physical work and those who could control their emotions would manage. This force or power acts in ways Foucault might describe as 'relational', as opposed to that which 'acquired, seized, or shared' (Foucault, 1981: 94). It might seem natural or even power-free, but power becomes very apparent when it is exercised.

Turning to Kracauer (1998: 33–9), we see the impact of this non-scientific 'scientific' selection and the way in which it regulates, disciplines and recreates the subject. As Kracauer suggests, the problem with selection is that it is not enough to feel the call; one also has to be chosen. So from the outset the relationship is skewed. One outcome of this is the madness of certification: for example, the office workers with certificates who need to 'know nothing' because knowledge is built into the technology, the protocols and the routines (see also Mills, 1951: 190–2). The second outcome Kracauer notes is the increasing science of selection via intelligence tests, personality tests and research from universities on the 'correct' characteristics required for different roles. These 'objective' measures supposedly enable employers to put 'the right person in the right place'. The third outcome is the dismissal of anything that might challenge the employer's right to choose as irrelevant: for example, management science is a pseudo-science and an encroachment on the private individual sphere.[6]

As Kracauer (1998) demonstrates, different scientists – graphologists, psychologists, personnel experts – have been increasingly enlisted to select employees 'objectively'. And here is the punch line – we end up in the economy of today. 'Science' leads us back to emotion (Mills, 1951: 182–8). Drawing on research conducted prior to Hochschild's (1983) important study on the commodification of emotion, Kracauer highlights the way in which managers employ experts and their tests to establish a veneer of science and objectivity in order to objectify the body and sexualize the workforce of the commercial world. To quote extensively from him:

> I try to learn from him [an official at a job centre] what magical properties a person's appearance must possess in order to open the gates of the firm. The terms 'nice' and 'friendly' recur like stock phrases in his reply. Above all employers want to receive a nice impression. People who appear nice – and nice manners are naturally part of the appearance – are taken on even if their references are poor. The official says, 'We have to do the things the same way as the Americans do. The man must have a friendly face' …
>
> I ask him what he understands by 'pleasant' – saucy or pretty?
>
> 'Not exactly pretty. What's far more crucial is … Oh, you know, a morally pink complexion.'
>
> I do know. A morally pink complexion – this combination of concepts at a stroke renders transparent the everyday life that is fleshed out by the window displays, salary-earners and illustrated papers. Its morality must have a pink hue, its pink a moral grounding. That is what people responsible for selection want. They would like to cover life with a varnish concealing its far-from-rosy reality.
>
> *(Kracauer, 1998: 38–9)*

Just as Marx, Foucault and others would have anticipated, people resisted, altered and fitted into the new relations within which capital was attempting to constrain them:

> Employees must join in whether they want to or not. The rush to the numerous beauty salons springs partly from existential concerns and the use

of cosmetic products is not always a luxury. From fear of being withdrawn from use as obsolete, ladies *and* gentlemen dye their hair whilst forty year olds take up sports to keep slim.

(Kracauer, 1998: 39; emphasis in the original)

It all sounds so familiar, but it was happening a hundred years ago. Indeed, in Kracauer's (1995) account of the 'Tiller Girls' – a chorus-line whose routines were based on mimicking working-class life as mass production (similar to the use of mass synchronized swimming in Hollywood films starring Esther Williams) – he notes the increasing emphasis on the body and the knock-on impact on the self brought about by photography and illustrated magazines. He also observes that the quest for association, which he argues is made more difficult by capitalism and modernity, is altering how we relate to others, ourselves, our own and other bodies and our emotions. We are being both individualized and standardized – reconfigured by science and planning (Panzieri, 1961).[7] Mills (1951: 183), in his discussion of the 'personality market', makes similar observations, commenting:

> Many salesgirls are quite aware of the difference between what they really think of the customer and how they must act toward her. The smile behind the counter is a commercialized lure. Neglect of personal appearance on the part on the employee is a form of carelessness on the part of the business management. 'Self-control' pays off. 'Sincerity' is detrimental to one's job, until rules of salesmanship and business become a 'genuine' aspect of oneself. Tact is a series of little lies about one's feelings, until one is emptied of such feelings.

Mills (1951: 187) then goes on to state:

> The literature of self-improvement has generalized the traits and tactics of salesmanship for the population at large. In this literature all men can be leaders. The poor and the unsuccessful simply do not exist, except by an untoward act of their own will.

Failure is individual even if alienation is universal:

> Still it is conformed to as part of one's job and one's style of life, but now with a winking eye, for one knows that manipulation is inherent in every human contact. Men are estranged from one another as each secretly tries to make an instrument of the other, and in time a full circle is made: one makes an instrument of himself, and is estranged from it also.

(Mills, 1951: 188)

As such, science – and especially the flawed' science of management theorists like Taylor and Mayo – is not an answer or an escape, not some neutral moment. Rather, through this dubious science, management sought to alter practices and hence subjectivities: that is, to influence and shape the diffuse intellectuality of the general intellect in order to posit some desires and potentialities as more important than others. With this comes the increased importance of age, attractiveness, amenability, the body, communicative capacity, affective skills and cognitive outlook – all are central in the personality market.

Having used constant capital and deskilling to create a flat division of labour, capital and the capitalist state aim to alter the cognitive and affective skills of labour so that 'personal traits become part of the means of production' (Mills, 1951: 225). These altered skills will then provide more free gifts to capital through the general intellect because they will disperse ways of being – gifts of socialization, education, the family, consumption, mass media and public opinion – and ideally the total subsumption of society to capital (Smith, 2013). It is unsurprising that this shift is accompanied by the (welfare) state's role as the planner of the economy, wherein it takes ever more responsibility for areas of cognitive and affective skill development – for example, education, social security, old age, health and employment. This all generates an increased emphasis on the creation and management of worker/producer/consumer subjectivity.

What this detour into Weimar Germany and the United States indicates is that consumption (and the production of it) becomes a more important element in shaping subjectivity as monotony takes hold at work and services grow within the economy as a whole. Bloomfield (1915) notes that this shift will create different requirements and hence a requirement for new subjectivities as the need for increasingly affective workers (touched upon by both Kracauer and Mills – see above) grows. But this also takes us back into subjectivity and Mayo, because it was he who developed these central themes in contemporary labour management.

As we saw earlier, Mayo (1924a) was interested in the 'psychology of the total situation'. Thus, one had to look at the worker as a whole person both inside and outside of work. Mayo recognized an element of subjectivity that was then important – namely, that work and life cannot be entirely separate entities. As was noted in the previous chapter, he went so far as to suggest that work could mitigate those disappointments of life that occurred outside of the corporation. The second issue for Mayo (1937) was that the human subject was inherently social, not individual. Thus, the individuation that was taking place at work was a problem. It was this that had led to the breakdown of apprenticeships and hence the loss of socialization as a mechanism of control; it was capitalism's incessant change that created dislocation or something like Durkheim's 'anomie'; and it generated a situation where workers no longer had a function. All of these shifts had made the subject – especially the working-class subject – irrational, and this had to be altered. The way to achieve this was through new routines, new emotional attachments, recreating groups, analysing the total subject, opening communication avenues and incorporating one or two suggestions from workers as regards working life – always in 'prudently homoeopathic doses', to steal from Marx (1976: 484). As we have seen, this also implied overseeing the world outside of the work organization.

By so doing, and through greater 'objective science', selection, analysing and rotation, mass industrial workers would no longer be parts of a mass and they would be reconciled to their individual situations – situations to which they were naturally condemned by their inability to learn and by their failure to control and understand their emotions without the leadership and authority of managers. However, if managed correctly, the new subject could be socially skilled and could adjust to their appropriate level; hence, they could be happy in a small-group work situation managed from above.[8] Management's authority would be both accepted and welcomed because of the 'natural' right of managers to lead, and the new worker–subject would be politically adjusted so that he or she would be assimilated via the group into capitalism's working life.

This is my interpretation of Mayo's vision of worker subjectivity. Hence, I disagree with Illouz's provocative and interesting book *Saving the Modern Soul*. Illouz (2008: 58–104) credits Mayo with initiating a feminizing of management through his stress on communication, emotions and controlling the self. One can see why this might be inferred by looking at his guidance for those interviewing workers in the Hawthorne studies. Mayo (1949: 65) suggests that they:

1   Give your whole attention to the person interviewed, and make it evident you are doing so.
2   Listen – don't talk.
3   Never argue; never give advice.
4   Listen to:

   (a)   What he wants to say.
   (b)   What he does not want to say.
   (c)   What he cannot say without help.

5   As you listen, plot out tentatively and for subsequent correction the pattern (personal) that is being set before you. To test this, from time to time summarise what has been said and present for comment (e.g. 'Is this what you are telling me?'). Always do this with the greatest caution, that is clarify but do not add or distort.
6   Remember that everything said must be considered a personal confidence and not divulged to anyone. (This does not prevent discussion of a situation between professional colleagues. Nor does it prevent some form of public report when due precaution is taken.)

This interviewing technique might look like empathy, but it also looks like the flawless Foucauldian confessional that is so prevalent in contemporary human resource management (Townley, 1993). At no point does the interviewer intercede to resolve anything or initiate any change – that comes to the worker on his or her own account simply through communicating frustration, or powerlessness, and being made to feel valuable (however briefly).

I disagree with this 'feminized' corporate management position in a number of ways. First, did Mayo feminize management or did he feminize workers? I accept this may seem an odd question but, as was highlighted in the Introduction, Federici (2004) shows that once the knowledge of females and colonized peoples was violently expropriated they were made dependent and vulnerable and more easily subject to physical and psychological violence. In light of this, we should bear in mind that management, in the past and in the present, has often opted for female labour because it is perceived to be – and often is – more vulnerable and dependent and hence more manipulable as a result (dependant children are often at the centre of this). One could argue that, in management's terms, feminizing workers is an advantage that makes control of the labour force easier. Talking and having talk accepted as a form of resolution might be a better strategy for management – if not necessarily for workers.

Federici (2004: 85–103) also observes that expropriation of the female body and female knowledge was perhaps seminal in the Enlightenment as women became the 'new commons', providing free labour and necessary but devalued labour to employers, the state and men. Feminizing management may reflect this: workers experienced the disciplining of their bodies, the expropriation of their knowledge, the dividing of their work into more minute tasks and the increasing necessity of providing free labour or bringing to work free gifts of personality in the emerging affective economy of monopoly capitalism. Women had already experienced this transition as violence, a forcing into the private sphere, exploitation, vulnerability and an unwarranted dependency on and centrality to the family. Mayo was seeking to assign workers to a similar set of experiences, except he sought to shift the dependency to the private corporation, which, alongside the family, could be loving or cruel, depending on one's acquiescence to one's allotted role and profitability.

Bendix (1956: 319–40), for example, points out that interviewers could listen to and elicit concerns, but they could not actually change the worker's circumstances. The interview process was quite simply a talking shop to make people feel included in a private sphere they did not control. He also suggests that management's hard side – targets, quotas and disciplining – never went away. The private corporation could be cruel. Finally, as should be obvious, Mayo was no industrial democrat: he believed in leadership's right to lead because managers, like patriarchs, could control their emotions, or at least their display, which is exactly the argument Illouz makes for the modern corporation: that management increasingly has to manage emotions in a rational system. (However, as Roediger and Esch, 2012: 46 highlight, so too did the slave overseer.) Illouz (2008: 197–238) contends that this is an improvement, although, to be fair, she has reservations about who wins and who loses.

In Illouz's argument, an increasing ability to control emotions, control communication, express empathy, manage one's body and cooperate more has altered how power works in an organization; and, in some sense, it is progressive. But is it? Michels (1915: 1–12) also endorses the control of emotion, dialogue and communication, but as means of dissembling and maintaining the elite in power in a sophisticated bureaucracy with an extended division of labour. Imagine being involved in a meeting wherein an employee with children is fired because of some situation beyond her control and, after all of the rules and regulations have been followed, people calmly explain what will happen next, tell her that a reference may be provided, and then she shakes the manager's hand and leaves the room. All very calm and well communicated; no one feels good, but at least it was not unpleasant; emotions were managed, perhaps so much so that we can be mildly pleased. Or can we? Surely there is fear, humiliation, anger, powerlessness, anxiety, panic, loss, shame, isolation and a sense of being stunned in this scenario. Perhaps these reach such a peak that the worker returns to the office to collect her belongings only when she knows her former colleagues will not be there. The science Illouz discusses is the expertise of the psychologist or manager who enables workers – the disempowered – as individuals, to adjust to an environment they cannot control. It is dehumanizing if to be human is to wish to exercise some control over one's life.

As we saw in Chapter 4, Mayo feels that such moments will increase, not decrease, as capitalism develops. But, in reality, the employee probably wanted to behave very differently towards the manager, despite the humane way in which the inhumanity was delivered; and she might have felt much better if she had done so. Having not behaved differently, to whom does she now take her anger and her feelings of humiliation, inadequacy or fear? To the company counsellor or to the private sphere and her friends, partner and children, who have to deal with the after-shock? As Deleuze (1983) suggests, dialogue is often a problem; and here he, not Mayo, is correct. Corporate dialogue, like objective science, always takes place within capitalist social relations; hence, whether feminized or masculinized, it is not liberating. There is something very inauthentic about Mayo's dialogue and about human relations because once the interview strays into politeness, it becomes a pure capitalist exchange; one of calculation. (Drucker, 2007a: 241 accuses human relations of being manipulative.) One can see the seeds of Mayo's control (and indeed some of Michels's ideas) in the following quote from today's leadership studies field:

> We believe leaders will be relatively transparent in expressing their true emotions and feelings to followers, while simultaneously regulating such emotions to minimize displays of inappropriate or potentially damaging emotions. That is, as authentic leaders come to know and accept themselves, they will display higher levels of trustworthiness, openness, and willingness to share (when appropriate) their thoughts and feelings in close relationships.
>
> *(Gardner et al., 2005: 358)*

This chimes with Mayo and his communication. Some leader gets to decide what is communicated, what is appropriate, what is inappropriate, what is revealed to the other person and what is not. Mayo's management is not a liberating meeting or in any way authentic. As Mills (1951: 183) suggests, in the emerging work regime, sincerity was sacrificed early.

Mills (1951), Hochschild (1983) and Kracauer (1998) have all demonstrated that controlling one's emotions and science do not equate to progress. The end result might be a build-up of emotion in the private sphere, as any display of emotion at work – a place of violence – is deemed 'irrational'; hence the emotional worker is usually viewed as unfit for leadership and indeed often for work itself. This may mean that Weber's power, wherein a manager can get a worker to do something without negotiation, is replaced by a seemingly more negotiated form of power relations, but this occurs only because, as Illouz (2008: 84) states,

> We arrive at the following astonishing paradox: 'real' psychological strength consists in being able to secure one's interests without defending oneself by reacting or counterattacking. In this way, securing self-interest and power in an interaction is established by showing self-confidence, which in turn is equated with a lack of defensiveness or aggressiveness. Power has become divorced from an outward display of hostility and from the defence of one's honour. Responses which have traditionally been central to definitions of masculinity.

This is Michels's (1915) form of organizational elitism and the creation or maintenance of an aristocracy who rule.

Illouz then recounts a tale of what I term 'disempowerment', wherein a boss dismisses an employee's idea, agrees to take the responsibility if the employee's prediction occurs, then shirks that responsibility and lands the employee in trouble. After this, she tells us how different interviewees suggested they would deal with this managerial pressure:

> *All* fifteen respondents whose age was below sixty answered they would not confront their boss and several suggested they would simply try to leave the company. However, all three of the respondents who were above sixty-five said they would raise the issue as a matter of principle.
>
> *(Illouz, 2008: 85 emphasis in original)*

The younger workers who simply absorbed the management onslaught represent the increasingly anxious worker of today. They may have reacted through a variety of resistances – sabotage or flight – or they may have acquiesced, but this 'new' management is *not* progressive. Many issues spring to mind here – gender, race, class, age and experience of job security, certainly – but also that this 'feminized' workplace may be less rule-bound, less bureaucratic, less 'scientific' and more managerially capricious so that the workers know not to complain. All of this might have more to do with the worst male accounts of 'feminization' as disempowerment (Du Gay, 2013a, 2013b). This objectivity, science, expertise, psychology or Taylorist time and motion is always *capitalist* objectivity, science, expertise, psychology and time and motion, and it is always seeking to alter the subject.

Reshaping the organization

Through his insistence on the increasing division of labour, deskilling, written or codified instructions, the separation of brain work from execution (Taylor, 1903:

1390), his emphasis on the worker's moral nature, piece rates and individualization, Taylor represents a form of organization and management that is very prevalent today – what Ritzer (1993) has termed McDonaldization. Taylor sought the active destruction of the existing organizational form and society, the creation of a world where linear, authoritarian hierarchies were prevalent, alienation was almost guaranteed (Mills, 1951: 224–9), refusal, sabotage, strikes, conflict and resistance were endemic (Benyon, 1973) and pleasure was derived only from outside work – hence the necessary Fordist link between mass production and mass consumption because only through this link could capitalism survive the 1930s (Mills, 1951; Tronti, 1971; Harvey, 1989; Kracauer, 1998). As we saw in Chapter 3, the work organization and the struggles around it meant that, for skilled workers, the world looked completely different by the Second World War: the average organization had perhaps ten workers in 1850; by 1937, General Motors had 150,000 employees. As Mills (1951: 224) puts it, 'The model of craftsmanship has become an anachronism.' Subdividing tasks, time and motion, piece rates, increased management, the argument that management was now productive and internal labour markets were all implicated in this organizational shift. As Stone (1973) observes, much of the modern corporate form is located in the rationalization processes recounted by Taylor and, indeed, Weber.

Mayo also sought to alter the organizational form. He rejected the state in favour of private corporations; he sought a taming of what he viewed as the destructiveness of competition; and he aimed to avoid the democracy of the masses with their irrational political choices (see Chapter 6). However, he was Durkheimian enough to realize that a planned private economy without some intermediary forces might overwhelm the individual. (Durkheim, 1957, 1984 pointed to a similar danger in the event of a lack of intermediary bodies between the state and the individual; see Appendix.) The individual needed smaller, more intimate and everyday forms of association. As is well known, Durkheim advocated guild-like professional associations to meet this need. Mayo never espoused these. Instead, he sought to recreate socialization and association in the private company through small groups, new routines and new attachments. Hence a worker might be encouraged to view himself as one of a dozen in the bank wiring room rather than one of the 100,000 who were employed by the firm as a whole. In so doing, Mayo tried to recreate the large corporation as a more intimate space. In one sense he tried to recreate the craft work group with its socialization processes, blurring of life and work, and mutual obligations (Mills, 1951: 220–4), but in a space organized by the bureaucratic elite rather than one of self-organizing workers, and increasingly a space where the skill hierarchy of the division of labour would become obsolete. He sought to recreate the organization as simultaneously an unknowable place of capitalist authority and planning *and* a small, disciplined, intimate space of worker socialization and identification.

He did so in new terms because, in light of the conflicts of the 'American Terror', management was now a legitimate authority. For Mayo, labour could talk but it was the group without a voice. Mayo sought the sociality of worker self-organization without its knowledge or its politics. He wanted to mask the scale of capital via small, uninformed, depoliticized groups. He wanted to establish a system where

> These things are not their [workers'] own act, but the act of capital that brings them together and maintains them in that situation. Hence the interconnection between their various labours confronts them, in the realm of ideas, as a plan drawn up by the capitalist, and in practice as his authority, as the powerful will of a being outside of them, who subjects their activity to his purpose.
>
> *(Marx, 1976: 449–50)*

Mayo wanted to mystify the organization through a manufactured cooperation that would appear spontaneous. To do so, the Cartesian conscience had to be reshaped.

Kracauer (1998: 74–80) notes a similar tension in Germany. Thus, large firms sought to recreate community but on a small scale, and by so doing to hinder the emergence of a mass community that could then easily turn into a working-class politics (see Chapter 6). So firms simultaneously isolated workers via the piece rate, by separating salaried employees from wage workers, by gender, by race and by internal career ladders, and sought to integrate them into smaller firm-based communities via sports clubs, smaller departmental groups, and welfare provision designed to shift the loyalty of the individual to the small collectivity and then to the firm. As such, 'community was a sham' as firms strove to 'confiscate the soul and guide everybody in a particular direction'. This confiscation was a necessary outcome of rationalization because 'Instead of working conditions being the fruit of proper human relations, rationalisation engenders a neo-paternalism that seeks to manufacture such relations subsequently' (Kracauer, 1998: 75). In this the firm achieved limited success and certainly grew some 'blood-oranges' who were 'yellow on the outside,[9] red within' (Kracauer, 1998: 79). Mayo's sense of small-group community is very much of this ilk. If the solidarity of the family, small group or local community could not be inspired by a mass corporate rally or get-together, then perhaps the small-scale socialization of disempowered workers could engender loyalty. But hindering 'mass community' also required the moulding and shaping of the spaces wherein it might occur. This included the general intellect, which had to be particularized, privatized and made passive in ways Adorno and Horkheimer (1997) suggested in the 'administered society'.

Generating new lines of authority

At the centre of these changes were class recomposition and the desire to make workers submit to the authority of capital, management and the division of labour (Michels, 1915; Mills, 1951). This was the overall agenda of creating new lines of authority. The changes described above were instrumental in creating the mass industrial worker. Through the deskilling of the craft worker, the generation of finely subdivided factory work, the hiring of immigrant, African-American, female and other sources of labour, and the spurious shift away from skill to education, these alterations enabled new forms of authority and power to emerge at work. Domination was increasingly rational; workers and work itself were increasingly rule-bound and based on the legitimacy of education and 'brain-work' rather than craft skill; and 'brain-work' was increasingly folded into procedures, rules, technology, science and human resource policies. When Taylor separates conception from execution, or when Mayo argues that workers are now without a function and need to be led by managers so they can adjust themselves to their new – if stunted – role, they are arguing that the new lines of authority, hierarchy and the division of labour are natural phenomena. Furthermore, both suggest that in a world of large-scale enterprise it is pathological to reject these new rationally functional roles. In their writings, they both pursue their version of the class recomposition that was already taking place (Michels, 1915; Mills, 1951: 109–11; Panzieri, 1961; Marx, 1976: 439–54).

They both endorse and encourage the emergence of a finely sub-divided labour process wherein some should lead or manage and others should follow. This is a world where self-organizing will not be permitted until 'proper' discipline can be assured. That the factory located in the labour of the vulnerable, the use of immigrant labour for large infrastructure projects and the destruction of craft had already taken place was perhaps unfortunate, but it also meant the world had science and objectivity rather than the rule of thumb – the planning and authority of capital (Panzieri, 1961). Increasingly, managers and management were to be university trained, and so obviously not working class (Mills, 1951; Stone, 1973; Kracauer, 1998). However, as we saw in the Introduction, this denies Smith's (1981: 28) fear of the division of labour being used to create illegitimate hierarchy.

Taylor and Mayo had no such qualms. For both schools of management, the worker was incapable of managing because of his or her political, moral and character failings. In light of these failings, the worker should be reduced and any authority based on skill should be replaced by the authority of position in an endless and meaningless organizational division of labour. Yet, as we have seen, the worker had to be beaten into the factory and even then was still capable of self-organizing and producing. Indeed, the nineteenth century was partly built upon this fact and its destruction. Although Mayo (1933: 15–18) bemoans the shift from a knowledge-of-acquaintance to a knowledge-about or from a practical skilled way of working that led to reflexivity and then to abstract thinking, he then wholeheartedly endorses it in his emphasis on 'social skills', the need for an elite, more communication and control of emotions, and through his active involvement in training a managerial elite at Harvard. In so doing, he places emotion and affect at the core of rationalization and management. Taylor, as we have seen, was even more explicit and did not want the worker to do any intellectual work at all. Thus, their attempts to create new lines of authority were absolutely positions of class – they were attempts to make natural the authority and hierarchy that Smith had astutely observed as unnatural (even though he endorsed it). For example, Robert Merton (1947: 81; emphasis in original), who, like Mayo was a member of the Harvard–Pareto circle, acknowledges this when he comments:

> To the extent that opportunities for higher education are socially stratified, moreover managers come increasingly to be drawn from social strata remote from those of workers. Also, since technically trained personnel enter industry at a relatively high level, they have little occasion to share the job experience of workers at an early stage of their careers and tend, accordingly, to have an *abstract knowledge* about rather than a concrete *acquaintance with* the perspective of workers. Finally, with the increasing rationalisation of managerial procedures, the relations between operating executives and workmen become increasingly formalised and depersonalised.

Another element of these new lines of authority was the fact that management was recreated as a productive enterprise. Indeed, as value producers, one could argue that the worker became secondary to the manager (Drucker, 2007a: 97). For Taylor, in any productivity drive that increased output by 100 per cent, workers would receive only a fraction of this. The rest went to management or owners, or was ploughed back into the firm. As we saw in Chapter 3, Taylor argues that the increased costs of management have to be factored in because these are an investment in current and future profitability and productivity. Mayo goes one step further to argue that management is not only productive in itself but will save civilization. Again, this is about giving legitimacy to the capitalism that was developing at the time. The emerging organizational division of labour, bureaucratic lines of authority and hence the class system that they underpinned were all deemed rational, meritocratic, productive, civilizing and enabling. To think otherwise was a sign of individual pathology. As such, the working class either agreed to this class recomposition or consigned itself to the irrational.

It is important to state here that these are the origins of management knowledge and its claims to the scientific, and that this management knowledge is really about managing and legitimating the redistribution of wealth from one class to another.

Conclusion

This chapter challenges the idea that Taylor and Mayo are contrasting rather than complementary management theorists. Indeed, if one looks at human resource management, which is often linked to Mayo (see Barley and Kunda, 1992; Jacques, 1996; Bruce and Nyland, 2011), one can see strong similarities between it and scientific management (see Guest, 1987; Townley, 1993; O'Connor, 1999a). Furthermore, both theorists were interested in issues that overlap very strongly: the moral and political role of management; management based in objective science; the moulding of the subject; the organization culture; and, finally, the creation of new lines of authority. Taken together, these are the management building blocks of social reproduction and the composing and recomposing of class relations:

management could not be further away from science and objectivity, nor could it be closer to politics. This seeming contradiction between management's moral/ political role and its scientific objectivity is denied by the claim that there is a 'one best way' or that other views are irrational and pathological. This often becomes most obvious in the issue of organizational change, wherein management derides any workers who refuse change. (Capital is only ever interested in its own valorization.) These workers are accused of being attached to anachronistic thinking or of irrationality, and are told they should adapt to the new environment and their new function within it. Not to do so demonstrates our old friends pathology and recalcitrance. The failing is individual not structural.

Obviously, mainstream management thinking has moved on since the days of Taylor and Mayo. However, it has not moved on very far. The issues they examined to apportion authority, power, blame, knowledge, skill, views of productivity and the role of management as productive remain absolutely central to management thought. Management seeks control and discipline. However, it also stresses other issues. Taylor stressed a finely planned, subdivided labour process that was developed by Ford into one where technology played a central controlling role. Mayo emphasised the total subject inside and outside the workplace and the capturing of sociality and the general intellect to enhance productivity and control. Both writers, and management more generally, sought to use capitalist planning to control and manipulate social relations, to increase the division of labour, to ensure that the elite kept control and to recreate the subject as a neo-liberal subject. We conclude by focusing on these issues in the final chapter.

Notes

1 This term is taken from Siegfried Kracauer (1998: 75).
2 The quote here is slightly different from that which appears in Taylor (1947).
3 To read a rather weak contemporary management endorsement of Taylor's thinking, see Locke (1982). When questioned by the Special Committee, Taylor (1947: 261) expressed doubts about his own 'science'.
4 Bell opens his piece with a note that the Ford Motor Company had just donated $500,000 to human relations research.
5 In this sense it links to issues of personalization and 'Big Data' today. We are individualized, monitored and tracked in order to be spliced and standardized into consumer, terrorist, subject of no value and other groups.
6 German trades unionists – presumably irrational working-class members – had more scientific reflection than their own compatriots or Mayo's colleagues and interviewers at Harvard because they protested against much of this in the name of privacy, among other things. Anyone with an email or Facebook account might appreciate this.
7 See Kracauer (1995), especially the essays 'Photography', 'The Mass Ornament' and 'Those who Wait'.
8 Hence money – which was never a primary motive for Mayo – becomes rather unimportant. A happy worker is a poorer worker, perhaps?
9 In 1920s German socialist circles, 'yellow' was a slang term for those who collaborated with the company.

6

MANAGEMENT

The first neo-liberal 'science'

We began with a discussion based on the division of labour, forms of authority and hierarchy, the free gift of sociality, and the nature of the general intellect, with both its shaping of and its shaping by capitalism. We then examined how the knowledge, recalcitrance and acquiescence of labour were central drivers in the attempts by capital and management to simultaneously eradicate its dependence on labour and to subsume it totally. However, as has been stressed throughout, capital and management need labour and cannot refuse it, hence the necessity to regulate it externally and discipline it internally. Management has always had this violent relationship to labour. Such a genealogy is largely one of class struggle from above, but it is also a very contemporary story.

The most noteworthy element of the 'new' economy is its obviously parasitic and unequal nature. Whether it is a Kirzner-like entrepreneurship located in capturing value created by others (Hanlon, 2014), the rise of open innovation (Ettlinger, 2014), the portrayal of the totally consumed, hardworking and creative artist as the ideal worker subjectivity that everyone should aspire to be (Graw, 2010; Brouillette, 2014), the rise of an affective economy wherein workers are supposed to innovate a response without it being scripted by bringing certain appropriate and ready-made potentials and behaviours to work (Dowling, 2007), the emergence of a world where one dreams about one's job (Lucas, 2010), the centrality of oligopoly to the global economy, wherein powerful companies leverage their economic clout to extract value from supply chains (Appelbaum and Lichtenstein, 2006), the rise of unpaid (family) subsidized internships, the expansion of global labour market forms such as Mechanical Turk, the extraction of value from seemingly non-economic activities and routines as epitomized by Google (the centrality of routines to neo-liberalism will become apparent later in this chapter), the provision by willing subjects of 'free' labour to major corporations – for example, every minute labourers/customers/users of YouTube upload forty-eight hours of material (Soar,

2011: 6) and volunteers translated Facebook from English to French in a few days and from English to Spanish within two weeks (Afuah and Tucci, 2012) – or the increasing 'co-creation' of value inherent in marketing and branding, which were themselves initially driven by the desire for greater control of the market through standardization (Lury, 2004: 18–20) – in all these forms one can point to a capturing of value created elsewhere and increasingly the capturing of value from beyond the organization. Each activity is parasitic because each in some sense feeds off the free gifts of sociality introduced at the beginning of this book. Each of these activities contains a free gift to capital, but each also appears as though it is organized by capital.

Although the contemporary economy is obviously different from the one studied by Taylor and Mayo, the two share many fundamentals. In particular, capital and management still need to access the free gifts of sociality, they still feed off the general intellect and they still seek to shape subjectivity so that the subject becomes a subject of value. Companies such as Threadless highlight these issues in stark fashion. Threadless is explicitly located in the free gift of cooperation and the general intellect. It uses its 500,000-strong community of designers, customers, voters and employees to create and evaluate the designs the company should go on to produce. Between 2000 and 2008, it received more than 133,000 design submissions from 41,666 community members. These designs were then voted on and the winning ones were produced. This enabled the company to develop 899 unique designs and sell over 1.5 million T-shirts. More recently, Threadless has enhanced its capability to reach further afield and drill down deeper by using a blog to enable its 'community' to comment on the designs in progress of potential submitters. Winners receive $2,000 in cash and $500 in Threadless vouchers. T-shirts sell for between $15 and $17, and cost between $5 and $7 to produce, making the business highly profitable by casual designer retail standards (Lakhani and Kanji, 2008). However, the company coordinates its 'community' (the customers/people who actually design the T-shirts) by exploiting a space that was already formed by new ways of being social – the internet, open-source software, social media, the rise of mass intellectuality or the desire for creativity. Threadless simply accesses the gifts provided by the social, creative, skilled people within this space who are capable of self-organizing electronically and remotely.

Equally, it is no surprise that the current model for the future of innovation is 'open innovation'. In contrast to the past, when firms sought integration and wanted to maintain strong R&D (research and development) departments, the future model is called C&D – connect and develop. In this model the powerful corporation does not do its own research. Rather, it encourages suppliers, subcontractors, smaller firms, groups or individuals to submit ideas for development on secure platforms where the intellectual property rights are handed over to the corporation or shared on a disproportionate basis – what Taylor might have called 'an almost equal division of work and responsibility'. Procter & Gamble has stated that it wants 50 per cent of its innovation to come from such a model. While the model is built on the format of open-source software, it contains the important twist that the powerful keep the knowledge and the profits (Ettlinger, 2014). We could compare and contrast this model of innovation with the inside contract. In both systems, management have accepted that they are not the bearers of know-how or innovation. However, across the two forms the power relations between management and labour are different. The large corporation today has the power to extract value from elsewhere in a model of rent-seeking, whereas, as we saw in Chapter 3, the knowledge workers of yesteryear had more control. Today, knowledge does not easily equate with power. In light of this, one can see why three-quarters of large US and European firms now practise open innovation.

Or we could point to the necessary skills of an experience-based economy. In such an economy the universal skills of the general intellect – language, affect, cognition, creativity and emotion – are required. As Mills so eloquently pointed out, these skills are located within the subject, so they are given to capital as free gifts – here we can think of the hospitality, education, retail and creative sectors. However, as was highlighted in the Introduction and Chapter 4, these skills are developed through cooperative interaction between the particular and the social individual – a cooperation that is influenced and modulated by the logic of capital accumulation and management. As the violent history of management demonstrates, the importance of these skills developed in cooperation ensures that the subject has to be managed, modulated and made acquiescent to capital's authority. In short, the subject has to be turned into a subject of value, certain potentials are stressed and others rejected or denied. The world outside of work has to be recreated in preparation for being selected to work.

In ways that also bear some resemblance to the past, we might examine the corporate accessing and shaping of non-paid and non-traditional consumption as activities and routines that will bear value or potential value in the future. For example, a central development of business practice has been the growth of personalization or 'Big Data' (Pariser, 2011). This entails the development of a corporate memory of the individual consumer so that previous non-paid activity is put to work in order to market and design personalized services, data mining and advertising. One aim of this is to shape and reinforce behaviour – in short, to modulate the subject so he or she becomes a subject of value (or more value) to capital. For example, on joining SKY Broadband in the UK in 2014, each new customer was offered the opportunity to sign up for personalization, which gives SKY permission to analyse their usage in order to tailor adverts, services or products to their tastes. Similarly, every time a user clicks on Google's search engine, uses Gmail or reads Google News, the company gathers and stores that data, then analyses it to provide individualized results for that user's next search in an attempt to keep them locked-in and content. In this manner it alters and shapes users' thoughts and practices to persuade them to come back for more (Fuchs, 2011; Halpern, 2011; Lanier, 2011; Pariser, 2011). SKY and Google both hope to create a quasi-monopoly over the provision of non-paid activities and routines of media viewing, internet searching, email use and news consumption because every happy click reveals a marketing secret from which to extract fees from advertising, keep users content and lock them in so they self-discipline and return for further valorization (Pariser, 2011; Soar, 2011).

In these examples, activities are provided for free and from beyond (or sometimes within) the workplace so that the organization extracting the value is simultaneously interested and uninterested in the where, when, how and under what conditions these activities are performed, and each individual's activities and routines are moulded and modulated. Today, ever more of our activities and routines are structured to generate value for capital – as data, as purchases, as ideas and so on. But this is also creating us anew as subjects – subjects of value moulded and modulated to seek out and engage in ever more commoditized or commoditizable routines and forms of conduct. As a result, it is reshaping our sociality and the general intellect. Our conduct and behaviours are increasingly rationally objectified so that we are regulated and disciplined to act as subjects of value (Hennis, 1988: 90–104; Skeggs, 2011, 2014). In many respects this is a continuation of, rather than a break with, management's dark interest in external regulation and internal discipline and its desire to expropriate knowledge, create new forms of capitalist authority and planning, recast subjectivity and totally subsume society to capital under the influence of elite guidance. Management has long attempted to achieve all of this.

This attempt to collapse society into the economy links management directly with neo-liberalism and raises the question of the relationship between the two. Both have long shared the same assumptions and agenda. Indeed, the managed organization is a central tool for delivering neo-liberalism's main ambition – the collapse of life into work and the polity into the economy. In this sense, management is the first neo-liberal 'science'. It is a clear tool in the neo-liberal class struggle from above that has been waged for over a century.

Neo-liberalism and management

Like management, neo-liberalism is ultimately a political rather than an economic project because its aim is to generate a new form of subjectivity. Neo-liberalism suggests that positive social and cooperative bonds are fostered through the market and that this generates new forms of positive subjectivity. However, it also argues that these bonds must be nurtured through constant vigilance and the maintenance of competition, because interest groups always seek to avoid the market. This vigilance is organized around three concepts: active intervention to ensure spontaneity in the market/society; the prioritization of competition; and the necessity of elite leadership (see, e.g., Hayek, 1948: 92–118). Intervention and competition necessarily look different in different social situations, so there is no one universal neo-liberalism (just as there is no universal management). Within neo-liberalism there are disputes about what exactly these should look like at any given moment (Brown, 2003, 2006; Peck, 2008; Gane, 2013). Neo-liberalism necessarily alters across time and space as societies are structured and then recomposed (Röepke, 1992: 48–52). As a result, we get ordo-liberalism, upon which much of the German post-war economy was built; or Lippmann's (1938/1943) 'good society', the 'American individualism' of President Herbert Hoover and the 'entrepreneurial man' of Hayek, Mises and, indeed, Drucker. These variants of neo-liberalism differ in their details but they all contain the themes of elite-led, institutional intervention to ensure competition from which springs the moral rejuvenation of the subject. In short, intervention is necessary because people need to be constantly moulded and modulated to capitalist society. This shaping of subjectivity then gives rise to the importance of authority and leadership because some visions of the present and the future are better – indeed, more normal (Brown, 2006: 699) – than others (Hayek, 1948: 108; Peck, 2008; Gane, 2013, 2014; Mirowski, 2013: 72–83).

As outlined throughout this book, these issues also lie at the heart of management thought. Management has always been informed by what today we call neo-liberalism. The genealogy demonstrates that neo-liberalism and management thought emerged simultaneously and developed the same solutions to the social crisis of the early twentieth century – a time when capitalism and markets were both growing and coming under threat from wider social forces. Thus, rather than seeing management planning and authority in large – even monopolistic or oligopolistic – organizations as antithetical to neo-liberalism, we should view them as the same because, in their origins, they are both responses to these social forces and to the collective challenges that were waged against the emerging forms of capitalist planning and authority.

Both neo-liberalism and management have stressed active intervention in institutions, the moral necessity of competition and the need for the elite to structure these two activities in light of the tendency of some groups to avoid competition. Both have done so because they are in essence the same project. The working class are especially accused of seeking protection from the market and, following on from this, they are deemed unable to know what is in their own best interests (Gane, 2013). In one sense, they are irrational because they refuse the logic of governmentality bound up in the market (Brown, 2003). Like Mayo, neo-liberals argue that this irrationality developed because of the social dislocation unleashed by industrial society. This dislocation is one reason why the elite need to control society and order it according to particular political rationalities based on the principles of market competition (Brown, 2006). Although not solely aimed at the working class, workers became the main target of such intervention because they were both numerically strong and morally undisciplined, hence they were either unable or unwilling to ensure their own 'self-care' through the market individually (Brown, 2003: 6). In short, they were a threat to the competitive principle that the elite sought to foist on to the majority. This threat meant that at a fundamental level democracy became problematic and needed to be tempered with other forms of regulation – the market, the law, the state and, importantly, the private organization.[1]

The two early schools of management thought also stressed the need for active planning, competition, elite leadership, the irrationality of the working class and the problematic issue of democracy. As with neo-liberalism, for these schools, intervention was necessary if competition, moral rejuvenation and indeed capitalism itself were to be safeguarded. Management theorists shared the same fears as neo-liberals and proffered active intervention, competition and elite leadership as the solutions. Thus, in their origins, the two projects shared fundamental beliefs. Furthermore, each project informs the work of the other: for example, Weber is a key influence on the neo-liberals (Mommsen 1974; Gamble, 1996; Foucault, 2008: 105; Gane, 2013, 2014); Mayo (1937) begins his essay on cooperation with an acknowledgement of the importance of Lippmann's *Method of Freedom*; the Dean of Harvard Business School between 1919 and 1942, Wallace Brett Donham (1933, 1936), was also informed by Lippmann; and the Harvard–Pareto circle, of which Donham and Mayo were members, was influenced by the neo-liberal President Hoover in their desire to deradicalize labour, create management as a legitimate authority and make it more scientific (Scott, 1992: 58–60). The two projects clearly addressed similar issues and proposed similar solutions for society, the market, the organization and the individual. Davies (2014: 108–47) highlights the link to contemporary management and neo-liberalism, but, crucially, my argument suggests the neo-liberal role of management is not new. Rather, it is an intensification of aspects of the subject area's origins.

Neo-liberalism and 'the social crisis of our time'

In 1938, the group later known as the Mont Pelerin Society (created in 1947) met in Paris to celebrate the French translation of Walter Lippmann's *The Good Society*. Although by no means the first neo-liberal tract, it highlighted the issues that still dominate neo-liberal thought (Dardot and Laval, 2013). The book, and neo-liberalism generally, was preoccupied with the crisis of social and political life reflected in the maladjustment of many to the emergence of organized capitalist society, and with the need for new forms of leadership and authority to intervene actively in the state, institutions and organizations so that the masses could be morally readjusted as new individualized subjects within the emerging society. It also reaffirmed the centrality of competition and the maintenance of private property rights to this societal programme.

As a project, neo-liberalism emerged from the belief that many facets of liberal thought, and especially laissez-faire, were no longer relevant to capitalism. Indeed, liberal ideas, which had been progressive in the nineteenth century, had become a source of many social and political problems (Foucault, 2008; Peck, 2008; Dardot and Laval, 2013; Gane, 2013, 2014). For example, Lippmann (1935: 25) argued that 'the pure doctrine of non-intervention in production and trade has never in fact been practiced anywhere' and thus laissez-faire was the 'cardinal fallacy' that allowed collectivists to point to the social and economic costs of capitalism as originating directly from market relations, competition and private property rights (see also Lippmann, 1938/1943: 184–92). Röepke (1992: 22) echoed these themes in *The Social Crisis of Our Time*, as did Hayek (1944: 14; 1948: 109–10) in his work. As such, neo-liberalism argued that liberal calls for laissez-faire rang hollow and became a conservative demand to return to a society that had never existed. Such a demand appeared to be an endorsement of ascribed inequality and thereby enabled collectivists to turn the masses against the market.

In this rendition, the key capitalist battleground was not whether to intervene but what form the intervention should take. Neo-liberals argued that capitalism needed saving because the spontaneous order of the market was threatened by the collectivism that had developed as a reaction to the negative effects of laissez-faire (Hayek, 1948: 107; Röepke, 1948: 24–34; Gane, 2013, 2014). Under the rubric of 'American individualism', Hoover (1922: 1–2) argues for many of the central tenets of this project. He suggests that a retreat to liberalism would create ever-stronger collective challenges to the market as an organizing principle. Indeed, one-third of the world was already engulfed in conflict and was listening to 'dreamers', and the 'Great masses of people had flocked to their banners in hopes born of misery and suffering.' Hoover (1922: 11–12) further states that the United States had already abandoned laissez-faire because of the ideology's reliance on 'the notion that it is "every man for himself and the devil take the hindmost"'. Rather than liberal laissez-faire, Hoover (1922: 9) calls for an active interventionist state that would use competition to structure market relations so

> that while we build our society upon the attainment of the individual, we shall safeguard to every individual an equal opportunity to take the position in the society to which his intelligence, character, ability and ambition entitle him; that we keep the social solution free from strata of classes; that we shall stimulate effort of each individual to achievement; that through enlarging a sense of responsibility and understanding we shall assist him to his attainment; while he in turn must stand up to the emery wheel of competition.

Hoover (1922: 48–62) then argues that the state should regulate the economy to ensure competition pervades society, nationalized industries are kept to a minimum, private initiative is allowed to flow and private property is secured.[2] Hoover was an interventionist who argued that institutions needed managing and that, if they were managed correctly, they would morally rejuvenate the individual and society. The management of institutions and organizations was to be carried out to prioritize the voluntary, the private, the competitive and the cooperative via the market. Crucially, this was to be an elite-led process so that the actions of the working class, the collectivist, the undisciplined and the irrational were to be tightly regulated to ensure that they were made to secure their own individual futures (see Roediger and Esch, 2012 on the elitist and race management aspects of Hoover's thought). Without naming it, Hoover, like the management thought examined throughout this book, outlined the essence of what we now understand as neo-liberalism's exhortation of self-care (Foucault, 2008).

The working class as social crisis

The crisis neo-liberals envisaged manifested itself in new forms of worker collectivism and in calls for protection from the marketplace. As we saw in earlier chapters, in different ways these forms of collectivism were created because the majority of the society sought security and protection from the market (Mises, 1944; Polanyi, 1944/1957). Such collectivist threats were widespread – from farmers, to capitalists, to professionals. Indeed, a key argument of neo-liberalism was that there were many interest groups who sought to foist the market on to others while pushing it away from themselves. Nevertheless, they correctly (see Chapters 2, 3 and 4) suggested the single greatest collectivist threat was the working class because it was both maladjusted to organized capitalist society and able to use its numerical voting power to capture the state and provide itself with protection against the market and thereby threaten freedom (Lippmann, 1935: 74–9, 1938/1943: 45–54; Hayek, 1944: 89–113, 1948: 107–18; Mises, 1944: 4–5; Röepke, 1948: 132–7).

Democracy was dangerous because it enabled the majority not simply to vote communist or socialist but to maintain the 'modest ethical gap between economy and polity' upon which liberal democracy was built but which neo-liberalism opposes (Brown, 2003: 9; see also Gane, 2013). If capitalism – but not necessarily democracy – was to be saved, the working class had to be moulded and modulated to the market's form. Management theorists were espousing this, too. The economy had to be collapsed into a neo-liberal polity where economy and society were one and the same – society had to be totally subsumed to capital (Mirowski, 2013: 89–157). The working class's pursuit of security and its numerical advantage in a democratic state meant that the world could descend to 'its lowest common denominator' (Lippmann, 1935: 24; Hayek, 1948: 109). Indeed, Mises (1944: 1–19) explicitly cites the New Deal as evidence of the mass voting against their own interests. To avoid this, labour had to be made to compete for work and the state had to ensure such competition (Lippmann, 1938/1943: 198–9). In management thought, too, the proposal was that labour had to be made to compete for work and the organization was central to ensuring such competition (see Chapters 2, 3 and 4).

Ensuring this required active and never-ending neo-liberal intervention in the institutions of society. As regards the impact of such intervention on the individual, it should operate on two levels – to regulate behaviour externally via rules, rewards and punishments, and to instil new values and ways of being internally so as to engineer a new subject. Necessarily, such a project is a work in progress because of both the recalcitrance of the majority and the dynamism of capitalist society (Lippmann, 1935: 73). Activity, planning and management by the elite can never end. Once in place, the resulting competitive thrust would force activity, planning and management on to organizations to ensure their ability to compete and, from there, on to individuals through selection, training, promotion and career ladders. Capital and management become the organizing authority which then morally rejuvenates people as new neo-liberal subjects. Crucial here is the idea of selection, which Taylor, Mayo and indeed Weber (1994: 283) all understood was fundamentally reshaping society through its creation of new forms of 'discipline'. This discipline meant that labour would not only heed the call for work but that it would adapt in order to be chosen in the competition to work. Neo-liberalism would trickle down through the institutions of management and organization once the elite had structured society along competitive lines.

Creating possessive individualism

Importantly, the condition of the working class and its desire for security came about because of the mistakes of liberalism. This flawed condition emerged from the errors of a transition period and, as such, it was unnatural and therefore incapable of remedy. Indeed, not only is collectivism not normal within a developed capitalist society but the competitive market itself becomes the most normal, most free and most spontaneous way of being (Hayek, 1948: 1–32; Gamble, 1996; Brown, 2006; Foucault, 2008). Because of this, collective security needs to be replaced with individualized competitive relations. In the nineteenth century, the need to destroy the regulatory system of the earlier order encouraged the collectivism or cartelization of the capitalist class. This capitalist collectivism undermined the market and then impoverished the working class and generated its inability to gather or maintain its property rights and its traditions of socialization. All of this forced the working class towards a collectivism that had to be reversed (Lippmann, 1938/1943: 23–4). Here, *contra* the workerist position, the capitalist class formed the collectivism of the working class. Workers do not naturally form a class collective; rather, they meet as individuals and through traditions, customs or ways of being form communities based on trade, place, religion, nationality or some other common interest. Famously, Tronti (1964) argues that individual capitalists compete against each other but are forced to form as a class because of collective labour's refusal of capitalist valorization (see Chapter 2).

Neo-liberals accept that the transition to capitalism led to the 'proletariat', by which they mean people who are 'dependent, property-less, urbanised wage-earners, and made to fit into the hierarchy of the commercial and industrial mammoth concern' (Röepke, 1948: 139; see also Lippmann, 1935: 92–5). They argue the drive to establish the freedom of market societies moved too quickly for social traditions to keep pace and thus generated the false urge to collectivize. This drive proletarianized much of the population and made them potentially unmanageable. Hence, these groups needed to be both externally regulated through institutions and organizations with incentives, punishments and individual property rights and internally disciplined through the creation of new desires, ambitions, motivations and ways of being if the social order were to be maintained (Lippmann, 1935: 91–7). New governance through new regulations would form new subjectivities housing new desires. Society needed to eradicate any collectivist threats through widening private property rights, markets, independence, competition and (limited) welfare provision. If collectivism were to be broken, the world of possessive individualism had to be opened up to all. This was the management task that neo-liberalism set itself.

Embracing this project meant that the working class – indeed, anyone who rejected market discipline – had to be morally reconstructed, re-educated, individualized and created anew as bourgeois subjects. Yet again, this is the stuff of management. Such an endeavour could not be accomplished easily because the working class was unthinking, prone to 'drift' (Lippmann, 1914/1985: 101–12), exponents of a 'mismanaged life' (Brown, 2003: 6) and hence easily led by Hoover's 'dreamers'. Indeed, their susceptibility to demagoguery was one reason why many neo-liberals felt uncomfortable about democracy – something Lippmann (1935: 74–9) termed the tyranny of 'transient majorities'. The will of the people was a fundamental problem because, as we saw in Chapter 2, the people sought security and hence favoured the 'wrong' forms of collectivist intervention – Keynesianism or worse (Hayek, 1944; Mises, 1944; Röepke, 1948). Collectivism necessarily led to war economies and undermined freedom (Lippmann, 1938/1943: 54–90, Mises, 1944; Röepke, 1948: 1–40; Gane, 2013, 2014). In this analysis, if the spontaneous market is to deliver freedom for people (Gamble, 1996: 26–49), it must be led by the elite, who will carry 'the Schmittian burden *to decide on behalf of others*' (Davies, 2014: 133; emphasis in original).[3] In light of this, public opinion and the mass become a focus of attention because the conditions of mass existence had made the worker incapable of thought. As Lippmann (1922: 75) puts it:

> The mass of absolutely illiterate, of feeble minded, grossly neurotic, undernourished and frustrated individuals, is very considerable, much more considerable than we generally suppose. Thus a wide popular appeal is circulated among persons who are mentally children or barbarians, people whose lives are a morass of entanglements, people whose vitality is exhausted, shut-in people, and people whose experience has comprehended no factor in the problem (i.e. the ability to think) under discussion among persons who are mentally children or barbarians. The stream of public opinion is stopped by them in little eddies of misunderstanding, where it is discoloured with prejudice and far fetched analogy.

This inability to think created a societal crisis. While neo-liberals acknowledged that this lack of thinking sprang from socialization and was a direct result of the development of capitalism on an ever larger scale, they nevertheless held the working class accountable for the problem and feared them. As advocated by Taylor, Mayo and management thought more generally, labour was to be policed and manipulated to fit the new society. This meant it became the role of the elite actively to shape public opinion and social institutions in order to mould and modulate the working class along neo-liberal lines (Lippmann, 1922: 107–8; Bernays, 1928; Röepke, 1992: 176–94; Peck, 2008: 11–18). Indeed, to overcome 'loose thinking' (Röepke, 1992: 151–3) or the 'drift' that emerged from organized capitalism's 'scattering of the soul' of labour (Lippmann, 1914/1985: 128), neo-liberals had to manage opinion and intervene in institutions as a moral endeavour. Institutional restructuring and moral reform merged so that the citizen had to be worked on through rules, desires and ways of being (Röepke, 1948: xxii).

In this emerging society, new forms of leadership and authority were required because older forms of authority – craft, age and status – were both uncompetitive and in the process of being eradicated. While this eradication was positive because it was unleashing human potential and allowing competitive merit to win out, it also threatened society. Hence, in order to save society and the subject, a restructuring that exposed people to the 'emery wheel of competition' was required. Indeed, competition must come before democracy, because of the latter's potential to give in to demands for protection from the market:

> The kind of self-education which a self-governing people must obtain can be had only through its daily experiences. In other words, a democracy must have a way of life which educates the people for the democratic way of life. The pioneers of democracy, particularly in America, dimly apprehended but never, I think, fully comprehended this truth. They had the great discovery that henceforth the people would rule, that they have the right to rule, and that the government through which they rule must be made truly representative. But what they did not master was the corollary of their discovery: that *if the people rule, they must rule in a particular way.*
>
> *(Lippmann, 1938/1943: 263; emphasis in original;*
> *see also Mises, 1944: 1–19)*

People were incapable of ascertaining their own interests or of organizing either themselves or society (see Lippmann, 1938/1943: 294–7). Therefore, they had to be led, enlightened and perhaps even deceived (Hayek, 1944: 117) into new daily experiences so that democracy would rule in particular ways. Echoing Chapter 2, constituted power needed to be asserted over constituent power because the constituents could not be trusted (Negri, 1999).

Because the sustaining of a competitive environment required constant vigilance to ensure that exposure to competition, the pursuit of efficiency, the sanctity of private property, the use of the market and price as the arbiters of worth were put forward above all other values, all human action was to become economically driven and hence the polity and the economy would become one and the same thing (Gane, 2013, 2014). That is, the environment had to be recreated and monitored to swing the great transformation firmly towards the market despite the wish of the majority for security. If the 'intellectual leaders of the modern world can recover their intellectual habit of looking for a solution to social problems by the readjustment of private rights rather than by public administration' (Lippmann, 1938/1943: 282), they would create competition, restore authority to society, ensure fairness and secure individualism. These are the essential and radical features of neo-liberalism (Peck, 2008) and indeed, as this book has attempted to demonstrate, of management thought. At their core is the need for constant elite intervention to ensure that the institutions of society are subject to competition. Intervention is ultimately aimed at morally reconstructing the individual so that he or she embraces the need for 'self-care', seeks out individualism, accepts competition, and values both work organizations and the market as institutions that could fulfil his or her ambitions, desires and daily experiences. Such processes would secure private property, liberty and peace.

Because neo-liberalism believes competition trickles down to mould and modulate behaviour, the institution of the managed organizational form becomes central, alongside the institutions of the market and the state. Significantly, the essential role of self-care in neo-liberal thought makes the organization pivotal to creating competition as the foundation stone of society because, if organizations have to be competitive, then so too does the human capital housed within them (Drucker, 2007a). Through state regulation the subject would be moulded and modulated in both the market and the work organization; he or she would be managed so as to become a neo-liberal subject, a human capital or an enterprise man/woman. It is because of these shared concerns that management, in its origins, is neo-liberal.

Neo-liberal themes and management

As we have seen, ever since its inception, management thought has analysed and/or described ways within which it might actively intervene and plan, push competition on to labour and provide the leadership to structure the organization in ways that will ensure labour is externally regulated, rewarded and punished, and internally disciplined so that it embraces new behaviours, desires, ambitions and ways of being. In this way labour will both hear the call to work but also need – or, better still, desire – the prospect of being chosen for such work and hence adapt accordingly.

This led to the reinvention of management. One of the key features of early management thought was the transition from management as an expense – as 'mere superintendence' (Pollard, 1965: 250) – to management as a (or indeed the most) productive activity within the organization (Drucker, 2007b: 97). In this transition, management, like the market, was to become a new form of authority or normation. As we saw in Chapters 2 and 3, elements of this included the shift away from a labour theory of value, deskilling, and reconfiguring work and organization so that management knowledge was deemed productive and its leadership central to the organization, the economy and society. Thus, Taylor's project is structured around the productive gains of 'good' management. Management becomes an active intervention into the struggle for the knowledge of production on behalf of capitalist accumulation – knowledge of production could be used for good only if it was management knowledge of production. Management was not merely about coordination; it was also about redistributing knowledge from one group to another. This redistribution was important because Taylor (1903: 1412), along with the neo-liberals, felt workers did not know their own best interests. Like colonized peoples, women, non-whites or children, the necessity of greater effort and the benefits of good management had to be explained to them.

Without an interventionist management, the organization would fail because workers would use their knowledge to seek protection from individualized competition, the security of collectivity and to control the pace of work (soldiering) to lower competition and productivity. Competitiveness could trickle down from the market to the organization and then to the individual worker only through management intervention. Although they did not know it, workers needed management to strip them of their knowledge if they were to be individualized, made competitive, made to be neo-liberal and hence given the opportunity to become fulfilled and free. Individuals, organizations and society needed management because it would deliver a neo-liberal world of competition, markets and freedom. As such, management bore the burden of responsibility for competition, authority and leadership (Taylor, 1919: 37).

To create such a world, craft production, putting-out systems, the inside contract and worker knowledge all had to be used and then traduced. Furthermore, many of the most vulnerable groups in society had to be corralled into factories, and the state had to ignore the democratic will of the people. Only then could management use this knowledge to set worker against worker, break up collectivity and indivi-dualize the workplace. This would be done through constant intervention in the organization via piece rates, internal labour markets, new reward and punishment systems and career ladders.

Competition would deliver all of this; hence, it is central to Taylor's thinking. These ideas went on to structure the organizational form of the twentieth century (see Chapter 3). Management became a necessary, productive and constant elite-led activity. But, of course, Taylor was not alone in stressing the need for constant intervention.

Elton Mayo, neo-liberal thought and the working class

Chapter 4 demonstrated the striking similarities between the role played by the 'spontaneous' in neo-liberals' concept of the market (Gamble, 1996; Gane, 2014) and Mayo's idea that work organization is based on 'spontaneous cooperation'. Mayo (1937) stresses that, in market societies, spontaneous, unthinking or semi-thinking routine creates a form of collaboration that generates positive social bonds and cooperative benefits. Although he (Mayo, 1939: 335) cites Malinowski, he also reflects Hayek (1948: 1–32), because he stresses the importance of 'custom, tradition, and non-logic' in routine cooperation. As we saw in Chapter 4, he argues that our limited knowledge – an immensely important concept in neo-liberal thought (see Hayek, 1945, 1948: 92–106) – by necessity leads to a society that should be administered and managed through a small state with a large private sector if individual freedom is to flourish. For Mayo, the collectivist state – unlike the market or the firm – is a(n) (im)moral entity that inevitably forces an unnatural cooperation on to people. For freedom and spontaneous cooperation to flourish, the (democratic) state must be limited. However, spontaneous cooperation will come about only through the creation of elite-led new routines:

> It must be insisted that the intelligent development of civilisation is impossible except upon the basis of effective social collaboration and that such collabora-tion will always be dependent upon semiautomatic routines of behaviour made valuable by personal association and high sentiment. The most intelligent adaptation will remain ineffective until transformed from logic and the abstract into the human and actual routine with deep emotional attachment.

> Here then is the problem for the sociologist and administrator that I propose
> to illustrate as best I may from personal experience.
>
> *(Mayo, 1939: 336)*

The role of elite administration was to create new routines and new emotional attachments that would reshape social collaboration and the general intellect in particular ways. These ways would be located in the habits of the market and of competitive organizational life; over time, they would form deep emotional meanings for people. Quite simply, Mayo wanted to re-engineer the subject. It was the moral duty of the educated elite to create these new liberating, non-state-driven routines and ways of being.

Again in a neo-liberal turn, Mayo suggests that 'spontaneous cooperation' is impossible without management because of the disruptive birth pangs of capitalism, which created a 'seamy side' that eradicated the traditional socialization and knowledge transfer capacities of the working class. This created a 'rabble' who were not to be trusted and were a threat to society (see Chapters 4 and 5; but see also Mayo, 1949: 3–50, 1923a, 1923b, 1924b). Therefore, labour needed to be moulded and modulated, and it was management's duty to do this through the development of new routines and socialization processes that supported private property, competitiveness and the market (Bendix and Fisher, 1949: 316). While acknowledging that the transition to industrial capitalism undermined the working class, Mayo (1922c: 159) goes on to accuse it of being incapable of developing the learning skills necessary for contemporary life.

Indeed, he further argues that one of the problems of capitalism is that it forces the processes of socialization on to the nuclear family, which is inadequate for the task. Consequently, other institutions need to take up the moral role of developing individual 'social discipline' (Mayo, 1937: 829–30). Neither the family nor the dying traditions of labour could discipline the individual into the new society, hence the work organization must become a central place for such moral and disciplining activity. He places the work organization at the heart of the neo-liberal drive to subsume society totally to capital. Here, work and life are collapsed so that life becomes the competitive discipline of work or of the competitive preparing for such a competitive discipline – of being selected for work and of waiting and altering in order to be selected for work. In this vision, we simply become human capital and all our life becomes work. (Chapter 5 highlights this with regard to Taylor, too.) This makes the role of management central because the work organization becomes a – if not the – major site for such reconstruction of the subject.

As we saw in Chapter 4, Mayo also suggests that one of capitalism's fundamental problems is laissez-faire liberalism, which he explicitly rejects. In his vision, society needs competition and individualism, it must reject the 'false individualism' (Hayek, 1948) of laissez-faire, and it should be fundamentally concerned about the working class and democracy. He argues that the working class will always try to use the state to undermine the market and hence civilized society. In light of this, democracy is potentially tyrannical. The way to circumvent this is to reconstruct the subject by understanding the 'total situation' of the subject and collapsing work and life or economy and politics. The neo-liberal Mayo is sceptical of democracy, sees the working class as corrupted and easily led, and suggests that society and the organization need elite intervention to restructure the worker–subject morally and secure competition, private property, the market and freedom. His is a neo-liberal project based on externally regulating while also internally disciplining people through new routines and other forms of spontaneous cooperation to which they will have 'deep emotional attachment'.

Donham (1933, 1936) – perhaps Harvard Business School's most influential dean – reflects these views, too. Like the neo-liberals, he argues that democracy is a potential danger because of the population's susceptibility to demagogues. The mass media and public opinion need to be manipulated because the old routines of the nineteenth century have been undermined and the population comprises an increasingly 'heterogeneous mixture' (Donham, 1936: 262). The demagogue could appeal to the emotions of the populace so that they question the current 'routines, habits, customs, institutions'. He goes on to reject the New Deal as state interference and argues for the training of new leaders – in business schools, of course (see Donham, 1922, 1933) – who 'understand social routines and their relations to the emotional nature of men' (Donham, 1936: 263).

Along with Hayek (1948: 1–32) and Mayo (1937), Donham argues that leaders can create emotional attachments for people and hence the necessary stability of capitalism by generating and then managing positive routines. To achieve this, in a Hoover-like manner, he argues society must reject the 'dreamlands' of planned Utopias because society is an 'evolutionary' or spontaneous project. Once routines are broken the mass becomes confused and vulnerable to political irrationalities – hence the problem of democracy. Leaders need to stabilize emotions through routines because 'Our primary jobs are to maintain enough strong social routines to keep stability and to preserve a moving equilibrium by making compensatory adjustments and building new routines which cure difficulties or prevent their recurring' (Donham, 1936: 267). In so doing, management will lead society towards neo-liberalism through active 'compensatory adjustment'. Yet again, external and internal management of the subject are essential if competition, property rights, markets and freedom are to be secured.

Max Weber: a reluctant neo-liberal

Although not a management thinker in the style of Taylor, Mayo or Donham, Weber is interesting because of his subsequent influence on Schumpeter, neo-liberals and core management areas such as leadership, entrepreneurship, innovation, public choice theory and organization studies. He also takes up some of these issues and aligns with neo-liberal thought. However, such a view is controversial because, while Weber certainly influenced neo-liberals (Mommsen, 1974; Gane, 2013, 2014; Gordon, 2014), he stresses the idea of a calling or a vocation in his work. A vocation is a form of conduct wherein different spheres of activity produce their own ethics, forms of behaviour and an ideal individual 'personality' type where those who embody the best of the sphere's ethics and conduct are lionized in their separate vocations – be they politics, science or art (Merton, 1940, Weber, 1948, 1994: 309–69; Hennis, 1983; Du Gay 2013a, 2013b; Gane, 2013, 2014). As we saw in Chapter 1, Du Gay (2000, 2013a, 2013b) has eloquently argued that Weber's work is opposed to the totalizing project of neo-liberal post-bureaucracy because such a project prioritizes the 'ethic' of private market-based competition above all others. However, I believe Du Gay is mistaken and will suggest that large elements of Weber – and hence of management thought – are fundamentally neo-liberal.

For instance, the opening pages of his essay 'Suffrage and Democracy in Germany' outline many of the tenets of neo-liberalism. Weber (1994: 90–1):

- stresses the moral imperative of work and attacks rentiers;
- demands votes for the productive elements of society (namely, workers and capitalists);
- calls for a small but effective state;
- argues that the state should enable the market and expose people to competition rather than protect groups from the market;
- bemoans the necessary expansion of state corporatism during the First World War and endorses its dismantling after the war;
- protests that a Durkheimian (see also Weber, 1978: II: 1396–7) – or any other – form of occupational corporatism is a regressive step that will damage the competitive dynamism of the market;
- comes out strongly in favour of the 'free' spontaneous association of unions and political parties as opposed to the state-driven forced association of some occupational grouping; and
- forcefully supports the view that the market ensures individual ethical behaviour because to act unethically would damage a person's competitive position – hence, a state-driven economy is unethical.

Many of the foundations of neo-liberal thought are present in these arguments. However, as usual with the 'bourgeois Marx' (Mommsen, 1974: 46), there is a twist. Unlike much neo-liberal thought, Weber argues for universal suffrage because he rejects the idea that the working class is a threat to capitalist society. He agrees that it is a powerful force, but is not convinced that it can – or even wishes to – abolish capitalism. His nationalism makes him suggest that, because the working class made up the bulk of the armies decimated in the First World War, it must be empowered with the vote, commenting: 'It is simply an extraordinary impertinence, however, to single out *equal* suffrage for slander as "democracy by numbers", as opposed to other elections as those based on "occupational groups"' (Weber, 1994: 102; emphasis in original).

However, Weber's defence of universal suffrage is made for neo-liberal reasons that are bound up with his fear of bureaucracy rather than democracy (Loader and Alexander, 1985: 4). So he argues that the working class, both as labour and as consumers, will ensure that the market is more, rather than less, competitive. But he also argues that, because labour is susceptible to being led, its organizations and protests will be reformist rather than revolutionary in nature. In other words, labour might be open to the demagoguery feared by other neo-liberals. Hence, competitiveness and interventionist leadership are central to his defence of democracy, and he sees democracy as opposed to bureaucracy. Instead of labour, he argues that the real threat to the market is an alliance between capitalist and state bureaucracies. This would give rise to 'robber capitalism' (Weber, 1994: 89) and allow capitalists and state bureaucrats to avoid competition, thereby undermining freedom. Weber's call for universal suffrage is made precisely to weaken the push towards corporatist protection from the market. He argues that the two great sources of privilege in capitalism – property ownership and education – are already in the hands of those groups that would most benefit from a state-dominated economy, and they would use these privileges to entrench their power and their capacity to avoid the market further. For Weber, the enfranchised majority working class acts as a bulwark against these anti-market groups:

> Thus the method of organising the economy is imminent, it is absolutely imperative, *before* it begins to function – which means immediately – for us to have a parliament elected on the principle that the *needs* of the masses must be represented, and *not* one which represents the way an individual is employed in the production of goods – in other words, a parliament of equal suffrage, wholly sovereign, in its power, which can take an independent stand in relation to this type of economic organisation [Weber is discussing corporatism here]. Parliament must be much more sovereign in its powers than hitherto, for in the past its position of power has *not* sufficed to break the power of vested commercial interests nor the inevitable rule of fiscal interests in state-run-industries. This is the *negative* reason for equal suffrage.
>
> *(Weber, 1994: 105; emphasis in original)*

For Weber, labour is as much – if not more so – a consuming entity searching for value as it is a producer interest (itself a neo-liberal view).

As we saw in Chapter 1, this analysis is linked to Weber's concerns about bureaucracy and his ideas about the necessity and desirability of 'Caesarist' leadership and demagoguery (Weber, 1978: 1452). For Weber, the power of bureaucracy is limited through charismatic leadership in a democratic state (Burawoy, 2013: 752–3). But his work on leadership also demonstrates a typically neo-liberal scepticism about democracy. The idea that democracy was about 'the realization of the principle of self-determination of the people … was in his opinion, ideological trash' (Mommsen, 1974: 87). (For a contrasting view, see Hennis, 1983.) Indeed, on the issue of democracy and leadership, he is alleged to have expressed the following to General Ludendorff: 'In a democracy people choose a leader in whom they trust. Then the chosen leader says "Now shut up and obey me". People and party are now no longer free to interfere in his business' (Gerth and Mills, 1948: 42).

Weber's reassertion of charismatic leadership in the face of bureaucratic societies is thus explicitly about enabling some to maintain their creativity while others are inevitably (if unfortunately) subject to the rules and regulations of bureaucracy – so much so that Mommsen (1974: 93–4) argues his views veer close to fascism and, indeed, display an affinity with Michels (see Chapter 1). In a democracy, the mass is driven by 'purely emotional and irrational influences' (Weber, 1978: II: 1459–60), but fortunately these emotions and irrationalities are controllable through demagoguery and charismatic leadership. Central to this charismatic leadership is the competitive struggle through which the few come to lead. Weber's example of this competitive individualism is the UK's parliamentary committee system (Weber, 1978: II: 1416–31, 1994: 127–9). This leadership style shifts to become more authoritarian so that society is run by the elite individuals with 'Caesarist features' (Mommsen, 1981: 114). This is a neo-liberal argument because it places power in the hands of the executive rather than among the parliamentary representatives who are more answerable to the electorate. A strong leadership or executive weakens the responsiveness of democracy to calls for protection from the market (Lippmann, 1935: 79–87). We might think of this as a de-democratizing tactic (Brown, 2003, 2006) or as the prioritization of constituted power. Here, charismatic leadership and bureaucracy potentially combine to enable the domination and authority of the competitively tested elite. Indeed, Thomas (2006: 154) asserts that Weber's role in creating the Weimar Constitution in Germany weakened the power of parliament and strengthened that of the executive, thereby benefiting Hitler. Weber and Chief Justice of the Supreme Court John Marshall have much in common (see Chapter 2).

For Weber, then, the twin features of bureaucracy and charismatic leadership – the 'double nature of what may be called the capitalist spirit' (Weber, 1978: II: 1118) – could potentially alter people's subjectivity in two neo-liberal management ways: bureaucracy will externally regulate them through its rules, rewards and punishments; and charismatic leadership will alter them internally by giving them new ambitions, desires and beliefs (Weber, 1978: II: 1115–17). Thus, if led by the right elite, bureaucratic rules and charismatic leadership will shape society, buttress competitive markets and protect individual freedoms. Here, Weber's charismatic leadership and bureaucracy combine and dominate society – a domination Weber never considers illegitimate (Mommsen, 1974: 78–83). (Although more favourable, Burawoy, 2013: 752 presents a similar argument.) Some will intervene and lead while others will follow and act in a prescribed and disciplined manner. All of this should take place in a market society with competitiveness, individualism and private property as its foundations. In this analysis, the charismatic leader is the dynamic force for change who intervenes to disrupt the bureaucratic rules, alter society and maintain competition. Here, the leader could act as Schumpeter's elite innovator–entrepreneur or as the 'enterprise man' proposed by Hayek, Mises and Drucker. Both are liberatory because they break static hierarchy. Although he was concerned with the issues of new elites and searched for ways out of the iron cage of bureaucracy, ultimately – like Michels, although with less enthusiasm – Weber felt only a few could achieve such a position and thereby lead, innovate and lend dynamism to capitalism (Titunik, 1997).

Thus, for Weber, restricting competition was a threat not because of the working class who could be led by charismatic leaders – or even labour leaders, although they would normally be from a non-working-class background (Weber, 1994: 336). Rather, competition was threatened by the newly emerging corporatist 'aristocracy' (see Weber, 1994: 121, 1978: 1139). Weber expresses real fears in a variety of essays and in *Economy and Society* about the emergence of property- and education-based elites who could avoid competition. These elites were already creating a pliant working class – an argument also put forward by Lippmann (1935: 94–5). Weber (1994: 68) sees the influence of this new aristocracy

> in America's 'benevolent feudalism', in Germany's so-called 'welfare provisions', in the factory system of Russia, and it is just waiting for certain conditions to make the masses 'compliant' enough to enter it ['the housing for the new serfdom'] once and for all.

This alliance between a dominant new aristocracy and a subservient labour was sure to undermine freedom. Weber was an elitist theorist who believed there would always be a gap between the ruled and the rulers, but he was also fundamentally concerned with how the relations between state bureaucracy and capital could corrupt the competitive nature of the market, return society to ascribed status, lead to economic stagnation, usher in the re-emergence of rent as an important category, create 'new castes' and thereby undermine freedom (Titunik, 1997).

In this reading, Weber is a neo-liberal theorist who favours competition, active intervention and elite leadership, and the same could be said of much of the management thought that emanates from his work. Where Weber nuances other neo-liberals is that he sees the worker as a partial solution to the emergence of new aristocracies and the undermining of the principle of market competitiveness. He believes labour is more in favour of freedom than the educated or propertied elite. In particular, he argued that the US worker had a tradition of resisting bureaucracy, maintaining his individualism, believing in his own worth or quality, and stressing the lack of importance of ascribed privilege. (Mises, 1944: 10, n1 exaggerates this view by arguing that bureaucracy itself is un-American.) But he also believed that this was coming to an end as America was 'Europeanised' (Weber, 1930/1985, 1994: 278–9). Central to this transition was the decline of 'free land', the growing power of the bureaucracy within the state and the private corporation, the role of education and the shift away from competition to corporatism (see Weber, 1948: 363–85, 1994: 272–303). A return to competition both in the marketplace and in leadership was required to reverse this European drift. To achieve this, the state had to act as a neo-liberal state by expanding the market and competition. Within all of this, the market, competition, private property and self-care were to be preferred over a planned collectivist economy. It was by advocating this that Weber was able 'to influence the neo-Liberalists of the 1950s so greatly' (Mommsen, 1974: 64).

To sum up, neo-liberalism and management thought share the same foundations, emerged as similar responses to the social crisis of legitimacy and authority that came about with the transition to corporate capitalism and saw the necessity of active intervention, the expansion of competition and elite leadership to recast social relations and reshape the subject through new forms of external regulation and internal discipline. Quite simply, management is a key element of neo-liberalism. It is the first neo-liberal 'science'.

Conclusion

In the final analysis, management is about recasting subjectivity through human resource management, human capital, marketing, operations management and logistics, strategy, 'Big Data', routines and activities, innovation, creativity, entre-preneurship and so on. This recasting is necessary if the subject is to be turned into a subject of value. But management is also parasitic in its relationship to labour. It needs to feed off of labour's free gifts in order to thrive. This means that management must reach beyond the organization and into society, culture or the general intellect. The ultimate goal is to alter social relations so that they become *capitalist* social relations or to subsume society totally to capital. Management attempts to achieve this subsumption through the expropriation of knowledge via deskilling, open innovation, co-creation, crowd sourcing, intellectual property rights and so on; by turning capital and management into the elite authority and planner of society (e.g. Threadless or the nineteenth-century factory); through the regulation of labour via rewards, punishments and the necessity of the wage; and by creating new desires, ambitions, ways of being, activities and routines so that we develop deep emotional attachments to capitalism as a way of life (e.g. motivation theories, leadership, marketing, branding and the personalization of data). Management uses violence against us physically, through cognition and through affect. Ultimately, it is neo-liberal class struggle from above.

Notes

1 As suggested, neo-liberal theory does not simply single out the working class; it also focuses on the concentration of capital and capital's tendency to avoid competition through monopolies, cartels, intellectual property rights and collusion. For example, Lippmann (1935: 91–7) accuses the 'plutocrats' of aligning with the working class to undermine the competitive nature of the market, Röepke (1992: 227–35) seeks a strong state to break up any tendencies to use various tactics to weaken the market and Hayek (1948: 107–18) is wary of the market power of large corporations, limited liability and intellectual property rights. While such a focus is rarely as strong as the emphasis on the working class, it is certainly present, and, as we shall see, Weber uses it to propose his neo-liberal solutions to the problem of social order.
2 Indeed, Hayek's papers 'The Meaning of Competition' and 'Free Enterprise and the Competitive Order' would echo these points some twenty years later.
3 It is in light of this that one can see why undermining liberal democracy is a central element of neo-liberalism today (see Brown, 2003, 2006; Du Gay and Morgan, 2013).

APPENDIX

Management, Durkheim and discipline

Management, and in particular human relations, is sometimes associated with Emile Durkheim. However, although there is such a link, it is very tentative. It is true that Mayo invoked Durkheim and, like Durkheim, he certainly rejected laissez-faire and the rational calculating subject; and both men also endorsed the need for the individual to be embedded in meaningful social and community relations (Mayo, 1919, 1933, 1937, 1949; Durkheim, 1951, 1957, 1984). Indeed, one of Durkheim's most important concepts – anomie – arises precisely because of a lack of meaning in the emerging social relations of capitalism, with its extended division of labour or what he called 'organic society' (Durkheim, 1984). He explicitly locates the necessity for social life to have meaning in 'the harmonious community of endeavours when minds and will come together to work for the same aim' (Durkheim, 1957: 17). He relates the undermining of this back to a change in how we interact and think, so that the economy comes to be seen as an end in itself rather than simply a means to a more important and worthwhile end – which, for Durkheim, is social harmony and community – as did Mayo, albeit for different reasons.

Durkheim argues that the growing division of labour, new forms of organization and an emphasis on possessive individualism caused the social disharmony he observed. As such, he endorses a renewal of something like, but ultimately different from, the guild structure (Durkheim, 1957, 1984). He argues forcefully that capitalism led to a dislocation that undermined society and isolated people – hence his concern with suicide, mental health, loneliness and anomie. His solution is to put social institutions between the individual and the state. He explicitly locates these institutions in the realm of work. He seeks out these institutions because, like Weber, he fears that a powerful bureaucratic state would swamp the individual and render the state oppressive to the citizen. These intermediate institutions would bolster civic morality and professional ethics. Thus, professional groups should organize production so that each economic sphere elects local, regional and national councils to oversee its specific industry. (Weber strongly rejects such a proposition, as we saw in Chapter 6.) As Durkheim puts it:

> An administrative council, a kind of miniature parliament, nominated by election, would preside over each group. We go on to imagine this council or parliament as having the power, on a scale to be fixed, to regulate whatever concerns the business: relations of employers and employees – conditions of labour – wages and salaries – relations of competitors with one another, and so on … And there we have the guild restored but in an entirely novel form.
>
> *(Durkheim, 1957: 37)*

Durkheim recognized that the systematic destruction of 'mechanical society', with its guilds and their socialization functions, had left a vacuum that needed to be filled (a vacuum the division of labour was in the process of creating and human relations was legitimating; see Chapters 2, 3, 4 and 6). Put simply, on its own, the state could not replace the guild or professional/trade/work group because it was too distant from working life. Like Mayo, he argues working life is the most suitable site to restore socialization and community because of its centrality to people's everyday existence and hence they should be given a voice in it via elections. Crucially, he also suggests that capitalist industry could not perform this function on its own because its origins were outside the guild system – for example, the non-guild factory was created through the use of migrant women in Massachusetts and Manchester alongside and in connection with the maintenance of the male-dominated guild craft system in non-factory settings (a theme discussed in Chapters 2 and 3). In light of this, Durkheim (1957: 49) argues that we need both the state – which acts as the 'the very organ of social thought' – and labour to work alongside private capital in order to develop institutions that could act as buffers between the large state, the large organization and the isolated individual.

Unlike Mayo, for Durkheim, the state is the organizing principle of society. If society is the collective conscious (Durkheim, 1957: 50, 1984), the state acts as the guarantor of the good of the collectivity over and above that of any one group – especially private capital. (This is a determinedly anti-neo-liberal stance.) If the collective consciousness is located in myth, religion and legend, the state, as a planner, is more reflexive and conscious of its own thinking and decision-making. Durkheim (1957: 50) has a Hegelian vision of the state, wherein it 'is a special organ whose responsibility it is to work out certain representations which hold good for the collectivity. These representations are distinguished from the other collective representations by their higher degree of consciousness and reflection.'

The guilds Durkheim seeks to create are to be independent of this state, but closely aligned to – and involved with – it. Importantly, so too is labour:

> A more important matter is to know what the respective place of the employer and employed would be in the corporative structure. It seems to

me obvious that both should be represented in the governing body responsible for supervising the general affairs and well-being of the association.

(Durkheim, 1957: 39)

However, Durkheim goes even further in terms of the state. He recognizes the unequal power structures of guilds and organizations. He fears the rise of elite fiefdoms of power, authority, dominance and control. He expressly raises this issue, arguing

> there must be no forming of any secondary groups that enjoy enough autonomy to allow of each becoming in a way a small society within a greater. For then, each of these will behave towards its members as if it stood alone and everything would go on as if full scale society did not exist.
>
> *(Durkheim, 1957: 61)*

He goes on to reiterate his fear of individuals being 'curbed and monopolised' and of groups gaining 'mastery over their members and mould[ing] them to their will' (Durkheim, 1957: 62). Hence, the state must intervene to limit the power of guilds and private bureaucratic organizations in their relations with individuals – in short, it must limit their power to discipline. Here, the state cannot act on the special local conditions of each and every individual, but it must

> liberate the individual personalities. It is solely because, in holding its constituent societies in check, it prevents them from exerting the repressive influences over the individual that they would otherwise exert. So there is nothing inherently tyrannical about state intervention in the different fields of collective life; on the contrary, it has the object and the effect of alleviating tyrannies that do exist.
>
> *(Durkheim, 1957: 62)*

Durkheim (1957: 12) further argues that capitalism or business (private bureaucracy) is at best amoral:

> Hence it follows that those in this *milieu* [the industrial and commercial sphere] have only a faint impress of morality, the greater part of their existence is passed divorced from any moral influence. How could such a state of affairs fail to be a source of demoralisation?

As we have seen, Mayo's view of the state and the private capitalist organization is entirely different, but he goes far beyond Durkheim and rejects any role for labour or industrial democracy:

> Cole [the guild-socialist]'s suggestion that workers in any industry should control it after the fashion of 'democratic' politics would not only introduce

all the ills of partisan politics into industrial management but would also place the final power into the hands of the least skilled workers. In many industries this would give the unskilled labourer control over the craftsmen properly so-called. And, more generally, the effect would be to determine problems requiring the highest skill by placing the decisions in the hands of those who were unable even to understand the problem. The principles of full publicity and moral control by 'the people' are sound: but there is no good reason for confining 'sovereignty' conceived thus to the workers in a particular industry.

(Mayo, 1919: 58–9)

Thus, Mayo violently diverges from Durkheim in terms of the state's role, the function of labour, how organizations should be managed, the role of the private work organization in developing new routines and ways of being, and their authoritarian tendencies. Mayo embraces the private bureaucratic elitism and leadership of Michels and Pareto and the neo-liberalism of Lippmann or Weber. For him, it is right that there are both leaders and led. In contrast, Durkheim appears to have feared three things: anomie in various forms; the lack of genuine collectivity and meaning in life under capitalism; and the oppressiveness of discipline within institutions and organizations. As we have seen, these issues are central to management because at their core is a view of life as an ever-increasing circle of obedience. This process and its attendant struggles appear nowhere more than in management's right to manage and in labour's role as a factotum that is accepting of authority. As we saw in Chapters 4, 5 and 6, Mayo is far removed from Durkheim on these issues. Indeed, he believes in management's right to manage; in the state as a repressive and negative force if it is ruled by the 'rabble' under democracy (Mayo, 1949: 31); in labour as a group to be listened to simply as a therapeutic exercise; in the elite leadership qualities of managers; in the worker as an object of control; and in the need to extend obedience into the general intellect. Consequently, Mayo and the human relations school align themselves more to elite and neo-liberal theorists than to Durkheim. The latter's corporatist vision is a more egalitarian one that values individuality as much as discipline, even if, like all forms of corporatism, it has the potential to create exclusionary tendencies. Mayo is inherently authoritarian, is closer to neo-liberal elitism and, importantly, widens the reach of managerial discipline beyond the factory and office to the worker's soul.

BIBLIOGRAPHY

Abbott, A. (1988) *The System of Professions: An Essay on the Division of Expert Labor*, London, University of Chicago Press.

Abrahamson, E. (1997) 'The Emergence and Prevalence of Employee Management Rhetorics: The Effects of Long Waves, Labor Unions, and Turnover, 1875–1992', *Academy of Management Journal* 40:3, 491–533.

Adorno, T. and Horkheimer, M. (1997) *The Dialectic of Enlightenment*, London, Verso.

Afuah, A. and Tucci, C. L. (2012) 'Crowdsourcing as a Source of Distant Search', *Academy of Management Review*, 37:3, 355–75.

Aglietta, M. (2000) *A Theory of Capitalist Regulation: The US Experience*, London, Verso.

Alexander, M. W. (1916) 'Hiring and Firing: Its Economic Waste and How to Avoid It', *Annals of the American Academy of Political and Social Science* 65:1, 128–44.

Appelbaum, R. and Lichtenstein, N. (2006) 'A New World of Retail Supremacy: Supply Chains and Workers' Chains in the Age of Wal-Mart', *International Labor and Working-Class History* 70:1, 106–25.

Armstrong, P. (1985) 'Changing Management Control Strategies: The Role of Competition between Accountancy and Other Organisational Professions' *Accounting, Organizations and Society* 10:2, 129–48.

——(1987) 'The Rise of Accounting Controls in British Capitalist Enterprises', *Accounting, Organizations and Society*, 12:5, 415–36.

Arrighi, G. and Silver, B. (1984) 'Labor Movements and Capital Migration: The United States and Western Europe in World-Historical Perspective', in C. Bergquist (ed.) *Labor in the Capitalist World-Economy*, Beverly Hills, Sage.

Bakan, J. (2004) *The Corporation: The Pathological Pursuit of Power and Profit*, London, Constable.

Baldi, G. (1972) 'Theses on Mass Worker and Social Capital', *Radical America* 6:3, 3–21.

Banaji, J. (2003) 'The Fictions of Free Labour: Contract, Coercion, and So-Called Unfree Labour', *Historical Materialism* 11:3, 69–95.

Barley, S. R. and Kunda, G. (1992) 'Design and Devotion: Surges of Rational and Normative Ideologies of Control in Managerial Discourse', *Administrative Science Quarterly* 37:3, 363–99.

Barnard, C. (1968) *The Functions of the Executive*, Cambridge, MA, Harvard University Press.

Bass, B. M. and Steidlmeier, P. (1999) 'Ethics, Character, and Authentic Transformational Leadership Behavior', *Leadership Quarterly* 10:2, 181–217.

Bauman, Z. (1998) *Work, Consumerism and the New Poor*, Milton Keynes, Open University Press.

Becker, G. (1962) 'Investment in Human Capital: A Theoretical Analysis', *Journal of Political Economy* 70:5(2), 9–49.

Bell, D. (1947) 'Adjusting Men to Machines: Social Scientists Explore the World of the Factory', *Commentary* 3, 79–88.

——(1973) *The Coming of Post-industrial Society: A Venture in Social Forecasting*, New York, Basic Books.

Bendix, R. (1956) *Work and Authority in Industry: Ideologies of Management in the Course of Industrialization*, New York, Wiley.

Bendix, R. and Fisher, L. H. (1949) 'The Perspectives of Elton Mayo', *Review of Economics and Statistics* 31:4, 312–19.

Benjamin, W. (2008) *One Way Street and Other Writings*, London, Penguin.

Benyon, H. (1973) *Working for Ford*, London, Penguin.

Bernays, E. L. (1928) *Propaganda*, www.whale.to/b/bernays.pdf, accessed 21 August 2012.

Blachly, C. C. (1839) 'Some Causes of Popular Poverty', in T. Branagan (ed.) *The Beauties of Philanthropy*, Albany, G. J. Loomis.

Blackford, K. M. H. and Newcomb, A. (1915) *The Job, the Man, the Boss*, New York, Doubleday, Page and Company.

Bloomfield, M. (1915) 'The New Profession of Handling Men', *Annals of the American Academy of Political and Social Science* 61, 121–6.

Bloomfield, M. and Willits, J. H. (1916) 'Foreword', *Annals of the American Academy of Political and Social Science* 65, vii–viii.

Boddewyn, J. (1961) 'Frederick Winslow Taylor Revisited', *American Journal of Management* 4:1, 100–7.

Bodnar, J. (1976) 'The Impact of the "New Immigration" on the Black Worker: Steelton, Pennsylvania, 1880–1920', *Labor History* 17:2, 214–29.

——(1980) 'Immigration, Kinship, and the Rise of Working-Class Realism in Industrial America', *Journal of Social History* 14:1, 45–65.

Bourke, H. (1982) 'Industrial Unrest as Social Pathology: The Australian Writings of Elton Mayo', *Australian Historical Studies* 20:79, 217–33.

Bramel, D. and Friend, R. (1981) 'Hawthorne, the Myth of the Docile Worker, and Class Bias in Psychology', *American Psychologist* 36:8, 867.

Braverman, H. (1974) *Labor and Monopoly Capital: The Degradation of Work in the Twentieth Century*, New York, Monthly Review Press.

Brody, D. (1965) *Labor in Crisis: The Steel Strike of 1919*, Chicago, University of Illinois Press.

——(1979) 'The Old Labor History and the New: In Search of an American Working Class', *Labor History* 20:1, 112–26.

Brouillette, S. (2014) *Literature and the Creative Economy*, Stanford, Stanford University Press.

Brown, R. D. (1972) 'Modernization and the Modern Personality in Early America, 1600–1865: A Sketch of a Synthesis', *Journal of Interdisciplinary History* 2:3, 201–28.

Brown, W. (2003) 'Neo-liberalism and the End of Liberal Democracy', *Theory and Event* 7:1, http://muse.jhu.edu/journals/theory_and_event/v007/7.1brown.html, accessed 6 March 2015.

——(2006) 'American Nightmare: Neoliberalism, Neoconservatism, and De-Democratization', *Political Theory* 34:6, 690–714.

Bruce, K. and Nyland, C. (2011) 'Elton Mayo and the Deification of Human Relations', *Organization Studies* 32:3, 383–405.

Burawoy, M. (1979) *Manufacturing Consent: Changes in the Labor Process under Monopoly Capitalism*, Chicago, University of Chicago Press.

——(2013) 'From Max Weber to Public Sociology', http://burawoy.berkeley.edu/PS/From%20Weber%20to%20PS.pdf, accessed 27 November 2014.

Burnham, J. (1943) *The Machiavellians*, London, Putman and Co.

Buttrick, J. (1952) 'The Inside Contract', *Journal of Economic History* 12:3, 205–21.

Byllesby, L. (1961) *Observations on the Sources and Effects of Unequal Wealth with Propositions towards Remedying the Disparity of the Profit in Pursuing The Arts of Life and Establishing Security in Individual Prospects and Resources*, New York, Russell and Russell.

Caffentis, G. (2011) 'A Critique of Cognitive Capitalism', in P. Micheals and E. Bulut (eds) *Cognitive Capitalism, Education and Digital Labor*, New York, Peter Land International.

Carlton, F. T. (1907) 'The Workingmen's Party of New York City: 1829–31', *Political Science Quarterly* 22:3, 401–15.

Chandler, A. (1977) *The Visible Hand: The Managerial Revolution in American Business*, Cambridge, MA, Harvard University Press.

Chesbrough, H. W. (2003) 'The Era of Open Innovation', *Sloan Management Review* Spring, 35–41.

——(2006) 'Open Innovation: A New Paradigm for Understanding Industrial Innovation', in H. Chesbrough, W. Vanhaverbeke and J. West (eds) *Open Innovation: Researching a New Paradigm*, Oxford, Oxford University Press.

Clawson, D. (1980) *Bureaucracy and the Labor Process: The Transformation of US Industry, 1860–1920*, New York, Monthly Review Press.

Commonwealth of Massachusetts (1837a) *Documents Relating to the Amherst Carriage Company*, Senate No. 53.

——(1837b) *Remonstrances Relating to the Amherst Carriage Company*, House of Representatives No. 38.

——(1838) *Petitions and Remonstrances Relating to the Amherst Carriage Company*, House of Representatives No. 33.

Cooke, B. (2003) 'The Denial of Slavery in Management Studies', *Journal of Management Studies* 40:8, 1895–918.

Crane, A. (2013) 'Modern Slavery as a Management Practice: Exploring the Conditions and Capabilities for Human Exploitation', *Academy of Management Review*, 38:1, 49–69.

Dardot, P. and Laval, C. (2013) *The New Way of the World: On Neo-liberal Society*, London, Verso.

Davies, W. (2014) *The Limits of Neoliberalism*, London, Sage.

Deleuze, G. (1983) *Nietzsche and Philosophy*, New York, Columbia University Press.

——(1992) 'Postscript on the Societies of Control', *October* 59, 3–7.

Della Costa, M. and James, S. (1972) *The Power of Women and the Subversion of the Community*, Bristol, Falling Wall Press.

Devinatz, G. (2003) 'Lenin as Scientific Manager under Monopoly Capitalism, State Capitalism, and Socialism: A Response to Scoville', *Industrial Relations* 42:3, 513–20.

DiMaggio, P. J. and Powell, W. W. (1983) 'The Iron Cage Revisited: Institutional Isomorphism and Collective Rationality in Organizational Fields', *American Sociological Association* 48:2, 147–60.

Donham, W. B. (1922) 'Essential Groundwork for a Broad Executive Theory', *Harvard Business Review* 1:1, 1–10.

——(1927a) 'The Emerging Profession of Business', *Harvard Business Review* 5:4, 401–5.

——(1927b) 'The Social Significance of Business', *Harvard Business Review* 5:4, 406–19.

——(1933) 'The Failure of Business Leadership and the Responsibility of the Universities', *Harvard Business Review* 11:4, 418–35.

——(1936) 'Training for Leadership in a Democracy', *Harvard Business Review* 14:3, 261–71.

Douglas, P. H. (1918) 'The Problem of Labor Turnover', *American Economic Review* 8:2, 306–16.

Dowling, E. (2007) 'Producing the Dining Experience: Measure, Subjectivity and the Affective Worker', *Ephemera: Theory and Politics in Organization* 7:1, 117–32.

Drucker, P. (2007a) *Innovation and Management*, London, Routledge.

——(2007b) *The Practice of Management*, London, Routledge.

Du Gay, P. (2000) *In Praise of Bureaucracy*, London, Sage.

——(2013a) 'New Spirits of Public Management "Post-Bureaucracy"', in P. Du Gay and G. Morgan (eds) *New Spirits of Capitalism? Crises, Justifications, and Dynamics*, Oxford, Oxford University Press.

——(2013b) 'Notes on Aspects of the Conceptual Architecture of the "New Spirit": Weber and Hirschman', in P. Du Gay and G. Morgan (eds) *New Spirits of Capitalism? Crises, Justifications, and Dynamics*, Oxford, Oxford University Press.

Du Gay, P. and Morgan, G. (2013) 'Understanding Capitalism: Crises, Legitimacy, and Change through the Prism of the New Spirit of Capitalism', in P. Du Gay and G. Morgan (eds) *New Spirits of Capitalism? Crises, Justifications, and Dynamics*, Oxford, Oxford University Press.

Durkheim, E. (1951) *Suicide*, New York, The Free Press.

——(1957) *Professional Ethics and Civic Morals*, London, Routledge.

——(1984) *The Division of Labour in Society*, Basingstoke, Macmillan Press.

Edwards, R (1979) *Contested Terrain: The Transformation of the Workplace in the Twentieth Century*, New York, Basic Books.

Endnotes (2010) 'The History of Subsumption', http://endnotes.org.uk/articles/6, accessed 29 February 2012.

Englander, E. (1987) 'The Inside Contract System of Production and Organization: A Neglected Aspect of the History of the Firm', *Labor History* 28:4, 429–46.

Esch, E. and Roediger, D. (2009) 'One Symptom of Originality: Race and the Management of Labour in the History of the United States', *Historical Materialism* 17, 3–43.

Ettlinger, N. (2014) 'The Openness Paradigm', *New Left Review*, 89, 89–100.

Federici, S. (2004) *Caliban and the Witch: Women, the Body and Primitive Accumulation*, New York, Autonomedia.

Ferguson, A. (1995) *An Essay on the History of Civil Society*, Cambridge, Cambridge University Press.

Fleming, P. (2009) *Authenticity and the Cultural Politics of Work: New Forms of Informal Control*, Oxford, Oxford University Press.

——(2013) 'Down with Big Brother! The End of "Corporate Culturalism"?', *Journal of Management Studies* 50:3, 474–95.

——(2014) *Resisting Work: The Corporatization of Life and Its Discontents*, Philadelphia, Temple University Press.

Foner, E. (1995) *America's Reconstruction: People and Politics after the Civil War*, New York, HarperPerennial.

Foucault, M. (1981) *The History of Sexuality*, Vol. I: *The Will to Knowledge*, London, Penguin.

——(2004) *Society Must be Defended: Lectures at the College de France 1975–1976*, London, Penguin.

——(2007) *Security, Territory, Population: Lectures at the College de France 1977–1978*, London Palgrave.

——(2008) *The Birth of Biopolitics: Lectures at the College de France 1978–1979*, London, Palgrave.

Fuchs, C. (2011) 'Cognitive Capitalism or Informational Capitalism? The Role of Class in the Information Economy', in M. A. Peters and E. Bulut (eds) *Cognitive Capitalism, Education and Digital Labor*, New York, Peter Lang.

Gall, G. J. (1982) 'Heber Blankenhorn, the LaFollette Committee, and the Irony of Industrial Repression', *Labor History* 23:2, 246–53.

Gamble, A. (1996) *Hayek: The Iron Cage of Liberty*, London, Polity Press.

Gane, N. (2013) 'The Emergence of Neo-liberalism: Thinking through and beyond Michel Foucault's Lectures on Biopolitics', *Theory, Culture and Society* 31:4, 3–27.

——(2014) 'Sociology and Neoliberalism: A Missing History', *Sociology* 47:1, 1–15.

Gantt, H. L. (1915) 'The Effect of Idle Plant on Costs and Profits', *Annals of the American Academy of Political and Social Science* 61, 86–9.

Gardner, W. L., Avolio, B. J., Luthans, F., May, D. R. and Walumbwa, F. (2005) 'Can You See the Real Me? A Self Based Model of Authentic Leader and Follower Development', *Leadership Quarterly* 16:3, 343–72.

Gerth, H. H. and Mills, C. W. (1948) 'Introduction', in H. H. Gerth and C. W. Mills (eds) *From Max Weber*, London, Routledge and Kegan Paul.

Gill, R. and Pratt, A. (2008) 'Precarity and Cultural Work in the Social Factory? Immaterial Labour, Precariousness, and Cultural Work', *Theory, Culture, and Society* 25:7–8, 1–30.

Gitelman, H. M. (1967) 'The Waltham System and the Coming of the Irish', *Labor History* 8:3, 227–53.

——(1973) 'Perspectives on American Industrial Violence', *Business History Review* 47:1, 1–23.

——(1988) *Legacy of the Ludlow Massacre: A Chapter in American Industrial Relations*, Philadelphia, University of Pennsylvania Press.

Gordon, C. (2014) 'Plato in Weimar: Weber Revisited via Foucault: Two Lectures on Legitimation and Vocation', *Economy and Society*, http://dx.doi.org/10.1080/03085147.2014.956464, accessed 6 March 2015.

Gordon, D. M., Edwards, R. and Reich, M. (1982) *Segmented Work, Divided Workers: The Historical Transformation of Labor in the United States*, Cambridge, Cambridge University Press.

Gordon, R. W. (1984) 'Critical Legal Histories', Faculty Scholarship Series, Paper 1368.

Gorz, A. (1999) *Reclaiming Work: Beyond the Wage-Based Society*, Cambridge, Polity Press.

Gramsci, A. (1971) *Selections from the Prison Notebooks*, London, Lawrence and Wishart.

Graw, I. (2010) 'When Life Goes to Work: Andy Warhol', *October* 132, 99–113.

Green, J. R. (1974) 'Comments on the Montgomery Paper', *Journal of Social History* 7:4, 530–5.

Grey, C. (2013) *A Very Short, Fairly Interesting and Reasonably Cheap Book about Studying Organizations*, London, Sage.

Guest, D. (1987) 'Human Resource Management and Industrial Relations', *Journal of Management Studies* 24:5, 503–21.

Gumus-Dawes, Z. (2000) 'Forsaken Paths: The Organization of the American Textile Industry in the Nineteenth Century', Ph.D. dissertation, Yale University.

Gutman, H. G. (1973) 'Work, Culture, and Society in Industrializing America, 1815–1919', *American Historical Review* 78:3, 531–88.

Halpern, S. (2011) 'Mind Control and the Internet', *New York Review of Books* 23 June.

Hamper, B. (1986) *Rivethead: Tales from the Assembly Line*, New York, Warner Bros.

Hanlon, G. (2008) 'A Re-theorization of Corporate Social Responsibility: On the Denial of Politics', in A. Crane et al. (eds) *Oxford Handbook of CSR*, Oxford, Oxford University Press.

——(2014) 'The Entrepreneurial Function and the Capture of Value: Using Kirzner to Understand Contemporary Capitalism', *Ephemera: A Journal of Theory and Politics in Organization* 14:2, 177–95.

Hanlon, G. and Mandarini, M. (2015) 'On the Impossibility of Business Ethics: Leadership, Heterogeneity, and Politics', in C. Rhodes and A. Pullen (eds) *The Routledge Companion to Ethics, Politics, and Organization*, Abingdon, Routledge.

Hardt, M. (2010) 'The Common in Communism', *Rethinking Marxism* 22:3, 346–56.

Hardt, M. and Negri, A. (1994) *Labor of Dionysus: A Critique of the State-Form*, Minneapolis, University of Minnesota Press.

——(2000) *Empire*, London, Harvard University Press.

Harvard Law Review (1989) '"Editorial" Incorporating the Republic: The Corporation in Antebellum Political Culture', *Harvard Law Review* 102, 1883–903.

Harvey, D. (1989) *The Condition of Postmodernity*, Oxford, Basil Blackwell.

——(2007) *A Brief History of Neoliberalism*, Oxford, Oxford University Press.

Haug, W. F. (2010) 'Historical–Critical Dictionary of Marxism: General Intellect', *Historical Materialism* 18, 209–16.

Hayek, F. A. (1944) *The Road to Serfdom*, London, Routledge.

——(1945) 'The Use of Knowledge in Society', *American Economic Review* 35:4, 519–30.

——(1948) *Individualism and Economic Order*, London, Chicago University Press.

Hechter, M. (1999) *Internal Colonialism: The Celtic Fringe in British National Development*, New York, Transaction Publishers.

Hennis, W. (1983) 'Max Weber's "Central Question"', *Economy and Society* 12:2, 135–80.

——(1988) *Max Weber: Essays in Reconstruction*, London, Allen and Unwin.

Hessen, R. (1974) 'The Bethlehem Steel Strike of 1910', *Labor History* 15:1, 3–18.

Hill, C. (1974) 'Fighting the Twelve Hour Day in the American Steel Industry', *Labor History* 15, 19–35.
Hirschman, A. O. (1977) *The Passions and the Interests: Political Arguments for Capitalism before Its Triumph*, Princeton, Princeton University Press.
Hochschild, A. R. (1983) *The Managed Heart: Commercialization of Human Feeling*, London, University of California Press.
Hodgskin, T. (1825) *Labour Defended against the Claims of Capital, Or the Unproductiveness of Capital Proved with Reference to the Present Combinations amongst Journeymen*, http://avalon.law.yale.edu/19th_century/labdef.asp, accessed 11 August 2012.
Hoover, H. (1922) *American Individualism*, New York, Doubleday, Page and Company.
Hoxie, R. F. (1918) *Scientific Management and Labor*, New York, D. Appleton and Company.
Huthmacher, J. J. (1962) 'Urban Liberalism and the Age of Reform', *Mississippi Valley Historical Review* 49, 231–41.
Huxley, A. (2007) *Brave New World*, London, Vintage.
Illouz, E. (2008) *Saving the Modern Soul: Therapy, Emotions, and the Culture of Self-Help*, Berkeley, University of California Press.
Invisible Committee (2009) *The Coming Insurrection*, New York, Semiotext(e).
Jacoby, S. M. (1983) 'Union–Management cooperation in the United States: Lessons from the 1920s', *Industrial and Labor Relations Review* 37, 18–33.
Jacques, R. (1996) *Manufacturing the Employee: Management Knowledge from the 19th to the 21st Centuries*, London, Sage.
James, C. L. R. (1970) 'The Making of the Caribbean People', *Radical America* 4:4, 36–50.
——(2001) *The Black Jacobins Toussaint l'Ouverture and the San Domingo Revolution*, Harmondsworth, Penguin.
Keller, R. T. (1984) 'The Harvard "Pareto Circle" and the Historical Development of Organization Theory', *Journal of Management* 10:2, 193–204.
Kelley, F. (1899) 'Aims and Principles of the Consumers' League', *American Journal of Sociology* 5:3, 289–304.
Keyssar, A. (1986) *Out of Work: The First Century of Unemployment in Massachusetts*, Cambridge, Cambridge University Press.
Kracauer, S. (1995) *The Mass Ornament: Weimar Essays*, Cambridge, MA, Harvard University Press.
——(1998) *The Salaried Masses: Duty and Distraction in Weimar Germany*, London, Verso.
Lakhani, K. and Kanji, Z. (2008) *Threadless: The Business of Community*, Harvard Case Study 608–719, Harvard Business School.
Land, C. and Taylor, S. (2010) 'Surf's up: Work, Life, Balance and Brand in a New Age Capitalist Organization', *Sociology* 44:3, 395–413.
Lanier, J. (2011) *You Are Not a Gadget*, London, Penguin.
Lazzarato, M. (1996) 'Immaterial Labour', in M. Hardt and P. Virno (eds) *Radical Thought in Italy: A Potential Politics*, Minneapolis, University of Minnesota Press.
Lears, T. J. (2000). 'From Salvation to Self-realization: Advertising and the Therapeutic Roots of the Consumer Culture, 1880–1930', *Advertising and Society Review* 1:1, http://muse.jhu.edu/login?auth=0&type=summary&url=/journals/advertising_and_society_review/v001/1.1lears.html, accessed 16 March 2015.
Lenin, V. I. (1913) 'A "Scientific" System of Sweating', www.marxists.org/archive/lenin/works/1913/mar/13.htm, accessed 23 March 2011.
——(1914) 'The Taylor System: Man's Enslavement by the Machine', www.marxists.org/archive/lenin/works/1914/mar/13.htm, accessed 23 March 2011.
——(1918a) 'The Immediate Tasks of the Soviet Government', www.marxists.org/archive/lenin/works/1918/mar/x03.htm, accessed 23 March 2011.
——(1918b) 'Session of the All-Russia CEC', www.marxists.org/archive/lenin/works/1918/apr/29.htm accessed 23 March 2011.
Lincoln, A. (1861) *State of the Union Address to the Houses of Congress*, www.infoplease.com/t/hist/state-of-the-union/73.html, accessed 21 February 2010.

Lippmann, W. (1914/1985) *Drift and Mastery*, revised edition, Madison, University of Wisconsin Press.

——(1922) *Public Opinion*, New York, Harcourt Brace.

——(1935) *The Method of Freedom*, New York, Macmillan and Company.

——(1938/1943) *The Good Society*, third edition, London, George Allen and Unwin.

Litterer, J. A. (1963) 'Systematic Management: Design for Organizational Recoupling in American Manufacturing Firms', *Business History Review* 37:4, 369–91.

Loader, C. and Alexander, J. C. (1985) 'Max Weber on Churches and Sects in North America: An Alternative Path towards Rationalisation', *Sociological Theory* 3:1, 1–6.

Locke, E. A. (1982) 'The Ideas of Frederick W. Taylor: An Evaluation', *Academy of Management Review* 7:1, 14–24.

Lucas, R. (1988) 'On the Mechanics of Economic Development', *Journal of Monetary Economics* 22, 3–42.

——(2010) 'Dreaming in Code', *New Left Review* 62, 125–32.

Lury, C. (2004) *Brand: The Logos of the Global Economy*, London, Routledge.

Lyons, F. S. L. (1971) *Ireland since the Famine*, London, Weidenfeld and Nicolson.

Marens, R. (2013) 'What Comes Around: The Early 20th Century American Roots of Legitimating Corporate Social Responsibility', *Organization* 20:3, 454–75

Marglin, S. A. (1974) 'What Do Bosses Do? The Origins and Functions of Hierarchy in Capitalist Production, Part I', *Radical Political Economy: Explorations in Alternative Economic Analysis* 6:2, 60–112.

Marx, K. (1973) *Grundrisse*, Harmondsworth, Penguin.

——(1976) *Capital: A Critique of Political Economy*, Vol. I, Harmondsworth, Penguin.

——(1981) *Capital*, Vol. III, Harmondsworth, Penguin.

——(1988) *Economic and Philosophical Manuscripts of 1844*, New York, Prometheus.

——(2000) *Theories of Surplus Value*, Books I, II, III, New York, Prometheus.

Mayo, E. (1919) *Democracy and Freedom: An Essay in Social Logic*, Melbourne, Macmillan and Co.

——(1922a) 'Industrial Peace and Psychological Research I', *Industrial Australian and Mining Standard* 67, 16.

——(1922b) 'Industrial Peace and Psychological Research II', *Industrial Australian and Mining Standard* 67, 63–4.

——(1922c) 'Industrial Peace and Psychological Research III', *Industrial Australian and Mining Standard* 67, 159–60.

——(1923a) 'The Irrational Factor in Human Behaviour: The "Night Mind" in Industry', *Annals of the American Academy of Political and Social Science* 110, 117–30.

——(1923b) 'The Irrational Factor in Society', *Journal of Personnel Research* 1:10, 419–26.

——(1924a) 'The Basis of Industrial Psychology: The Psychology of the Total Situation is Basic to a Psychology of Management'. *Bulletin of the Taylor Society* 9:6, 249–59.

——(1924b) 'Civilization: The Perilous Adventure', *Harper's Monthly Magazine* October, 590–7.

——(1933) *The Human Problems of an Industrial Civilization*, London, Routledge.

——(1937) 'Psychiatry and Sociology in Relation to Social Disorganization', *American Journal of Sociology*, 42:6, 825–31.

——(1939) 'Routine Interaction and the Problem of Collaboration', *American Sociological Review* 4:3, 335–40.

——(1949) *The Social Problems of an Industrial Civilization*, London, Routledge.

McGregor, D. (1957) 'The Human Side of Enterprise', *Management Review* November, 41–9.

McKenzie, J. (2001) *Perform or Else: From Discipline to Performance*, London, Routledge.

McKinlay, A. and Wilson, J. (2013) '"All They Lose is the Scream": Foucault, Ford and Mass Production', *Management and Organizational History* 7:1, 45–60.

Meadows, P. (1947) 'The Motivations of Industrial Man', *American Journal of Economics and Sociology* 6:3, 363–70.

Merlin, S. (1943) 'Trends in German Economic Control since 1933', *Quarterly Journal of Economics* 57:2, 169–207.

Merton, R. K. (1940) 'Bureaucratic Structure and Personality', *Social Forces* 18:4, 560–8.

——(1947) 'The Machine, the Worker, and the Engineer', *Science* 24 January, 79–84.

Meyer, Stephen, III (1980) 'Adapting to the Immigrant Line: Americanization in the Ford Factory 1914–21', *Journal of Social History* 14:1, 67–82.

Mezzadra, S. and Neilson, B. (2013) 'Extraction, Logistics, Finance: Global Crisis and the Politics of Operations', *Radical Philosophy* 178, 8–18.

Michels, R. (1915) *Political Parties*, New York, Hearst's International Library Co.

——(1949) *First Lectures in Political Sociology*, Minneapolis, University of Minnesota Press.

Mills, C. W. (1951) *White Collar Work*, New York, Oxford University Press.

Mirowski, P. (2013) *Never Let a Serious Crisis Go to Waste: How Neo-liberalism Survived the Financial Meltdown*, London, Verso.

Mises, L. von (1944) *Bureaucracy*, New Haven, Yale University Press.

——(1996) *Human Action: A Treatise on Economics*, Vol. II, Indianapolis, Liberty Fund.

Mommsen, W. J. (1974) *The Age of Bureaucracy: Perspectives on the Political Sociology of Max Weber*, Oxford, Basil Blackwell.

——(1981) 'Max Weber and Roberto Michels: An Asymmetrical Partnership', *European Journal of Sociology* 22:1, 100–16.

Montaigne de, M. (1958) *Essays*, London, Penguin.

Montgomery, D. (1968) 'The Working Class of the Pre-industrial American City, 1780–1830', *Labor History* 9:1, 3–22.

——(1974) 'The "New Unionism" and the Transformation of Workers' Consciousness in America: 1909–22', *Journal of Social History* 7:4, 509–29.

——(1987) *The Fall of the House of Labor*, New York, Cambridge University Press.

Moore, W. E. (1947) 'Current Issues in Industrial Sociology', *American Sociological Review* 12:6, 651–7.

——(1948) 'Industrial Sociology: Status and Prospects', *American Sociological Review* 13:2, 382–400.

Mosca, G. (1939) *The Ruling Class*, New York, McGraw-Hill.

Mount, F. (2013) *Power and Inequality in Britain Now: The New Few or a Very British Oligarchy*, London, Simon and Schuster.

Mumby, D. (2014) 'Organising beyond Organization: Branding Discourse and Communicative Capitalism', plenary paper presented at the 11th International Conference on Organizational Discourse, Cardiff Business School, July.

Negri, A. (1989) *The Politics of Subversion: A Manifesto for the Twenty-first Century*, Cambridge, Polity Press.

——(1991) *Marx beyond Marx: Lessons from the Grundrisse*, New York, Autonomedia.

——(1996) 'Twenty Theses on Marx: Interpretation of the Class Situation Today', in S. Makdisi, C. Casarino and R. E. Karl (eds) *Marxism beyond Marxism*, New York, Routledge.

——(1999) *Insurgencies: Constituent Power and the Modern State*, Minneapolis, University of Minnesota Press.

Nelson, D. (1995) *Managers and Workers*, second edition, Madison, University of Wisconsin Press.

Nelson, D. and Campbell, S. (1972) 'Taylorism versus Welfare in American Industry: H. L. Gantt and the Bancrofts', *Business History Review* 46:1, 1–16.

Nichols, E. M. (1916) 'The Employment Manager', *Annals of the American Academy of Political and Social Science* 65:1, 1–8.

O'Connor, E. (1999a) 'Minding the Workers: The Meaning of "Human" and "Human Relations" in Elton Mayo', *Organization* 6:2, 223–46.

——(1999b) 'The Politics of Management Thought: A Case Study of the Harvard Business School and the Human Relations School', *Academy of Management Review* 24:1, 117–31.

O'Neill, J. (1986) 'The Disciplinary Society', *British Journal of Sociology* 37:1, 42–60.

Orwell, G. (1946) 'Second Thoughts on James Burnham', www.orwell.ru/library/reviews/burnham/english/e_burnh, accessed 11 June 2014.

Panzieri, R. (1961) 'The Capitalist Use of Machinery', http://libcom.org/library/capitalist-use-machinery-raniero-panzieri, accessed 29 February 2012.

Pareto, V. (1991) *The Rise and Fall of Elites: An Application in Theoretical Sociology*, New Brunswick, Transaction Publishers.

Pariser, E. (2011) *The Filter Bubble: What the Internet is Hiding from You*, London, Viking Press.

Peck, J. (2008) 'Remaking *Laissez-Faire*', *Progress in Human Geography* 32:3, 3–43.

Perrow, C. (2002) *Organizing America: Wealth, Power, and the Origins of Corporate Capitalism*, Princeton, Princeton University Press.

Person, H. S. (1916) 'University Business Schools and the Training of Employment Executives', *Annals of the American Academy of Political and Social Science* 65:1, 117–27.

Pijl, K. van der (2012) *The Making of an Altantic Ruling Class*, London, Verso.

Polanyi, K. (1944/1957) *The Great Transformation: The Political and Economic Origins of our Time*, Boston, Beacon Press.

Pollard, S. (1965) *The Genesis of Modern Management: A Study of the Industrial Revolution in Great Britain*, Vermont, Gregg Revivals.

Prahalad, C. K. and Ramaswamy, V. (2004) 'Co-creation Experiences: The Next Practice in Value Creation', *Journal of Interactive Marketing* 18:3, 5–14.

Pred, A. (1966) 'Manufacturing in the American Mercantile City: 1800–840', *Annals of the Association of American Geographers* 56:2, 307–38.

Redfield, W. (1916) 'The Employment Problem in Industry', *Annals of the American Academy of Political and Social Science* 65: 9–14.

Reisman, D. (2001) *The Lonely Crowd*, London, Yale University Press.

Ricardo, D. (1996) *Principles of Political Economy and Taxation*, New York, Prometheus Books.

Ritzer, G. (1993) *The McDonaldization of Society*, Beverly Hills, Sage.

Rockefeller, John D., Jr. (1916) 'On Labor and Capital', *New York Times*, 9 January, http://query.nytimes.com/mem/archive-free/pdf?res=9500E2D61739E233A2575AC0A9679C946796D6CF, accessed 23 January 2012.

Roediger, D. and Esch, E. (2012) *The Production of Difference: Race and the Management of Labor in US History*, Oxford, Oxford University Press.

Röepke, W. (1948) Civitas Humana: *A Humane Order of Society*, London, William Hodge and Company.

——(1992) *The Social Crisis of Our Time*, New Brunswick, Transaction Publishers.

Roland, H. (1897) 'Six Examples of Successful Shop Management, V', *Engineering Magazine* 12, 994–1000.

Roy, A. (2011) *Broken Republic: Three Essays*, London, Hamish Hamilton.

Scaff, L. A. (1981) 'Max Weber and Robert Michels', *American Journal of Sociology* 86:6, 1269–86.

Schumpeter, J. (1943) *Capitalism, Socialism and Democracy*, London, Allen and Unwin.

——(1983) *The Theory of Economic Development*, New Brunswick, Transaction Books.

Scott, W. G. (1992) *Chester L. Barnard and the Guardians of the Managerial State*, Kansas, University Press of Kansas.

Scoville, J. G. (2001) 'The Taylorization of Vladimir Ilich Lenin,' *Industrial Relations* 40:3, 620–6.

Sellers, C. (1991) *The Market Revolution: Jacksonian America, 1815–1846*, New York, Oxford University Press.

Silver, B. (2003) *Forces of Labor: Workers' Movements and Globalization since 1870*, New York, Cambridge University Press.

Skeggs, B. (2011) 'Imagining Personhood Differently: Person Value and Autonomist Working-Class Value Practices', *Sociological Review* 59:3, 496–513.

——(2014) 'Values beyond Value? Is Anything beyond the Logic of Capital?', *British Journal of Sociology* 65:1, 1–20.

Skidmore, T. (1829) *The Rights of Man to Property: To Make it Equal among the Adults of the Present Generation*, New York, Alexander Ming.

Smith, A. (1776; 1981) *An Inquiry into the Nature and Causes of the Wealth of Nations*, 2 vols, Indianapolis, Liberty Fund.

Smith, J. L. (1998) 'The Enduring Legacy of Elton Mayo', *Human Relations* 51:3, 221–49.

Smith, T. (2013) 'The "General Intellect" in the *Grundrisse* and Beyond', in P. Thomas, G. Starosta and R. Bellsfiore (eds) *In Marx's Laboratory*, Amsterdam, Brill.

Soar, D. (2011) 'It Knows', *London Review of Books* 33:19, 3–6.

Sohn-Rethel, A. (1978) *Economy and Class Structure of German Fascism*, London, CSE Books.

Stacey, C. L. (2006) 'Finding Dignity in Dirty Work: The Constraints and Rewards of Low-Wage Home Care Labour', in D. Allen and A. Pilnick (eds) *The Social Organization of Healthcare Work*, Oxford, Wiley-Blackwell.

Stedman-Jones, G. (1974) 'Working-Class Politics in London, 1870–1900: Notes on the Remaking of a Working Class', *Journal of Social History* 7:4, 460–508.

Stewart, M. (2009) *The Management Myth: Debunking Modern Business Philosophy*, New York, W. W. Norton & Co.

Stone, K. (1973) 'The Origin of Job Structures in the Steel Industry', *Radical America* 7:6, 19–66.

Taylor, F. W. (1895) 'A Piece Rate System: A Step towards Partial Solution of the Labor Problem', *ASME Transactions* 16, 856–93.

——(1903) 'Shop Management', *ASME Transactions* 24, 1337–480.

——(1919) *The Principles of Scientific Management*, New York, Harper and Brothers.

——(1947) *Taylor's Testimony before the Special House Committee*, New York, Harper and Brothers.

Thomas, P. (2006) 'Being Max Weber', *New Left Review* 41, 147–58.

Thompson, E. P. (1967) 'Time, Work-Discipline, and Industrial Capitalism', *Past and Present* 38:1, 56–97.

——(1968) *The Making of the English Working Class*, London, Penguin.

——(1971) 'The Moral Economy of the English Crowd in the Eighteenth Century', *Past and Present* 50:1, 76–136.

——(1978) 'Eighteenth Century English Society: Class Struggle without Class?', *Social History* 3:2, 133–65.

Thompson, P. and McHugh, D. (2009) *Work Organizations*, Basingstoke, Macmillan.

Titunik, R. (1997) 'The Continuation of History: Max Weber on the Advent of a New Aristocracy', *Journal of Politics* 59:3, 680–700.

Torigian, M. (1999) 'The Occupation of the Factories: Paris 1936, Flint 1937', *Comparative Studies in Society and History* 41:2, 324–47.

Townley, B. (1993). 'Foucault, Power/Knowledge and its Relevance for Human Resource Management', *Academy of Management Review* 18:3, 518–45.

Tronti, M. (1964) 'Lenin in England', www.marxists.org/reference/subject/philosophy/works/it/tronti.htm, accessed 16 March 2015.

——(1965) 'Strategy of Refusal', http://operaisoinenglish.wordpress.com/2010/09/30/strategy-of-refusal/, accessed 23 January 2013.

——(1970) 'Social Capital', http://operaisoinenglish.wordpress.com/2010/09/social-capital.pdf, accessed 23 January 2013.

——(1971) 'Workers and Capital', http://operaisoinenglish.wordpress.com/2010/09/30/workers-and-capital/, accessed 20 November 2012.

Vercellone, C. (2007) 'From Formal Subsumption to the General Intellect: Elements for a Marxist Reading of the Thesis of Cognitive Capitalism', *Historical Materialism* 15:1, 13–36.

Virno, P. (2004) *The Grammar of the Multitude*, New York, Semiotext(e).

Volvo (2015) 'Quality as a Core Value', www.volvogroup.com/group/global/en-gb/volvo%20group/ourvalues/quality/pages/quality.aspx

Watson, B. (1971) 'Counter-planning on the Shop-floor', *Radical America Solidarity of Labour* 5:3, www.prole.info/texts/counterplanning.html, accessed 6 March 2015.

Weber, M. (1930/1985) *The Protestant Ethic and the Spirit of Capitalism*, London, Unwin Paperbacks.

——(1948) *From Max Weber*, edited by H. H. Gerth and C. Wright Mills, London, Routledge and Kegan Paul.

——(1978) *Economy and Society*, 2 vols, Berkeley, University of California Press.

——(1994) *Political Writings*, Cambridge, Cambridge University Press.

Webster, D. (1830) 'In Reply to Hayne', speech delivered in the US Senate, 26 January, www.bartleby.com/268/9/3.html, accessed 11 June 2012.

Weeks, K. (2011) *Feminism, Marxism, Antiwork Politics and Postwork Imaginaries*, Durham, NC, Duke University Press.

Wilentz, S. (2004) *Chants Democratic: New York City and the Rise of the American Working Class, 1788–1850*, twentieth-anniversary edition, New York, Oxford University Press.

Williams, J. M. (1917) 'An Actual Account of What We Have Done to Reduce our Labor Turnover', *Annals of the American Academy of Political and Social Science* 71, 51–70.

Williams, T. (1917) 'Mobilization of Population for Winning the War', *Annals of the American Academy of Political and Social Science* 78, 1–6.

Williamson, H. F. (1952) *Winchester: The Gun that Won the West*, New York, A. S. Barnes and Company.

Willis, P. (1977) *Learning to Labour: How Working Class Kids Get Working Class Jobs*, New York, Columbia University Press.

Willits, J. H. (1915) 'The Labor Turn-over and the Humanizing of Industry', *Annals of the American Academy of Political and Social Science* 61, 127–37.

Willmott, H. (1993) 'Strength is Ignorance; Slavery is Freedom: Managing Culture in Modern Organizations', *Journal of Management Studies* 30:4, 515–52.

——(2010) 'Creating "Value" beyond the Point of Production: Branding, Financialization, and Market Capitalization', *Organization* 17:5, 517–42.

——(2013) '"The Substitution of One Piece of Nonsense for Another": Reflections on Resistance, Gaming, and Subjugation', *Journal of Management Studies* 50:3, 443–73.

INDEX